THE SACRAMENT
OF TEACHING

VOLUME 1

Getting Ready

to Enact the Sacrament

Explorations in Religious Instruction

JAMES MICHAEL LEE

EXPLORTIONS IN RELIGIOUS INSTRUCTION is a series of books written by James Michael Lee in which he explores various extensions of the social-science approach that he set forth in his monumental trilogy on religious instruction. Each book in the series Explorations in Religious Instruction is devoted to examining at greater length one or another important aspect of religious instruction that was manifestly or latently covered in Lee's foundational trilogy. Every book in this series, then, fleshes out important points that by dint of space the trilogy was not able to cover extensively or in great detail. Like the trilogy on which it is consciously based, each book in the series Explorations in Religious Instruction is deliberately targeted to make religion teaching as effective as possible at all times and in all milieux.

Lee's trilogy, then, is the ecology in which the series Explorations in Religious Instruction is rooted. The titles of the groundbreaking trilogy are *The Shape of Religious Instruction*, *The Flow of Religious Instruction*, and *The Content of Religious Instruction*. The purpose of Lee's foundational trilogy is to present in a comprehensive and systematic manner the social-science macrotheory of religious instruction. The goal of the social-science macrotheory is to make all intentional religion teaching optimally effective by explaining, predicting, and verifying every phase of religious instruction activity.

THE SACRAMENT
OF TEACHING

VOLUME 1

Getting Ready
to Enact the Sacrament:
A Personal Testament

A SOCIAL SCIENCE APPROACH

James
Michael
Lee

REP

RELIGIOUS EDUCATION PRESS
BIRMINGHAM, ALABAMA

Library of Congress Cataloging-in-Publication Data

Lee, James Michael.
    The sacrament of teaching : a social science approach / James Michael Lee.
        p.   cm.—(Explorations in religious instruction ; 1)
    Includes bibliographical references and indexes.
    PARTIAL CONTENTS: v. 1. Getting ready to enact the sacrament.
    ISBN 0-89135-100-0 (hardcover : v. 1 : alk. paper)
    1. Religious education—Study and teaching. 2. Christian education.
    3. Religious education—Teaching methods. 4. Sociology, Christian.
    I. Title. II. Series: Lee, James Michael. Explorations in religious instruction ; 1.
    BV1471.2   .L4425 1999 vol. 1
    268—dc21   98-23812
                                                                                          CIP

Religious Education Press
5316 Meadow Brook Road
Birmingham, Alabama 35242-3315
10 9 8 7 6 5 4 3 2

Religious Education Press publishes books exclusively in religious education and in areas closely related to religious education. It is committed to enhancing and professionalizing religious education through the publication of serious, significant, and scholarly works.

PUBLISHER TO THE PROFESSION

TO MARLENE
uxor mea

A Deo vocata esse consors tota mea matrimonii nostri,
itaque ergo particeps adjutrixque tota mea
laboris apostolatus mei.

Volumes in the Series

EXPLORATIONS IN RELIGIOUS INSTRUCTION

by

JAMES MICHAEL LEE

1. THE SACRAMENT OF TEACHING, VOLUME 1

JAMES MICHAEL LEE'S FOUNDATIONAL TRILOGY ON RELIGIOUS INSTRUCTION

The Shape of Religious Instruction
The Flow of Religious Instruction
The Content of Religious Instruction

CONTENTS

Preface

This is the first volume in my series Explorations in Religious Instruction. It is my intention that all the major solo-authored books specifically on religious instruction which I will write for the remainder of my life will be volumes in this series.

Every volume in the Explorations series will flow directly from my foundational trilogy on religious instruction and thus can be properly understood as direct extensions and developments of points I raised in that seminal trilogy–*The Shape of Religious Instruction*, *The Flow of Religious Instruction*, and *The Content of Religious Instruction*. The ongoing expansion of my basic trilogy can be readily seen in each of the three volumes on the sacrament of teaching because the final endnote at the end of every meditation supplies a reference to the place in one or another books in the trilogy in which the issues raised in that meditation are treated.

I have chosen *The Sacrament of Teaching* to lead off this Explorations series because I firmly believe that the success or failure of the religious instruction enterprise as a whole and in all of its parts is principally determined by the way in which religious educators enact their divine call. Unless religious educators wholeheartedly and at all times live out concretely the very high degree of instructional competence intrinsically necessitated by their divine vocation, religion teaching will never attain authentic effectiveness.

The purpose of this book—and the next two volumes which also deal with the sacrament of teaching—is to render significant assistance to religious educators in what should be their untiring quest for truly outstanding instructional competence in every phase of their teaching activity, regardless of whether this teaching activity takes place in formal or informal settings, or with persons of every age and circumstance. This book, and the next two, endeavor to help religious educators enhance their competence by focusing on the glorious vocation of the religious educator as the enactor of the sacrament of teaching. Unfortunately in the history of Christianity, the sublime vocation of the religious educator has seldom been accorded it rightful due by ecclesiastical officials or even by religious educators as one of the two central missions of the church as explicitly commanded by Jesus in The Great Commission (Mt 28:19–20). In our own era, the exalted vocation of the religious educator has all too often been trivialized and marginalized, as, for example, when some ecclesiastical officials claim that anyone, regardless of talent or preparation, can be a religious educator or when some religious educators themselves prefer not to be called religious educators but instead wish to be known by such trendy flavor-of-the-month but substantively meaningless titles as pastoral minister or pastoral associate. It is only when religious educators truly realize their glorious, divine vocation to superexcellently enact the sacrament of teaching, and it is only when religious educators consciously tap into the full practical import of their divine vocation, that the actual teaching of religion will attain that lofty degree of effectiveness which Jesus commanded in The Great Commission.

While each meditation in this book, and indeed in the entire three-volume work *The Sacrament of Teaching* can be read independently of the others, nonetheless there is a definite and cohesive flow in the whole series from chapter 1 in this book to the last chapter in the final volume. The first volume deals with the personal/professional qualities that religious educators must possess in order to *get ready* to enact the sacrament of teaching. The second volume of meditations deals with the heart of religious instruction, namely, what religious educators must actually do to *effectively enact* the sacrament of teaching. The concluding volume examines of those personal/professional qualities that religious educators must have to *seal and confirm* their enactment of the sacrament of teaching.

There is an additional cohesive flow embedded in the basic structure of this three-volume meditation series, namely, the flow of temporality. Chapter 1 of the three-volume series deals with the time when the religious educator first accepted the divine call within a call to enter into instructional ministry. The final chapter in the final book, chapter 100, deals with the death and subsequent divine judgment of the religious educator.

In the first volume of this series, there is a definite and deliberate flow. The book opens with God's first call within a call to a person to become one of his corps of elite, one of his religious educators. The book moves on to vision, that essential requirement which all religious educators must have prior to engaging in of even beginning to think about engaging in religious instruction activity. The next few chapters center on the development of those priorities and set of commitments as the rock-bottom conditions that all religious educators must meet before beginning religious instruction work. Following this come two chapters highlighting the sacramentality of the religious instruction act and therefore the sacredness of the place in which it occurs. After these chapters the book moves on to key ingredients which religious educators must acquire if they are going to optimally enact the sacrament of teaching. The book closes with a chapter bidding religious educators to become converted in their minds, hearts, and actions to placing themselves totally and with no reserve at the disposal of facilitating religious outcomes in learners.

The most useful way for a religious educator to use this book, as well as the two other volumes in this series, is to prayerfully meditate on each chapter for a day or more, depending on what each chapter has to say to that person in her concrete existential situation. The religious educator should consciously place the meditation in a framework of action. By this I mean that the purpose of each meditation is to help the person doing the meditation to more effectively enact the sacrament of teaching all along the line. The action thrust of each meditation can be activated in two ways. First, the religious educator takes one or more points in the meditation that hold special appeal for him and then develops a concrete plan of action to activate these points in his own religious instructional ministry. Second, the religious educator enacts the particular performance objective that concludes every meditation in this three-volume series. Both ways can be used separately or, better yet, in complementary fashion.

The performance objective that I place at the end of every meditation clearly highlights the action orientation of this series of volumes on the sacrament of teaching. All my books are action oriented, and this one is no exception. Most meditation books in various areas of religion merely present the author's ideas and dreams; only a few give concrete ways in which these ideas and dreams can be put into action. This is regrettable, because I have always believed that it is the responsibility of an author, like that of any educator, to provide the reader or other kind of learner with concrete guidelines on incarnating the material into action. The performance objective at the end of each meditation represents a tangible and specific plan of action for concretizing the main point or one of the main points in the meditation. Only through a performance objective of one kind or another can the meditation become truly actualized in our personal/professional lives. I should note that these performance objectives are often not objectives in the very important original Mager sense of that term. Rather, the performance objectives at the end of each meditation are action objectives in the more general meaning of the word "performance".

Each performance objective deals with concrete things that religious educators can do to improve instructional effectiveness here and now, as well as in their current or future ministry. Though volume 1 of the series deals with getting ready to enact the sacrament, the performance objectives presented in volume 1 are not be confined to things that the religious educator should do in remote preparation for enacting the sacrament, but also include specific things the religious educator should do now in order to get ready to successfully enact the sacrament the next time. Getting ready is part of teaching, not an activity truly separate from it.

In order to make the performance objective as pointed as possible in the professional life of religious educators, the personal pronoun "I" is used to highlight the religious educator's own here-and-now task to incarnate one of the main thrusts of the meditation. This use of the word "I" stands in marked contrast to the way in which this personal pronoun is used in the body of the meditation.

In the latter case, the word "I" is used to indicate my own personal involvement, concern, or viewpoint.

The second subtitle of each book in the three-volume work on the sacrament of teaching is *A Personal Testament*. For the first time in all my writings I have overtly and extensively incorporated into a book my own deeply personal commitments and heartistic way of looking at things. This in no way implies that the books in this three-volume work on the sacrament of teaching are nothing more than my personal perspective on religious instruction. Nothing would be further from the truth. Underneath the second subtitle of this book appear the words which will constitute the overarching ecological subtitle for all my future books in the Explorations series: *A Social Science Approach*. This last-mentioned subtitle is placed in uppercase on the title page clearly indicating that I am deliberately inserting my own personal testament into the overall boundaries and specific operations of the social science approach, as opposed to presenting some free-floating views.

The fact that this three-volume treatment of the sacrament of teaching is both a series of meditations and also a personal testament does not in any way make it a low-level kind of devotional and inspirational book that is grounded primarily in some well-meaning thoughts of the author. *The Sacrament of Teaching* is indeed intended to be inspirational, but in the sense of inspiring religious educators to become optimally competent in the discharge of their religious instruction activities. Far from being sweet nosegays or untethered O Altitudos offered to religious educators, this three-volume work provides fundamental and sometimes hard-hitting challenges to religious educators to significantly enhance their level of competence. And far from being just a pastiche of well-meaning, loosely connected thoughts on my part, this series of meditations has a definite systematic flow and is solidly rooted in the best available theory and research. Basically, this three-volume work offers religious educators a generalizable, generative, evaluative, and research-based scaffolding on which to place the personal/professional dimensions of their religious instruction activity. Thus these three books are research-based and theory-grounded social-scientific treatments of the teaching process clothed in the form of deeply personal meditations.

In order to heighten the personal dimension of this three-volume series on the sacrament of teaching, I have included in some chapters particular events from my life. I had not intended to do this when I was outlining the contours and substance of the book prior to writing it. However, the more I thought of how to inject the personal dimension into this series, the more I came to the conclusion that it was necessary to bring in some personal life events if the book was to be a genuine personal testament. Nonetheless I was very hesitant and extremely apprehensive about doing this, since it might seem to some that I was seeking ego gratification by writing the series in this manner. After considerable soul-searching, I eventually decided to introduce selected incidents from my life, always making sure that I present these personal life incidents and life outlooks in a fashion that enhances the reality and instructional usefulness of the chapters.

The words "religious instruction", which I use in this book and in my other writings, should not be misconstrued. I have chosen the word "instruction" deliberately because this word primarily implies the kind of teaching that is intentional, as contrasted to that type of teaching that just "happens", is purposeless, or is otherwise nonintentional. The term "instruction" secondarily implies the kind of teaching that is consciously enacted out of a theoretical and research base as contrasted to that kind of teaching which is done off the cuff and with no solid explanatory, predictive, or evidential foundation. The word "instruction" is in no way coterminous with any one or several specific teaching procedures, such as lecture or group discussion. "Instruction" is a term that includes every kind of teaching procedure. Furthermore, the word "instruction" in no way implies school-based teaching. Rather, "instruction" is a term which describes the intentional facilitation of learning in any and all kinds of milieux, whether formal or informal.

Even a cursory glimpse at this book and each of the next two volumes in this series The Sacrament of Teaching instantly reveals that the chapters are of uneven length–some are short while others are long. As I was writing this book I saw no practical usefulness in placing each and every meditation in the selfsame procrustean bed of length. I made the length of each meditation fit its topic. Meditations such as the one on vision or the one on commitment are short because they make a single powerful point whose forcefulness would be diminished by making it longer. On the other hand, the main point of meditations such as the one on religious experience or the one on talking versus doing is significantly enhanced by all the material in that meditation, material which expands, reinforces, and incarnates in a different but complementary manner the major focus of the meditation, important points in other meditations in the book, and the overall theme of book as a whole.

The main thrust of this book, and indeed of the entire three-volume series on the sacrament of teaching, is a combination of two major elements. The first major element consists of my own passionate beliefs on what the life of a Christian and the life of a divinely called religious educator ought to be—in short, the things I preeminently stand for. The second major element is that which empirical research and theoretical formulations have found to be the personal and professional requisites of an effective teacher. Some of the many pivotal points of both of these combined elements, which thoroughly infuse all parts of this book and the two ensuing volumes, include love as both the radiating center and all the spokes of the religious instruction apostolate, intense hard work, ego-abnegating sacrifice, giving everything we have, courage in the face of adversity, unquenchable desire, constant striving to do the very best, unremitting attention to detail, reliance on solid research and theory rather than gimmickry or trendiness, red hot religion, persistence, and becoming a victim soul.

Throughout this book I have endeavored to use inclusive language. In those comparatively rare cases where such language would render the prose awkward and detract from its clarity, I eschewed such linguistically clumsy expressions as his/her or s/he, and instead alternated between the masculine pronoun and the feminine pronoun.

The seeds for this book were first sown in 1966, when I became director of the Graduate Religious Education Program at the

University of Notre Dame. At that time I decided to write a book like this and slowly began to accumulate notes. But the press of administrative and teaching duties, plus the great amount of time I spent writing my foundational trilogy in religious instruction, forced me to place this book of meditations on the back burner, though I continued to gather information and make notes in preparation for the time when I would be able to write it. I had hoped to write it at comparative leisure in a warm, humanistic Continental ambiance during my 1983–1984 sabbatical year in Rome—when the weather was cold writing in the historic and old-worldish Caffè Greco on the via Condotti while reflectively sipping espresso, and when the weather grew warmer, writing at an outdoor table at the Tre Scalini on the Piazza Navona as I would meditate while enjoying a dish of wonderful tartufo ice cream. But unfortunately I was not at all able to work on the book during that sabbatical year because all my time was consumed in finishing *The Content of Religious Instruction*, the final volume of my foundational trilogy. When I returned to Birmingham, all my time went to performing an ever expanding set of service duties at the University of Alabama at Birmingham where I teach, writing lengthy scholarly chapters in books whose editors could not find anyone else competent to write these chapters, and doing work in my capacity of publisher of Religious Education Press. In late spring 1994 I came to realize that I could no longer delay writing the meditation book and therefore decided to devote my full scholarly attention to it. Though my original goal all those years from 1966 until then was to write a two-hundred-page book, it soon became evident after I had finished five or six chapters that the book would be longer than I had initially projected. By the fall 1997 the manuscript had reached over seven-hundred pages. I decided at that point to divide what I had originally planned as one short meditation book into three somewhat lengthy volumes.

As in the case with every book or article I have ever written, I do all my research totally by myself. I never have had a research assistant or anyone else who does research for me. I believe that true scholarship is best served when scholars do their own research. Students, however able they might otherwise be, are still students;

research assistants, for all their talent, are still research assistants. In neither case do these persons have the breadth of experience or the requisite level of scholarly competence to engage in that kind of rigorous high-level research required of a first-class scholarly book. Additionally, I have made quite a few serendipitous but very important research discoveries over the years just by looking at the books in the library shelves surrounding the volume for which I was searching, which never would have happened if another person were doing my research for me. My respect for an author who claims to be a scholar is diminished when I find out that this individual made use of a student or research assistant to do the work that the author should have been doing.

Although the preponderance of this book was written in Birmingham, some other chapters or parts of these chapters were written in different localities. Wherever I go anywhere, for whatever reason I go anywhere, I am always on the job in one way or another; I am never ever on vacation from the religious instruction apostolate. In June 1994 I began outlining the book (which at that time was going to be one volume) while on my knees in The Church of Our Lady Before Týn, a haunting medieval edifice whose unforgettable eerie-looking twin spires brood over the Old Town of Prague. I deliberately chose the Týn Church in which to commence my book on the sacrament of teaching because this church was the scene of bitter fighting between Protestants and Catholics in the early modern period. Possibly the most searing example of this acrimonious intra-Christian strife was the affair of the gilded chalice. Around the middle of the fifteenth century King Jiří of Poděbrad had a gilded chalice, the symbol of the Hussites, majestically displayed high on the front gable of the Týn Church between the two towers. When the Hussites were defeated by the Catholic Habsburgs in 1620, the chalice was removed and replaced by a statue of the Madonna. As the crowning insult, the Hussite chalice was melted down and made into the Madonna's shimmering halo, where it remains today. My own writings, and indeed the totality of my professional religious instruction activities, have always stressed deep collaboration and collegueship among Catholic and Protestant religious educationists and educators. By beginning this book in a church that was for so long a deeply acrimonious source of contention between Protestants and Catholics I hoped that in some small way I would make reparation for the sins of the past, help point the way to greater cooperation and understanding among all the various types of Christian faith groups, and write a book that would assist religious educators from all sorts of Christian confessions to more successfully teach their learners to love and serve God better.

After a while, I arose and strolled to the nearby Old Town Square. I walked across the square and sat down on the grass on the opposite side. The plaza was dominated in the center by the powerful monument to Jan Hus. At some distance to the rear and sides of this large and imposing Secessionist-style statue were a group of very lovely historic buildings surrounding Old Town Square, one of the most dazzling and impressive town squares in all of Europe. In this wonderful setting I continued to outline the book. I developed the outline further in various cities, towns, and churches in the Czech Republic, notably in the wonderful old town of Český Krumlov, where I sat at an outdoor café for a full afternoon in the little jewel of a town square reworking and refining the outline of the book.

It was on the sacred Greek island of Delos that I penned the beginnings of the chapter on Socrates, whose trial began just as the holy ship bearing the annual thanksgiving offering to the shrine of Apollo on Delos was being prepared to sail from Athens to the sacred isle. A few other chapters were outlined and partially written in locales as diverse at the Greek island of Mykonos, the University of Oxford, and an outdoor dockside café overlooking fishing boats at Tarpon Springs, Florida. The chapter on Thomas More holds special memories for me because I wrote this chapter haltingly and slowly and in great anguish as I sat by the bedside of my dying mother for a couple of months. When my mother breathed her last just at sunset on September 25, 1994, it was a crushing blow to me, one that took me two full years to recover from. She was, and still is, the most influential force in my life personally, professionally, and most importantly, religiously. My mother was the most brilliant woman I have ever met, and she was by far the most hardworking individual I have ever encountered. I have never experienced anyone who could even come close to matching her uncompromising standards for excellence in life and in work. She was considered saintly by persons who knew her; I always knew her in this way. Everything worthwhile that I have ever done in my entire life is in a true sense just a footnote to her. Her love for the church and for me was incredibly great, so great in fact that it went far beyond what is reasonable—but she did it all for love, and true love is always unreasonable. At the inside of the entrance to my *auctorium* (the small booklined teakwood room where I write my books) hangs the crucifix that rested next to her head at the casket during her wake. Every day, when I enter and leave the *auctorium,* I pause for a little while by this crucifix and ask my mother, who to me is still as alive and as real now as she was when she walked this earth, to pray for her son and for the success of his apostolic work in the field of religious instruction.

I wrote this three-volume series on the sacrament of teaching for religious educators. But there is also a sense in which I also wrote this three-volume series as the soul of my own special legacy for my three sons, now in their teenage years. When they are grown and when, with the ripening of age, they come to understand things in a deeper light, I would like them to know what their father essentially stood for, what motivated his life, and how he tried to live his life.

Many persons were responsible for helping me with this book. The staff of the University of Alabama at Birmingham library was always on hand to lend me assistance. Especially noteworthy in this regard is Eddie Luster, the interlibrary loan officer whose cheerful demeanor was as ever present as his efficiency. I could never have gotten all the various books which I consulted if it were not for Eddie Luster at the interlibrary loan desk. Clint Bruess, the dean of School of Education at UAB, voluntarily with absolutely no strings attached encouraged me to get a computer (supplied by UAB) and write my books on it. This generous act brought me into a new era of writing, and I am grateful to him for his suggestion. I have been very fortunate to have served at UAB under the three finest department chairs I have ever had: Clay Sheffield, a ruggedly virile prototypical Southern gentleman; James S. Davidson III, a

Domer and one of the two most inherently fair and decent persons I have ever met anywhere; and Boyd Rogan, a courtly, beaming, and exquisitely diplomatic person. What united each of these three very different kind of men was a common philosophy of educational leadership, namely, that the central task of an educational administrator is primarily to do everything possible to enable faculty members to do their work. All three department chairs were fine examples of servant leadership, and all three did so many things in so many ways over the years to make it easier for me to do my research.

Authors often write in their prefaces that they stole time from their spouses and children to work on the book. I do not know how much of this is a cliché, how much is an exaggeration, or how much is actually true. In my case, it is more than true. Not just with this book but in all my scholarly endeavors in the apostolate over these last twenty two years since our marriage, I have more than robbed my wife Marlene and then my three sons of a considerable amount of my physical presence with them. Some individuals would say, and rightfully so, that I was unreasonable in the time I spent on the apostolate. I hope that Marlene and my three sons will understand. I hope that they realize that by giving me the time to spend on apostolic duties—time spent away from them—they were being genuine partners in my apostolic labors since it was their sacrifice that enabled me to devote more time to the Lord in the apostolate. To these four, my silent and real partners, I offer the chalice of my undying gratitude. I beg the Lord to forgive me for the time I was not physically with them. But I am comforted by the fact (or more accurately by the hope) that the Lord and they will realize that I had to be about the Father's business.

Prefaces are typically written when an author finishes writing a book. It is Holy Thursday as I compose the final lines of this first volume on the sacrament of teaching. Though it is sheer coincidence that I am completing this book on the anniversary of the establishment of the *sacramentum sacramentorum*, still I find it eminently fitting and possibly even providential that I am finishing this book on such a wellspring day in the Christian calendar. As the Eucharist is the primordial sacrament through which all other sacraments are enlivened and fulfilled, so too I hope that the substantive and structural contents of this book on the sacrament of teaching will have a share in their own special way in the all-giving sacrament of sacraments. As the foundational sacrament of the Eucharist is Jesus the salvific reality, so too I hope that this book on the sacrament of teaching will assist religious educators to help bring learners into a deep personal contact with Jesus the *Ursakrament* who religiously educates and saves us all. And as the fountainhead sacrament of the Eucharist has for two millennia bodied forth through time the flesh and blood of the preeminent suffering and dying servant of God, so too I hope that this book on the sacrament of teaching will show religious educators that unless they suffer much for learners and die to their egos, they will not be effective enactors of the sacrament of teaching.

Just as I finished the preceding sentence, my second son, Michael F. X., walked into the *auctorium* and asked me what I thought was a surprising question: "Dad, if you were able to go to only one Mass all year, what would that be?" Responding instantly from the heart, and without thinking, I responded: "The Mass of Holy Thursday." When my son left, I reflected on what I had said. Shouldn't I have responded "Easter," since this is the great day of the Lord's Resurrection? Or shouldn't I have answered "the Ascension" since this is the great feast of religious instruction, the day in which Jesus gave The Great Commission to teach all nations? But as I thought about this and tapped into my affects, I realized that my answer to Mikey was, for me, the right response. Holy Thursday has always been for me the most precious of all days—and evenings—in the Christian calendar. As I see it, the Eucharist that Jesus instituted that Maundy Thursday night almost two thousand years ago makes every new day an Easter day and makes every new day a Great Commission.

In just a couple of hours I will partake of the Eucharist during the annual Holy Thursday liturgy. As I do so, I will pray that this book, and also the next two volumes in my trilogy on the sacrament of teaching, will help each and every religious educator to enact this glorious sacrament in a manner worthy both of its inherent grandeur and of its potential efficacy in facilitating robust holistic religious outcomes in learners.

Birmingham, Alabama   *James Michael Lee*
Feast of the Institution of
The Sacrament, 1998

The First Call

From the limitless bounds of endless eternity we have been called. From the mists of time beyond all time we have been called.

From the ages before all ages we have been called. From the nowness of the now we have been called.

From the farthest reaches of sidereal space we have been called. From the inmost recesses of our whole being we have been called.

From out of the whirlwind we have been called. From all things and all persons we encounter we have been called.

Through all and in all we have been called.

God has called each one of us to be eternally present with him. To be eternally present with him is to do his will as he wishes his will to be done. It is up to us to accept God's call to accomplish his will here on earth. It is up to us to live the call. It is up to us to nourish the call.

All Christians have been called by God to be with him in a matchless manner now and for all eternity. All Christians have been called to live unto God in an enriched way and to serve him with all their hearts. All Christians have been called to lead grace-filled lives and to radiate this grace to all reality—to persons, to animals, to plants, to the mountains, to the seas, to the stars. This is the call God has given to each and every Christian.

In addition to this general call to be a Christian, some persons have been given a special call to be religious educators in the formal sense of the term. This call to be religious educators is a call within a call.

The call within a call shares fully in all the properties of the general call. But additionally and more importantly, the call within a call is a privileged divine invitation to devote one's whole consciousness and entire efforts to being a particular channel of God's grace. This channel consists in effectively teaching others how and why to walk with the Lord every day of their lives.

By giving us the call within a call, God has thrust his hands through the pages of history and says, "It's here, it's you!" By giving us the call within a call, God touches our whole being and says, "I want you to be one of my religious educators."

If the general call requires us to think, the call within a call requires us to think more deeply. If the general call requires us to love, the call within a call requires us to love more truly. If the general call requires us to serve, the call within a call requires us to serve more completely. If the general call requires us to work, the call within a call requires us to work more vigorously.

The call within a call to be a religious educator is one of the two highest Christian vocations because it existentially imitates the personal vocation of Jesus himself. Jesus' own vocation on earth was twofold: to save and to teach. He was a savior who also religiously educated, and he was a religious educator who also saved. Everything he did was directly geared to his twin goal of saving and teaching. The gospels are very clear on this point.

More than a thousand years before the birth of Jesus, a boy named Samuel received a call within a call to be a religious educator in the prophetic mode. Samuel's highly existential answer to the call within a call is a splendid model for our own response to God's call within a call to us. Samuel replied, "I am here!" This answer has two deeply interconnected dimensions. First, "*I* am here!" I, the complete I, the total I, the I without reserve. Second, "I am *here!*" Right here, right now, right here-and-now as I am in my present concrete situation and not in some fantasy land.

The call within a call is a vocation to donate ourselves totally and unconditionally to Jesus, for Jesus, in Jesus through the competent exercise of religious instruction ministry. In this exalted vocation there is no holding back. In this glorious vocation there is no looking for any direct or indirect reward for ourselves. In this magnificent vocation, our eyes are always fixed on Jesus as he is in himself and as he incarnated in the religious instruction task.

The vocation of religious educator is an especially intense act of religion. It is an act of deep and tireless and complete devotion. More than almost any other vocation, it involves a selfless giving of one's total life to the service of the Lord.

The vocation of religious educator is a twenty-four hour a day apostolate. Our vocation as religious educator means that we are always on call. We have a call to always be on call.

The vocation of religious educator is not essentially a sentimental or romantic sort of thing, though at times sentimentality and romanticism might be attached to it for some individuals. The vocation of religious educator is not living in some seventh heaven but rather living for a concrete task to be accomplished, the task of serving others by effectively facilitating religious learning outcomes. The vocation of religious educator is not for the dreamy, not for the scatterbrained, not for Don Quixote types. It is for persons who are eager and willing to engage in all the difficult, nitty gritty, and sometimes unpleasant aspects of teaching so that the guiding vision of helping people to follow Jesus more nearly can be successfully realized.

How faithful are we to our divine vocation of religious educator? Do we thank God every day and throughout the day for his supreme grace in calling us to be religious educators? How much do we treasure our divine vocation as a pearl of infinite price?

Do we pray often—not just meditative prayer but also prayer of the heart and prayer of deeds? Other than on Sunday, how much time do we spend each day participating in liturgy or in other forms of worship?

Are we head over heels in love with our religious education vocation? Are we completely and unreservedly in love with every dimension of religious instruction activity, large and small, pleasant and unpleasant?

Do we squander the magnificent gift of God's call within a call, or do we work unremittingly to nourish it with all the energy at our disposal? To what extent are we complacent in the greatness of our divine vocation or do we know in our minds and feel in our hearts that the magnificence of this vocation must be accompanied by total devotion and unremittingly hard work on our part?

Are we always on call whenever or wherever we are needed to do religious education instruction work? How often do we try to avoid or shirk the nitty-gritty aspects of the religious instruction task in favor of its more glamorous and recognition-filled dimensions?

To what extent do we cultivate our divine vocation by engaging in appropriate growth activities such as daily professional reading, or do we think we know enough? To what extent do we frequently engage in those professional skill-building activities that maintain and improve our instructional competencies, or do we just stand pat in the belief that our teaching is pretty good?

Performance Objective: Every day, immediately upon rising, I will thank God from the deepest region of my heart for having graced me with the call within a call to be one of his religious educators. I will immediately follow this prayer of thanksgiving by consecrating myself anew to the Lord's privileged service as a religious educator. I will then solemnly pledge to be with my call within a call throughout the day—to think often about it, to feel it frequently in the depths of my being, and to live it in everything I do, whether large or small.

2

Vision

I have always been drawn to stone quarries, probably because I greatly enjoy seeing the many and varied possibilities inherent in all reality, especially when the possibilities are not readily apparent. The great temples of antiquity, the magnificent cathedrals of the Middle Ages, the splendid modern buildings of the preconcrete era—all these had their beginnings and still maintain their ontic roots in stone quarries. As I wander around stone quarries, I am always dazzled at the possibilities and potentialities that lie silently and almost inertly there. The marvel of a marble sculpture, the poignance of a granite tombstone, the loveliness of a splendid building's limestone facing are, from one perspective, already present within the quarry.

I remember one early summer day many years ago. It was during my bachelor years, when I had time and money to travel often to Europe. Each summer I would bring about forty books with me from the United States so I could do serious professional reading while relaxing on the beach or after a day of intense cultural sight-seeing. On that particular day I was relaxing and reading on the beach at the Italian seaside resort of Viarregio. All of a sudden I got the urge to visit the nearby town of Carrara, the site of what is probably the world's most famous marble quarries. Its fame derives from the fact that Carrara marble has a seemingly immaculate white color with unequaled texture and purity. Only the great marble quarries at Paros in the southern Cyclades archipelago in what is now Greece can match the quality of Carrara marble. It was to Carrara that Michelangelo Buonarroti would come to personally select with extraordinarily exacting discrimination those marble blocks he would use in his sculptures. (Among modern sculptors who have visited the Carrara quarries to choose their marble was Henry Moore.) For Michelangelo, as for any great sculptor, the purity, texture, and luster of marble is a silent partner in producing the finished statue of great beauty and power. Echoing Aristotle and Thomas Aquinas, Michelangelo went as far as to assert that the form of the eventual statue already exists in the block of marble. The task of the sculptor is to release the form already dwelling within the marble—to bring potency to act, in philosophical terminology.

There is a tale told of a man who once visited a quarry. As he walked around, he came upon a worker cutting stone.

"What are you doing?" asked the visitor.

"I'm cutting stone." responded the worker.

The visitor continued his tour of the quarry. After a little while he happened upon a second worker cutting stone.

"What are you doing?" inquired the visitor.

"I'm making ten dollars an hour," replied the worker.

The visitor watched the worker for a while and then meandered down one of the paths in the quarry. Sometime later he saw another worker cutting stone.

"What are you doing?" asked the visitor.

"I'm building a cathedral," responded the worker.

The first two stonecutters saw their work solely in terms of immediacy. The third worker had vision. He saw his work in terms of its long-term consequences.

Vision is so essential for us religious educators. It helps us to perform our religious instruction apostolate with optimum effectiveness. And it helps us to avoid many of the problems and pitfalls that are an intrinsic part of our work.

Vision transforms and elevates ordinary tasks into tasks of great worth and significance. Viewed from the perspective of its long-term consequences, every religious instruction task, no matter how small or seemingly insignificant, has the power to become a mighty force in the learner's life over the long haul.

Vision gives meaning to our religious instruction work. The nitty-gritty, grinding tasks that necessarily form a major part of our work as religious educators are charged with meaning when seen in the light of vision, when viewed from the perspective of their long-term consequences.

Vision urges us to perform our tasks in the best manner possible because vision organically links what we are doing right now with what will occur in the long run as a consequence of what we are doing right now. When we religious educators do things with vision, we thereby will automatically be drawn as if by a powerful magnet to instinctively eschew every kind of low quality work.

Vision prevents burnout in the religious educator. I have never met a religious educator experience burnout who habitually does things in the light of abiding vision. In every single instance, the burned-out religious educators whom I have met either had little or no vision of their apostolate or somehow lost it along the line.

Vision is an intrinsic and organic dimension of our call within a call as religious educators. It is almost impossible to adequately fulfill our divine mission as religious educators without being constantly guided and illumined by vision.

How much vision do we religious educators possess in terms of our apostolate as a whole and in terms of each and every task tied in with our apostolate?

What is our vision of the religious instruction apostolate? Have we clearly enunciated this vision? How frequently throughout the day do we bring this vision to the forefront of our consciousness?

What is our vision of our role as religious educators?

To what extent are our eyes always fixed on the long-term consequences of all our activities in religious instruction?

To what degree do we make sure that vision thoroughly interpenetrates everything we do in religious instruction?

Without abiding vision, we will perish as religious educators, and our religious instruction work will perish along with us.

Performance Objective: Before the week is out, I will sit down and write a statement of my vision for religious instruction. I will then make two attractive copies of this vision statement, posting one copy in a prominent spot in my workplace and putting the other one in a conspicuous place in my home. Whenever I look at my vision statement, I will examine myself to ascertain the extent to which my religious instruction activities are in fact faithful to my vision statement. Every six months I will sit down again, review the vision statement, and revise it if necessary.

3

Priorities

For about two and a half millennia, the prototype of the thoughtful, concerned, in-depth educator has been Socrates. He was born around 469 B.C., the son of Sophroniscus the stonemason and Phaenarete who was a midwife. During the Peloponnesian War he served as an infantryman. He married when he was about fifty and had three sons. His wife Xanthippe was an acid-tongued termagant who had no sympathy or understanding for Socrates' supreme mission as a moral and religious educator, a man whose highest priority was to help others attain virtue through philosophical activity. Even to this day Xanthippe is regarded as the prototype of a nonunderstanding and shrewish wife.

Plato called Socrates "the best man of his time, in our opinion, that we have ever come across, and, in general, the wisest and the most just."

Socrates taught anyone who wished to learn. He was ever and always the teacher to all sorts of persons in all sorts of circumstances. As far as we can tell, he was engaged in the teaching task at every possible moment regardless of whether the pedagogical opportunity was immediately at hand or whether it could be brought into existence by his skillful instructional midwifery. His learners included poets, politicians, artisans, and especially young men from families both rich and poor. He was an untiring and outspoken opponent of any kind of teaching that was aimed primarily at ideological ends or was done primarily for financial or political advantage.

His teaching technique consisted of higher-order questioning carefully architected to assist his learners in exploring the ultimate basis and truly practical consequences of human conduct. Such probing, in-depth questioning necessarily included an open and searching examination of the foundations of the religious beliefs and practices of the day. This kind of rigorous inquiry, together with his open contempt of the lifestyle pretense and shoddy thinking with which so many high-ranking leaders cloaked themselves, brought him quite a few religious and political enemies, whose self-pride and self-justification he had offended. His enemies eventually brought him to court on two very serious charges, namely, heresy and corrupting learners by teaching them to honestly confront the bases and operations of their religious and political beliefs. An Athenian court condemned him to death. Rejecting pleas from his friends to let them bribe his jailers so he could escape to Thessaly, he drank the poison hemlock and died in 399 B.C.

To philosophers, theologians, and historians, Socrates is revered as the Western world's first great philosopher. To educated non-philosophers and even reasonably informed persons in the street, Socrates is remembered for such seminal and insightful statements as "Know yourself," "No evil can happen to a good person," and "A person should not think primarily in terms of living and dying but only of right and wrong."

Socrates considered himself as primarily a moral and religious educator. His instructional goal was practical in the foundational sense, namely, to teach persons what is for them the greatest good of all: the ultimate basis, nature, activities, and consequences of human conduct and virtue. Socrates endeavored to achieve this kind of practical instructional goal by teaching learners to engage in continuous and rigorous self-examination throughout their lives. "The unexamined life," declared Socrates, "is not worth living."

What made Socrates tick? What was his basic motivation for devoting his life so fully and so completely to being a moral and religious educator? Socrates is very clear about this. Over and over again he declared that he considered himself to be the direct recipient of a once and continuing call from God (or, more properly, the gods) to be a teacher—not just a teacher in general but a teacher who strives to touch the depth of human souls. Socrates uncompromisingly asserted that it was God who directly ordered him to be an educator, and as such he and his work constitute a priceless gift given by God both to individuals and to the state. As a religious man in the ancient Athenian sense of that word, Socrates was firmly convinced that he must continuously obey God's call to be an untiring moral and religious educator of the finest, deepest, and most skillful kind.

Socrates stated that the concrete and persuasive empirical proof of his divine mission as a moral and religious educator was to be found not just in what he said but far more importantly in what he did in terms of fulfilling his vocation. Socrates consciously and deliberately subordinated his personal concerns, including at the very end the continuance of his own life, to the divine call. So faithful was he to the call that he constantly placed the demands of his teaching vocation ahead of his family, his personal interests, his financial security—in short, ahead of everything. This was the divine voice that Socrates told us keeps murmuring in his ears, to place his teaching mission before all else. At various times throughout his career, he implied that other persons with a divine call to be moral and religious educators should do likewise. Socrates' own divine call to be a moral and religious educator determined his priorities.

As religious educators, we have been called by God. What are our priorities in life? Do we, like Socrates, manifest the strong tendency to place our divine call above all our other priorities? Can we honestly tell God and ourselves that we are being faithful to our divine call if, as a general rule, we put our own personal, social, and financial interests ahead of the concrete, practical, everyday demands of our religious instruction vocation?

There are times in our lives when family and personal matters are so truly momentous or calamitous that it is absolutely necessary for us to give immediate pride of place to these extraordinarily grave concerns—the imminent death of a parent, a child who has just got into very deep trouble, loss of house and property due to a violent storm, and so on. But these momentous or calamitous events are clearly the exceptions to the general rule that by virtue of our call within a call to be religious educators, we have to make our religious instruction apostolate our topmost priority.

The characteristically consistent subordination of our priorities to the divine call is very difficult at times. But it is the price we must pay if we are going to carry out our divine vocation, if we are going to be faithful to God's call within a call. By granting each of us the glorious call to be religious educators, God has extended to us one of his greatest gifts. Only by giving God the regular subordination of all our other priorities to the exigencies of religious instruction work can we say that we are in resonance with the divine call.

The regular subordination of personal interests to the religious instruction apostolate does not mean that we religious educators grossly neglect either our family or important personal matters. Priority is not exclusivity. Giving priority to the religious instruction apostolate means that we religious educators place our divine call within a call at the top rung of the rest of their priorities. This is what it means to have a divine vocation. The other rungs are still there and need to be attended to appropriately.

One of the greatest gifts that we religious educators can give to our families is to place our instructional mission at the top of our priorities because this very act of giving priority to the apostolate will be an especially powerful lesson to our family members of the supreme importance of religion in our own lives. And it well may be that the our concrete modeling of great dedication to our religious mission will teach and inspire other family members to themselves become a part of our apostolate, or at least to motivate them to put God first in their own lives. In such situations, the whole family will grow closer together in God because we religious educators have deliberately placed our call within a call at the topmost rung of our priorities.

In discoursing about the proper ordering of priorities for a moral and religious educator, Socrates told us to look at his own vocational deeds rather than just to his words about his vocation. It is easy, and in a sense glib, for us present-day religious educators to assert: "Oh yes, I will put my divine call as a religious educator ahead of all my other priorities." But do we in point of fact, in the here-and-now concrete order, place our religious instruction priorities first? If, for example, a conflict arises between nonemergency family interests and an important religious instruction exigency, which priority do we consistently choose? We rightfully expect obstetricians to get out of bed in the middle of the night to deliver the baby of one of their patients. Can we religious educators, whose ministry consists not only in the care of the body but more essentially in the care of souls, be less heedful of our call? In the beginning, middle, and end, it is our divine call within a call, and the thoroughgoing professionalism in which this call is clothed, that must dictate our priorities in large matters as well as in small ones.

Performance Objective: Whenever a conflict arises between my own personal interests and desires on the one hand and the demands of my religious instruction apostolate on the other hand, I will resolutely act in each and every case to give my priority to the apostolate unless the matter involves a serious personal emergency or constitutes grave neglect to my family.

4

Giving Everything We Have

In a far-off land a very long time ago, when history wore a rose, there lived a king who had three sons. They were fine boys and the king was exceedingly pleased at the thought that the young princes would someday rule the kingdom wisely and well.

When his sons had grown into their early twenties, the king decided to send them to distant countries so that they would bring back to the realm hearts and minds filled with fresh new ways of looking at things. Each son, he decided, would stay in a different country for two years before returning home.

The two years sped by swiftly, and before long the three young princes returned home. Overjoyed at having his sons with him once again, the king threw a lavish banquet in their honor. All the courtiers were present to publicly join with the king in welcoming home the three young men.

Toward the end of the banquet, the king asked his sons to tell him and all the assembled guests what they had learned from their two-year sojourn in the distant lands.

The first son rose from his seat and told of the many new sights and sounds he had encountered. As he was about to conclude his story, he drew out from his robe a clear round glass that was given to him by a wizard in the land he had visited. This, he told his father and the guests, was a magic glass. By looking deeply into it, one could see anything that was happening anywhere in the world.

The second son also recounted the marvelous things he had learned from his two years in the foreign land. As he was about to end his story, he picked up from the floor next to where he stood a

14

beautiful, intricately woven carpet that had been given to him by a shaman in the country where he had sojourned. This, he explained excitedly, was a magic carpet, and was capable of transporting whomever sat on it to domains far and near.

It was now the youngest son's turn. Like his brothers, he told of the inestimable treasures of heart and mind that he had acquired from his stay in the foreign land. As he was about to conclude, he drew from the fold in his garment nearest his heart a pomegranate that had been given to him by an old priest in that distant country. This pomegranate, he explained, was a magic fruit. Whoever ate it, no matter how near death, would be instantly healed.

After the banquet had ended and the last guest had bade farewell, the king invited his three beloved sons to join him in his private chambers. When they arrived there, the king said to his eldest son: "Look into your magic glass and tell us what you see."

The eldest son looked into his magic glass. There he beheld a beautiful and innocent-looking princess playing the lyre in a land beyond the sea. Excitedly he beckoned to his two younger brothers to look into the magic glass with him.

"She seems so lovely, so pure, so fresh," exclaimed the second son. "We must see her in person. Let us get on my magic carpet and we will surely be in her presence right away."

And so they all got on the magic carpet, and in less than an instant they were in the presence of the princess.

So captivated were they by the beautiful and innocent-looking princess that before they realized it a month had passed. By that time each of the young men had fallen deeply in love.

Fate so often seems to decree that there is a dark and hidden side to every rapturous reality. And so it came to pass that the princess told the three young men that she was suffering from an incurable illness and would die in three weeks.

At hearing this, the youngest prince pulled out the magic pomegranate from the place in his garment closest to his heart. "Eat all of this, fair princess, and you will be cured." The princess ate the pomegranate and felt instantly better. Shortly afterward the court physicians proclaimed the wonder of wonders—the princess was completely and wholly cured.

A week later, when the three young men were all together with the princess in an especially lovely part of the palace garden, the eldest son asked for her hand in marriage. "You are a wonderful prince," she replied, "and I am deeply honored by your expression of love. But my heart belongs to another." Saddened by the princess's reply, the young man stepped away.

The second son approached the beautiful princess and asked her to marry him. "You are a splendid person with a great many magnificent hopes and talents. But I must decline your offer because my heart belongs to another." So like his older brother, he stepped away.

The third son approached the lovely princess and gently asked if she would marry him. "Yes", replied the princess, "because my heart belongs to you." The young prince was overjoyed.

But his two older brothers were sorely vexed by the princess's choice. The eldest spoke first. "What does my youngest brother have that I lack? After all, if it were not for my magic glass, you never would have seen us and you never would have been cured of your fatal illness. Surely this should find great favor in your eyes."

It was now the second brother's turn to speak. "What does my younger brother have that I lack? After all, if it were not for my magic carpet, we never would have been able to come to you."

The princess nodded in a soft and understanding way to each of the two young men. "I am very fond of you both," she said, "and I am deeply grateful to you. And I always will have a very special place in my heart for each of you."

"But let me answer your questions very directly. The oldest brother did me a magnificent favor, and without him I would not have been in a position to be healed. But he still has his magic glass."

"And the middle brother also performed an inestimable service because he helped make it possible for me to be cured. But he still has his magic carpet."

"The youngest brother no longer has his magic pomegranate. He gave me everything he had."

So too it is with religious educators. Only when we religious educators give everything we have to the religious instruction apostolate will we be truly the religious educator God has called us to be. Everything we have—body, mind, heart, conduct, lifestyle, all in one harmonious emptying of ourselves into religious instruction work. We cannot, we must not, we dare not hold back anything.

Part and parcel of our call within a call to be religious educators is the complete giving of ourselves to each and every demand of the religious instruction apostolate. Are we faithful to this essential aspect of our call?

To what extent do we give everything we are and everything we have to each and every facet of our religious instruction apostolate?

Do we hold back, even if only a little, from giving everything we are and everything we have to our religious instruction activities?

Do we even want to give our complete selves without any reserve to the grinding demands of the religious instruction apostolate?

To what degree do we spur ourselves onward when we detect even the slightest flagging of our desire to give ourselves totally to each and every aspect of religious education ministry?

Do we realize in our mind and do we feel in our gut that the measure of our success as religious educators is directly proportional to the degree to which we give everything we are and everything we have to our call within a call?

Performance Objective: Each day I will resolve not to hold anything back, large or small, in mind or in heart or in overt action, but rather to empty myself completely in everything I do in the religious instruction apostolate. During the day I will periodically examine myself to ascertain whether I am indeed giving everything I have or am holding back, even a little. If I find that I am not giving everything I have, I will make sure that the next time I will indeed pour myself out totally on behalf of the religious instruction apostolate in all its phases and faces.

5

Commitment

All-out war between China and Japan began on July 7, 1937, when the Japanese precipitated an incident at Lukouchiao on the outskirts of Peiping (now Beijing) in northern China. Over the next eighteen months the imperial Japanese military forces swept southward and successively conquered Kiangsu, Shanghai, Nanking, Hangchow, Swatow, Sancian, Canton, and Hong Kong.

Over the centuries Christian missionaries from Europe and the United States had traveled to China in an effort to teach the Christian religion to the inhabitants. During the first third of the twentieth century these missionary activities intensified, and many thousands of missioners toiled fruitfully in this vineyard of the Lord. A goodly number of Chinese men and women were converted to Christianity. Often they were exemplary converts whose deep devotion to God was a source of great satisfaction and edification to the missionaries.

In the late 1930s the United States was still at peace with Japan, and so American missioners were able to continue their apostolic activities in China. Their efforts were made considerably more difficult because they sometimes had to work in an environment in which bombs rained down from the sky and fierce battles took place on the ground between Chinese and Japanese troops.

American war correspondents were also in China to cover the Sino-Japanese military conflict and report their stories back home. It was only natural that these war correspondents came upon Christian missionaries at work.

One day a seasoned war correspondent arrived at a medical clinic operated and staffed by a group of Catholic nuns. The correspondent had seen battles around the world and the sufferings of countless human beings. As a result he was gristled and hardboiled and pretty much used to everything, no matter how shocking. He walked into the crude ramshackle building that housed the clinic. On one side of the clinic he saw a nun. She was a thin young woman, almost fragile. Many of the wounded patients were in severe pain and crying out to her for help.

At that moment the nun was tenderly and lovingly washing the sores of a badly wounded Chinese soldier. His gangrenous leg was oozing with vile-looking pus and blood. It was a sight that sickened even the calloused correspondent. He turned away in horror and revulsion.

When he regained his composure, he said to the nun, "I wouldn't do that for a million dollars."

Without pausing in her work, the nun looked up at the correspondent, smiled softly, and replied, "Neither would I."

This nun was totally committed to her profession of physical healing, a profession in which she encountered God by gladly answering her own call within a call. To what extent are we religious educators committed to our profession, to our call within a call? Totally? Partially?

Are we committed, in the final analysis, primarily to our own selves in religious instruction ministry? Or are we unreservedly and completely committed to the wholehearted service of learners, no matter how difficult, grinding, or even at times revulsive this service might be?

It is easy to say, "Yes, I am totally committed to religious instruction work." But talk is not commitment. More than anything else, commitment is dedication and willing, competent action in the concrete here and now. How do we religious educators stack up against this standard of commitment?

It is easy to be committed to the "big" things, to the glamorous features of the religious instruction apostolate. The test of the totality and intensity of our commitment comes in our willingness to gladly engage in all the difficult, nitty-gritty, unappealing, and unsung aspects of teaching religion to others.

How fully do we realize that the strength of commitment is truly wondrous and can surmount virtually every obstacle?

To what extent does our commitment to religious instruction measure up to the nun's commitment to her apostolate? And what are we going to do about the level and intensity and constancy of our commitment to religious instruction ministry? Here? Now? In the concrete?

Performance Objective: Today I will write a letter to Jesus promising him that I will commit myself to do the very best as a religious educator. Every Sunday evening I will reread this letter and ask Jesus if he thinks I am totally and unreservedly committed to the religious instruction apostolate in everything I do, whether large or small, whether visible or hidden.

6

A Holy Act

Many world religions ranging from Hinduism to Christianity have what they themselves call sacraments. Though each major religion conceptualizes sacrament in a different way, there is a large zone of commonality among them. For these religions, a sacrament essentially is a ritual that enacts, focuses, and concentrates the distinctive beliefs, affects, and lifestyle of the particular religious tradition. A sacrament constitutes the surpassing exemplar and overarching paradigm for all other holy acts that take place in that religion. A sacrament bears a privileged relationship both to the religious tradition as a whole and to the specific activities that occur within that tradition.

In the phenomenological description of sacrament given in the preceding paragraph, religious instruction within the Christian tradition can be properly regarded as a sacrament. The religious instruction event is essentially a process that holistically enacts, focuses, and concentrates the distinctive beliefs, affects, and lifestyle of one or another Christian faith tradition. By virtue of The Great Commission (Mt 28:18–20), religious instruction constitutes *a* surpassing exemplar and overarching paradigm within which all other activities within Christianity take place. And by virtue of The Great Commission, religious instruction bears *a* privileged relationship both to Christianity as a whole and to all other activities within Christianity. It is in this larger sense that it is proper to give the name "sacrament of teaching" to religious instruction. By any account, religious instruction is intrinsically a very holy act.

The word "sacrament" derives from the Latin *sacra-mentum* which means a reality that is set apart religiously, a reality that is consecrated, a reality dedicated to religious use, a sacred pledge or bond. In Latin *sacra* means holy, while *mentum* is a generic suffix that denotes the result of something—in the case of *sacra-mentum*, the result of a holy or sacred reality. Surely in this sense religious instruction is a *sacra-mentum*, a reality formally consecrated to helping others know and feel and live Jesus, a reality dedicated exclusively to religious use, a reality that is very special in the church because it quintessentially shares in the central mission of Jesus, a reality that constitutes a sacred pledge made by religious educators that they will effectively teach Jesus to all learners.

In early Roman times a *sacramentum* was a pledge of money or property made by persons in a contract or a lawsuit. The money or property was deposited in the temple in a religious ceremony there. In this way, the contract or lawsuit was officially and publicly transformed into a holy act, a *sacra-mentum*. The money or property was forfeited by the party who broke the contract or lost the lawsuit.

Religious instruction is a *sacramentum* for religious educators in that, like the case of the earlier Romans, we have answered our call within a call and have thereby solemnly and officially contracted with God, with the local ecclesia, and with the learners to effectively facilitate desired religious outcomes. As in the case of the early Romans, if we fail to successfully perform our sacramental duties, we automatically break the contract, violate the *sacramentum* of religious instruction, and forfeit our call within a call, together with all the spiritual benefits that derive from this call.

In later Roman usage, the word *sacramentum* was frequently employed to mean a military oath, a sacred vow taken early in his career by a soldier in which he solemnly swore that he would be loyal and true and effective. Through this oath, through this *sacramentum*, the soldier hallowed his present and future military activities. This solemn oath took place in a religious ceremony in a designated sacred place.

Religious instruction is a *sacramentum* for religious educators in much the same sense as it was for ancient Roman soldiers because authentic religious educators explicitly or implicitly promise before God and church to be true and effective facilitators of religious living. By saying yes, and especially by doing yes to God's call within a call, religious educators sacrament themselves to the work of God in the teaching task.

A sacrament is an especially focused and charged channel of God's grace and assistance. Religious instruction serves as a converged and potent conduit through which God's grace and assistance pour forth in a sacramented way to teacher and learner.

In sacrament the finger of God touches our entire personhood, reaching even to our deepest selves. In religious instruction the finger of God reaches holistically into the inmost core of the learner's existence and thus sacraments that individual to wholeness and completion.

Sacrament is God's self-disclosure of his presence, his power, his existence. In the religious instruction act God reveals himself to learners in a concentrated way by meeting and greeting and sacramenting learners as they grow holistically unto him.

Sacrament gives immediate access in a privileged manner to an intimate union with the divine. Through the studying and the loving and the experiencing of God that take place in the religious instruction act, learners are given access to a close personal sacramented coupling with the Lord.

Sacrament is deeply enmeshed with all the events of a person's life—the manifestly decisive transitions such as birth and marriage and death, as well as the less salient but nonetheless incrementally important moments such as times of repentance or sickness. Life is an eminently concrete affair, and sacrament is a divine eruption into this processive concreteness. By its presence and power, religious instruction pervasively sacraments all moments in the life of the learner and universalizes them for the learner now and for the rest of time into eternity.

Sacrament is not a prelude to a holy act. Sacrament is a holy act in itself, and its result is holy. Religious instruction is not a vestibule leading to some later holy act, but is itself a house of holiness whose rooms and gardens all sacrament learners into holiness.

Through Christian sacrament the work of Jesus as savior (re-deemer and religious educator) is continued for all time. In the reli-gious instruction act, the work of Jesus—his life, his actions, his teachings, his death, his resurrection—is made present and potent in the lives of learners. The religious instruction act sacraments learners into the salvific activity of Jesus.

For many Christians, sacrament is an essential and necessary part of the whole divine economy of salvation because sacrament is the privileged way in which Jesus has willed to share his presence and grace with human beings. Religious instruction occupies a cen-tral and indispensable place within the divine economy of salvation because through it learners are sacramented to share in the pres-ence and grace of Jesus in a special way by learning to know him more clearly, love him more truly, and follow him more closely. Without religious instruction of one sort or another, it would be very difficult and maybe impossible to know, love, and follow Jesus even to a minimal degree.

The true nature and thrust of Christian sacrament is properly un-derstood only when it is seen within the entire eschatological con-text of salvation through Jesus. The true sacramented nature and thrust of religious instruction can be grasped only when it is en-acted in and through and for the whole eschatological context of salvation.

When the church through one of its appropriate ministers con-fects a sacrament, both it and its ministers thereby pledge that spe-cial grace will come to the cooperating recipient in and through the sacrament. When the broad ecclesia through one of its religious ed-ucators teaches religion, both it and the educator thereby pledge that through their cooperation with God's immanent presence in the competently enacted religious instruction event, graced learn-ings will come to the receptive learner in and through the sacra-mented religious instruction act.

The ultimate source and connective conduit of Christian sacra-ment is the incarnation of the Second Person of the Trinity here on earth. Jesus is the primal sacrament, the essential sacrament, the fundamental sacrament, the underlying sacrament. Each sacrament in its own way inheres in, emanates from, and flows back into the once and continuing incarnate Jesus. The ultimate source and ongoing power of the sacramented religious instruction act is the then and now incarnate Jesus. Sacramented religious instruction is a central and indispensable way in which the church helps make Jesus more fully incarnate in the thoughts and feelings and lifestyles of learners.

Because the Incarnation is the ultimate source and continuing wellspring of all sacrament, the central Christian sacrament has always been the Eucharist. In its authentic and full form, religious instruction flows from, shares with, and pours into the eucharistic Jesus. Additionally but just as essentially, the religious instruction act is itself always a eucharist because it is a sacramented personal existential communion between educator and learners.

For many Christian groups, sacrament is the most basic and most vital action of the church. Through sacrament the church is the church in its deepest, most authentic, and most salvific form. Religious instruction is an especially basic action of the church because without religious instruction the church would either cease to exist or become extremely feeble. And religious instruction is an extremely vital action of the church because it is through religious instruction that the sacramented relationship of a person with Jesus receives its necessary cognitive expansion, affective ripening, and lifestyle deepening.

Some Christian groups regard the church as the mystical body of Jesus which in a privileged manner embodies the Lord's abiding presence in the historical world. When the church is truly the church, it acts as a sacrament in Christ. In its own special way religious instruction acts as a sacrament in Christ in that it extends the presence of Jesus in the world. Additionally, through the religious instruction act learners are joined in sacramented communion with all those other members of the mystical body worldwide who are also learning how to know, love, and live Jesus better.

To what extent are we religious educators continually aware that religious instruction is a holy act—not just another holy act but rather a surpassing and overarching paradigm for so many other kinds of holy acts?

To what degree do we treat our teaching activity as a holy act? How much do we reverence our teaching?

Do we always prepare and enact and evaluate our religious instruction as befits the seriousness and gravity of a sacred reality?

Do we religious educators habitually sacrament ourselves by giving our sacred pledge to God that we will work as hard and as thoroughly as possible to effectively teach Jesus to learners?

To what extent do we structure our teaching activities so that the finger of God can touch learners in all phases of their existence?

How frequently do we work with consummate diligence to ensure that our teaching activities sacrament learners to grow holistically unto the Lord, not in some vague or ethereal way but in a concrete here and now fashion?

Is our vision of religious instruction as sacrament sufficiently farseeing in that we are deeply aware that our religious instruction activities are not simply marginal or temporary but are inextricably intertwined with the whole eschatological economy of salvation?

To what degree do we make our teaching activity a movable house of holiness?

How often is the beginning, middle, and end of our instructional work such that in its own processive way it brings Jesus to learners in a truly incarnate manner?

Our call within a call to be God's religious educators carries with it the responsibility to incarnate Jesus in the minds, hearts, and deeds of learners. What are we doing in the concrete here and now to make our teaching an ongoing eucharist?

Performance Objective: At the beginning of every religious instruction event, whether in a formal or an informal environment, the learners and I will begin by explicitly consecrating to God the time we spend together in the realization that what we will be doing is intrinsically a holy act and so therefore we should all consciously work together to help us grow concretely in holiness during the religious instruction event.

7

A Holy Place

In the early 1990s, my wife and I decided that our three young sons should enroll in a karate program in order to gain a high level of the kind discipline that is founded on a spiritual base and that holistically integrates mind, affect, and body. My wife and I firmly believe that holistic discipline is something our three sons urgently need if they are to fulfill their abilities now and especially later in life. Fortunately for us, Birmingham is the American Southeast headquarters for World Oyama Karate, one of the finest karate programs in the entire United States.

Our sons have been especially fortunate in having as their principal teacher Yasuhiko Oyama, who holds the rank of *Saiko Shihan* (grand master). Born, raised, and professionally trained in karate in Japan, he is a black belt 8th *Dan*, an All-Japan Full Contact Karate Champion, and a well-respected author of many books and articles about karate in Japan. In the mid-1980s he was received in the Oval Office of the White House by President Ronald Reagan, who awarded Yasuhiko Oyama an official certificate of recognition both for excellence as a karate master and for his skill as a teacher of karate. (His older brother, Soshu Oyama, a 9th *Dan* black belt, and author of a best-selling novel on karate, was recognized as the greatest Japanese karate grandmaster and international karate authority when he was selected to introduce into the United States traditional Japanese karate adapted to modern karate systems which had been springing up in various parts of the world. Soshu Oyama was undefeated throughout his career in tournaments in Japan. He fought the legendary hundred-man *kumite* in Japan during the mid-1960s, defeating all opponents consecutively. He currently directs the World Oyama Karate international headquarters located in New York City.)

The origins of karate are veiled in the mists of time. It is only through legends that we can gain even as much as a faint glimpse of how karate began. One version of the most famous of these legends revolves around a renowned Indian Buddhist monk named Bodhidharma Taishi (known in Japanese as Daruma Taisha). Sometime in the sixth century A.D., Bodhidharma made a long and extremely difficult overland journey through seemingly impassable terrain from southern India to China in order to teach the principles of Buddhism to the reigning Liang dynasty monarch. He remained in China, residing at the monastery of Shao-Lin-szu (Shorin-ji in Japanese), where he taught the tenets of Buddhism to the monks there. The unsparing discipline plus the rapid pace of learning that Bodhidharma exacted of the monks caused them one by one to pass out from sheer physical exhaustion.

On seeing this unfortunate turn of events, Daruma decided to gather his learners together. He reminded them that the goal of Buddhism is the salvation of the soul (enlightenment) and that an indispensable path for attaining this goal is the harmonious and energetic interaction of body and soul. He patiently explained that no person could possibly ascend the very steep and precipitous way toward spiritual enlightenment unless his physical condition was strong enough to perform highly demanding bodily ascetical exercises. Bodhidharma was not content merely to give a cognitive explanation of what was required to successfully proceed along the way toward enlightenment. Ever the religious educator, and drawing from his long study in India of the martial arts, Bodhidharma devised a new system of dynamically integrated physical, mental, and spiritual exercises. This new system provided a comprehensive training program for the Buddhist monks at Shao-Lin-szu. With the passage of time, the fame of the overwhelmingly superior martial arts skills of the Buddhist monks of Shao-Lin-szu spread throughout the length and breadth of China. As the centuries eased by, the Shao-Lin principles and techniques revolutionized and vitalized the ancient martial arts system of *kempo* which has been in existence in China since at least the time of the Chou dynasty (1122 B.C.–256 B.C.)

As the Shao-Lin training program became diffused throughout China over the succeeding centuries, the classical Buddhist principles that had originally formed the basis of this training program became gradually absorbed into *ch'an,* (a word derived from the Indian *dhyani* meaning meditation, and which later became Zen in Japan). Thus in its wellspring, set of procedures, and goal, karate is inextricably intertwined with Zen. (It should be underscored that Zen is not a religion. It is not even primarily a philosophy. Basically, Zen is a highly disciplined, systematic, and focused instructional method. This method does have some general foundational and operational principles. Because it is chiefly a method to attain enlightenment, Zen can be used by persons of any, all, or no religious persuasion. For example, there can be, and indeed is, such a thing as Christian Zen.)

As it is known and practiced today throughout the world, karate descends directly from Okinawa, the principal island in the Ryukyu chain in what is now southernmost Japan. For centuries Okinawa belonged to China. Probably *kempo* (and its generalized encasement in *ch'an*) found its way into Okinawa along with many other elements of Chinese culture. In the beginning of the fifteenth century, King Hashi of Okinawa united the Ryukyu Islands into a single kingdom. In order to ensure compliance with its laws, the government seized all weapons in the kingdom and decreed that the mere possession of a weapon constituted a crime against the state. Two centuries later the Satsuma clan from Japan occupied the island, and continued to prohibit the possession of weapons. Local resistance groups, first against Hashi and later against the Satsuma clan, sprung up and flourished. Because weapons were forbidden, the Okinawan resistance groups relied on *kempo*, practicing it, expanding it, and modifying it. All this was done in secret so that the governmental authorities would not know what the resistance groups were doing. Early in the nineteenth century the Okinawan version of *kempo* had evolved to a point where it became popularly known as karate. (In present-day Japanese, the word "karate" is written with two characters meaning literally "empty" (*kara*), and "hand" (*te*), denoting that the practitioner of karate carries no weapons such as guns or knives.)

In 1901 karate emerged from secrecy and became part of the curriculum in at least one middle school in Okinawa. Karate got its first really big boost when, in 1917 and again in 1922, Gichin Funakoshi (1869–1957) from Okinawa gave karate demonstrations in Japan proper on behalf of the Ministry of Education there. He spent most of his life popularizing karate in Japan, always placing greater emphasis on the spiritual nature of karate than on its specific techniques per se. From Japan karate spread rapidly to the rest of the world, usually by means of native Japanese karate masters who migrated to other countries in order to teach their special skills.

It is said that there are about one hundred different karate styles in existence throughout the world. World Oyama Karate can be described as a neoclassical style. It is one of the most demanding forms of karate in the United States. (Indeed, many other karate schools in America have severely watered-down versions of classical karate, and some have lax standards in terms of requirements for advancement in rank.) Karate styles that are truly authentic place great emphasis on the spiritual dimension of this martial art. For example, the traditional set of spiritual principles that undergirds and penetrates the World Oyama Karate style are grounded in the virtues of honesty, respect, and courtesy.

To properly appreciate karate, it is absolutely essential to bear in mind that karate is intimately admixed with Zen at all points. Zen is karate's inmost meaning and mainspring. In a certain sense karate can be considered as Zen done in a standing position and with vigorous movement. Indeed, if karate were no more than a fighting technique, it probably would not have survived as long as it has. The vitality and continued appeal of karate derive from its nature as a balanced fusion of formal martial arts physical techniques with a deeper spiritual way. Properly viewed, karate is not basically a fighting technique but a way of personal perfection and enlightenment. Thus every genuinely authentic karate class session, such as those conducted by the World Oyama Karate organization, begins and ends with meditation. During the class sessions, the teacher intervenes not only to help the learners perfect a particular physical technique but also to directly relate the technique and the accompanying physical exertion to an underlying spiritual principle.

Like Zen, of which it is a manifestation, karate seeks to assist its practitioners to completely free themselves from egoism. Zen regards egoism as the principal obstacle standing in the way of enlightenment, the way of attaining true selfhood. Egoistic desires in whole and in part inevitably spawn such evils as revenge, lust, jealously, envy, covetousness, competitiveness, and the like. One walks along the path to enlightenment in karate/Zen by dying to one's egoistic desires. In enlightenment, the person comes to what Zenists call impassivity, a state in which egoism disappears and is replaced by unity: unity of one's self with the universe, unity of body and spirit, unity of the self with time so that there is no past or present but only absorption in the present instant, and in the actual karate practice sessions unity with the opponent so that the practitioner not only coexists with the opponent but achieves unity with that person.

Mysticism, then, lies at the center and in the spokes of karate. As is true of every form of mysticism, the way of karate is achieved through austerities of body and spirit. And as is also true of every form of mysticism, karate in its fullest form bestows on its practitioners a kind of supernatural power that endows them with enormous inner peace and forcefulness.

Persons learn and perfect the karate way to enlightenment on the *dōjō*. It is a truism that the *dōjō* is the mother of karate. The Japanese word *dō* derives from the Chinese word *Tao*, which means The Way. The Japanese word *jō* means place. Thus the *dōjō* is the place where one trains in The Way of karate by means of formal exercises. The *dōjō* is thus a holy place because it is here that one learns the way to harmonious character development, the way to personal fulfillment, the way to enlightenment.

In the martial arts, there are many kinds of *dō*, many forms of The Way, such as, for example, karate-*dō*, ju-*dō*, ken-*dō*, kyu-*dō*, and the like. What gives all these forms of The Way, all these *dō*s, a single common ground is Zen.

In a Zen monastery, the training of a monk takes place at the *semmon dōjō* ("training hall for perfect wisdom"), which is specifically built for this purpose. This training hall for the monks exists in all major Zen monasteries in Japan. A person cannot become a full-fledged Zen monk until he goes through a minimum of several years at the *semmon dōjō*. Outside the monastery, where the vast preponderance of karate practice sessions take place, the *dōjō* is no less a place where a person learns the way to enlightenment.

The *dōjō* is always a holy place regardless of where it is located, whether in a monastery or in the world, whether indoors or outdoors, whether in the country or the city. The *dōjō* is always a holy place because what takes place on it is a holy act.

In karate, the *dōjō* is treated as a holy place by both the teacher and the learners. No one is allowed on the *dōjō* except the teacher and the learners because persons not engaged in the karate way of enlightenment would profane this holy place. Before entering the *dōjō*, the teacher and the learners bow in reverence to the *dōjō* because it is in this holy place that a holy act will soon occur. During the practice training session in the *dōjō*, the learners bow to their teacher whenever the teacher speaks to them because it is the teacher who is helping them proceed along the path to enlightenment in that holy place. During training in the *dōjō*, moreover, the learners bow to each other before and after they engage in karate because it is their fellow learners who are helping them along the way of enlightenment in the *dōjō*. Immediately before leaving the *dōjō* at the end of the class session, the learners, proceeding in single file, bow to the teacher and give him a two-hand shake signifying appreciation of the holy act that has just been completed in the *dōjō*. When the learners leave the *dōjō*, they bow at its perimeter, indicating their reverence for this holy place.

When the teacher and the learners enter the *dōjō* in the World Oyama Karate organization, they immediately bow to the *dōjō*. As they bow, they forcefully exclaim the Japanese word *Osu* (pronounced Oos). This exclamation, uttered from head and heart and body, is a holistic pledge of respect for the *dōjō*, the holy place where the holy act of teaching/learning will occur. By exclaiming *Osu*, the teacher and learners thoroughly commit themselves to undergo hardship and to persevere patiently in training while in the *dōjō*. During the training in the *dōjō*, the learners exclaim *Osu* whenever the teacher speaks to them . The learners also bow and exclaim *Osu* before and after engaging in karate against an opponent. After the training session is finished, the learners bow to their teacher while exclaiming *Osu*. As they leave the sacred precincts of the *dōjō*, each learner steps backward while facing the *dōjō*, bows, and at the same moment exclaims *Osu* to indicate profound respect for the holy place where the latest round of instruction has just occurred.

Once the learners and the teacher have entered the sacred precincts of the *dōjō* to begin the day's training session, the learners form a line and face their teacher. They put themselves into the preparedness stance (*yoi-dachi*), body erect, legs spread apart about eighteen inches, toes pointed out, arms bent at about twenty-five degrees at the elbow, and hands clenched in a fist. The preparedness stance is used whenever the learners receive instructions from their teacher. As soon as all students are in the preparedness stance, the teacher gives the command *mokuso*, meditation. (All regular group commands in the every *dōjō* operated by the World Oyama Karate organization are given in Japanese). The learners then sit down in the *seiza* position, back and head straight, forelegs tucked under the thighs and buttocks with both feet pointing toward each other, buttocks resting on the foreleg and heels, hands placed firmly on the thighs. For a period of thirty seconds to one minute the learners engage in meditation. The purpose of this Zen meditation is to empty the mind and heart of all distractions so that the students and the teacher can unite mind and heart and body, thus enabling them to concentrate totally on the training. An essential element of *mokuso* is breathing (*kokyu*). Proper breathing during meditation is to inhale slowly with the air going all the way down to the center, followed by slow exhalation. Meditation, grounded as it is in Zen, is an indispensable element *dōjō* training. It is through meditation that the learners and the teacher place themselves into the mode of integrating intellect, affect, and body in order to truly practice *dō*, The Way. It is through meditation that the learners and the teacher begin to achieve unity of mind and body, self and the training activity, self and the opponent.

After meditation has been completed, the learners, always under the vigilant direction of the teacher, begin a series of warm-up exercises that last about five to eight minutes. These exercises include twisting, turning, flexing, stretching, and the like. The warm-up exercises are designed to rejuvenate the body and spirit so that the students can get the most out the whole practice session. Following the warm-up exercises, the learners practice the two main ingredients of karate combat, namely, basic methods (*kihon*) and basic form (*kata*).

The basic methods that the karate learners practice include starting, thrusting, striking, kicking, blocking, and lunging. Each of these methods contain a variety of specific techniques. Some of the most common kicking techniques, for example, are the high kick, the side kick, the knee kick, the roundhouse kick, and the back kick.

Karate methods become effective when placed into a more generalized and overall form. A person deploys a specific karate technique within the matrix of form. In karate, form (*kata*) is the basic pattern of movement through which various techniques are performed. Form consists of a sort of ritualized pattern of movement from which and during which the karate practitioner kicks, blocks, strikes, and so forth. Thus exercises in which learners practice form constitute the central part of training in the *dōjō* because unless a technique is encased in a form, that technique will not be successful. *Kata* is the physical core of karate; all physical activities in karate are a corporeal extension of *kata*. When properly executed, there is no mechanistic aspect in *kata*. Thus, someone who truly watches a karate master do a particular *kata* will tend to be riveted by the beauty and power of the movements.

After the learners have finished their methods exercises and form exercises, they engage in free fighting (*kumite*) against each other. The purpose of free fighting is to help the karate learner integrate in a practical situation the methods and the form that he or she has learned.

After completing the free fighting portion of the training exercise, the learners and their teacher engage in a few minutes of cool-down exercises. Then, at the command of the teacher or of a learner designated by the teacher, the learners sit down in the *seiza* position and engage in about a minute of meditation (*mokuso*) during which they center themselves and ingest into their self-system those things they learned during the training class. At the end of the meditation period, the learners rise, proceed in single file to thank the teacher, and reverentially leave the sacred precincts of the *dōjō*.

At the World Oyama Karate Organization, as with every authentic karate association, the students thoroughly scrub the *dōjō* floor and carefully clean all other parts of the *dōjō* at regular intervals. This instructional activity is intended to teach the karate students to have profound respect for the *dōjō* because it is in the karate *dōjō* that they learn to travel The Way.

We religious educators all have our *dōjō*, the place in which we teach learners how to become holy. Sometimes the religious instruction *dōjō* is a classroom. Sometimes the religious instruction *dōjō* is a family room or a dining room in a home. Sometimes the religious instruction *dōjō* is the playground. Sometimes the religious instruction *dōjō* is the street corner. Sometimes the religious instruction *dōjō* is a church building. In every case, our religious instruction *dōjō* is a holy place because it is here that the work of the Lord is done in an especially focused and precious manner. It is in the religious instruction *dōjō* that the sacrament of teaching unfolds.

To what extent do we religious educators reverence our *dōjō*, the place where the holy act of teaching and learning religion takes place? The place where the holy act of religious instruction is done is an essential molar variable that intrinsically affects the outcome of religious instruction activity. If the act of teaching religion is holy, then automatically the place in which this act occurs is holy since environment is an intrinsic dimension of the act.

To respect the place in which the religious instruction act occurs is to recognize that the environment in which the teaching/learning of religion occurs is a major aspect of the religious instruction act.

All too often our religious instruction efforts are not truly successful because we neglect the environment in which this sacramental act occurs.

In the Catholic Church, the priest kisses the altar at the beginning of Mass out of veneration for the table on which the holy sacrifice of Jesus will shortly take place. When John Paul II visits a foreign country on an apostolic mission, the first thing he does after leaving the airplane is to reverentially kiss the ground because this ground, this country, is the place where he is teaching people to increase their love for God.

The religious instruction *dōjō* is the place where we educate others to live The Way. To what extent do we religious educators appreciate that our *dōjō* is, or at least should be, a laboratory for Christian living, a place where learners learn to actually live a deeper Christian life?

Our call within a call to be religious educators culminates and finds its fulfillment in what we do in the religious instruction *dōjō*. How much care do we habitually take to ensure that our work in the religious instruction *dōjō* is of the very highest quality as a whole and in every detail?

To what degree do we religious educators see the setting in which religious instruction takes place as an environment which promotes enlightenment—or do we just see it as a place to dispense information?

How frequently do we consciously endeavor to make enlightenment a major context and goal of our instructional work in the *dōjō*?

Do we expend every effort to assist learners in the religious instruction *dōjō* to free themselves from the shackles of their egoism so that they can become open to embrace the Lord on the Lord's own terms?

How often do we religious educators interweave meditation into the religious instruction act?

To what extent does our religious instruction activity in the *dōjō* integrate the learner's body, mind, heart, and overt behavior?

To what extent do we respect, reverence, and venerate the *dōjō* in which the holy act of religious instruction occurs? Only when we respect, reverence, and venerate the environment in which religious instruction occurs will we take this environment seriously as a key dimension of the religious instruction act.

Performance Objective: At the beginning and at the conclusion of every religious instruction event the learners and I will do something physical with respect to the place in which the event occurred. For example, I can touch the floor or a chair or a wall to tangibly remind myself that the specific location in which religion teaching/learning occurs is a holy site because it is here that I am helped in a special focused way to come to know, love, and serve God better.

8

Religious Experience

John Wesley was one of the most important, most dedicated, and most hardworking religious educators of the modern era.

Most people think of Wesley as a highly successful preacher. That he was. But preaching is, of course, one mode of teaching. A preacher, therefore, is essentially and undeniably a religious educator first and foremost.

Wesley's life stands as a shining testament to so many of those qualities that characterize every truly authentic religious educator: a sense of priorities that places the call to the apostolate above all personal interests, an unquenchable desire to overcome every adversity that might stand in the way of totally answering the call within a call at all times and in all circumstances, personal holiness placed at the complete disposal of the religious instruction apostolate, an abiding sense of providence and destiny with respect to one's own life, enormous self-sacrifice, incredibly hard and incessant work, wholehearted discipline, constant professional reading of first-class books, insistence on red-hot religion, and a deep interest in the process of effective communication and ways to perfect this process. In short, John Wesley was a man whose life was completely consumed by the Lord and by the Lord's religious instruction ministry of helping every person attain holiness.

The great religious educator John Wesley was born on June 17 (old style; June 28 new style), in the year 1703. His birthplace was in the small town of Epworth located in the rough fen country of Lincolnshire. He was the fifteenth child and second surviving son of Samuel and Susanna Wesley. His father, the somewhat impoverished rector of the local Anglican parish church, was a devout and well-read High Churchman. His legacy to John included unsparing self-discipline, uncompromising courage, unquenchable thirst for learning, and unswerving love of the Church of England. Like her husband, Susanna was widely read and acquitted herself well in learned theological and religious discussions that she had with her husband and with other clergymen. She educated her children at home; indeed, it was not until he was seventeen that John went out of his home to go to school. Susanna, the benevolent matriarch of the family, was pretty, saintly, scholarly, strong willed, and an efficient housekeeper. She was John's ideal woman, an idealization that probably contributed significantly to the consistent lack of success he had with women throughout his life in matters amorous.

When John was six years old, the rectory was torched, possibly by some Epworthians displeased with his father. All the Wesley children were barely rescued from the flames. Both John and his father regarded this deliverance as the direct work of divine providence. The sense that God spared him from the flames to engage in a special apostolic mission inspired John for the rest of his life. He often referred to himself as "a brand plucked out of the burning," a phrase borrowed, albeit somewhat out of context, from Amos (4:11) and Zechariah (3:2). So central in John's consciousness was this sense of divine providence calling him to a special mission that when he was fifty-one years old and thought he would die at any moment of pulmonary tuberculosis, he prescribed that this phrase would be put on his tombstone as his epitaph. (His premonition of death was premature, and he lived thirty-seven more years. Others wrote his eventual tombstone epitaph which, while alluding to special providence, did not use John's biblical self-descriptor.)

It was only later that John realized that the special mission for which divine providence had called him so dramatically was that of religious educator. As the distinguished Methodist theologian Albert Outler remarked, for John Wesley "evangelizing and theologizing were [but] two functions which formed major dimensions of his single chief endeavor: the effectual communication of the gospel" (which is to say, religious instruction).

In January 1714 John was sent to London to attend the Charterhouse School on a scholarship for poor students. Six years later he entered Christ Church College of the University of Oxford as a Charterhouse Scholar. He received his bachelor's degree in 1727 and his master's degree in 1729. John's years at Christ Church provided him with a superb foundation for his later religious instruction ministry. At Christ Church he led an austere life, arising daily at 4 o'clock in the morning. He retained this habit for the rest of his life. Academically John proved to be an excellent student. He read, in the original of course, the Greek classics including Homer and Xenophon, as well as the Latin classics such as Terence and Sallust. He learned Hebrew grammar and read the Bible in the original language. He also studied metaphysics, ethics, logic, physics, and Arabic grammar.

At Christ Church, the most distinguished college at Oxford, Wesley also read widely and well in theology. Strongly influenced by two devotional books on religious living and religious dying written in the mid-eighteenth century by the important English prelate and theologian Jeremy Taylor, Wesley underwent a powerful religious experience in 1725. While in the midst of this religious experience, Wesley instantly resolved to dedicate his entire life to God—all his thoughts and all his words and all his actions. Wesley made this wholehearted and unyielding resolution to dedicate every fiber of his being to the Lord's service because he was thoroughly convinced that there is no middle ground when it comes to consecrating oneself to God's work.

Because of his considerable academic proficiency, Wesley was elected Fellow of Lincoln College at Oxford in 1727. For the next few years he spent most of his time assisting his father in parish ministry, first as a deacon and then as an ordained Anglican priest. In 1729 he began to reside full-time at Lincoln. He quickly assumed the leadership of a religious study circle originally founded at Oxford by his younger brother Charles. This circle lived an almost semimonastic life. The members regularly prayed, fasted, and received the Eucharist together. Additionally they engaged in religious instructional and philanthropic works. Some persons nicknamed the circle "The Holy Club." Other persons, less friendly, derisively called members of the circle "the Methodists" because of its strong emphasis on ordered spiritual discipline and external organization. The period of "Oxford Methodism" ended in 1735 when the club disbanded.

Wesley was a voracious reader. Some of the books he read during his Oxford years helped his personal religious life and later professional religious instruction ministry enormously. In 1726 he read the writings of Thomas à Kempis (1380–1471) and as a result realized that giving his entire life to God was worthless unless he also gave his entire heart to the Lord's service. Wesley learned from reading Thomas à Kempis that true Christianity is Christianity of the heart. A year or two later Wesley read the works of another spiritual writer, William Law (1686–1761). From Law's writings Wesley became even more determined to become all-devoted to God and to his service in the full awareness of the absolute impossibility of being half a Christian. Wesley also began to read the Eastern Fathers of the Early Church. From these Fathers, especially Clement of Alexandria (c.150–c.220) Wesley gained familiarity and love of Christian mysticism. For the rest of his life Wesley endeavored to somehow meld the ancient Eastern tradition of holiness as disciplined love with the Anglican tradition of holiness as aspiring love.

In 1735 James Oglethorpe, founder and chief administrator for the British colony of Georgia, persuaded Wesley to return with him to America in order to be pastor to the colonists and to convert the Indians to Christianity. John accepted the offer. Together with Charles and two other members of the Holy Club, he set sail for the New World. The Georgia adventure proved to be a fiasco for all concerned. Charles turned out to be a bumbling secretary to Oglethorpe. The other two members of the Holy Club were also woefully ineffective. But it was upon John that the greatest calamity fell. The Indians rejected his missionary endeavors. Though he tried to serve his parishioners faithfully and sincerely, he alienated most of them with his uncompromising High Churchmanship and his prescriptions for highly disciplined conduct. Wesley's greatest disaster in Georgia came as a result of his falling in love with Sophia Christiana Hopkey, the eighteen-year old niece of the chief magistrate of Savannah. Wesley was not a model suitor by any stretch of the imagination, probably because he was painfully and awkwardly torn between his newly discovered feelings of love and his longstanding personal inhibitions. Having grown weary of John's indecisiveness and immature tenders of affection, Sophia eloped with a rival suitor. In retaliation, John barred Sophia from receiving the Eucharist. Her enraged husband sued Wesley for defamation of his wife's character. A grand jury indicted Wesley on twelve separate counts and sent the case to trial. After six months of harassment, Wesley fled Georgia in disgrace in December 1737.

It is characteristic of great persons that they convert both successful and unsuccessful experiences into long-term advantage. So it was with John Wesley. While in Georgia, Wesley organized fellowship meetings that met regularly. These meetings were to become the first rudiments of the Methodist societies that he later organized in England. And while in Georgia, Wesley came into contact with some Moravians and began to look deeply into the background and basic principles of this religious group.

From the perspective of divine providence, it sometimes happens that events which might seem to be unfortunate in the immediate term prove to be most fortunate over the long term. If John had a successful courtship with Sophia and had married her, he probably would have remained in Georgia for the rest of his life. He never would have had his great conversion experience at Aldersgate, he never would have been responsible for founding the Methodists, he never would have personally spearheaded one of the greatest religious revivals of the modern era, and he never would have taught those thousands upon thousands of moving religious instructional sermons throughout England.

When he returned to England in 1738, Wesley met Peter Böhler, the leader of the Moravians in that country. Not long afterward, he and Böhler organized the Fetter Lane Society, a religious fellowship group under the auspices of the Church of England with a membership consisting primarily of Moravians. The Moravian Church, whose formal name is *Unitas Fratrum* (Unity of the Brethren), underwent a major Pietist renewal in Germany during the early eighteenth century. Wesley's deep encounter with

Moravianism strongly influenced the core of both his personal religious life and his religious instruction ministry. In an era when arid and asphyxiating rationalism had risen to the ascendancy in much of Christianity, Moravianism stressed inner feelings and personal religious experience over abstract doctrine. For Moravians, authentic Christianity consists in living and experiencing faith. A strong element of Moravianism was a valence toward mysticism in general and mystical union with Jesus in particular. Additionally, Moravians thought of themselves as an overarching religious society founded on experiential religion and personal piety. Along this line, Moravians of that time regarded themselves not so much as a separate denomination but as an *ecclesiola in ecclesia*, a little church within a church, which would serve as leaven to revive and renew the larger institutional Protestant churches. Thus the eighteenth-century Moravians believed that organic fellowship with the Brethren neither involved nor demanded separation from any existing Protestant denomination.

May 24, 1738 turned out to be the most momentous day in John Wesley's momentous-filled life. After his early morning ablutions and other personal duties, he began his workday at five o'clock by reading and then reflecting in earnest on the Gospel passage "you are not far from the kingdom of God" (Mk 12:14). In the afternoon he was asked to go to St. Paul's Cathedral where he was deeply moved during the congregational singing of the *De profundis*, "Out of the depths I cry to you, O Lord . . ." (Psalm 130 in the B.C.P. Psalter that Wesley favored). In the evening he went unwillingly to a meeting of a local religious society that was convening regularly in Aldersgate Street. During the course of this eventful incident, a man stood up and began reading from Martin Luther's *Preface to the Epistle to the Romans*. At about a quarter before nine, while he was listening to Luther's description of the change that God works in the human heart through deep faith in Christ, Wesley felt his "heart strangely warmed," to use his own words. At that instant he underwent the most intense religious experience of his entire life, an experience which proved totally decisive for him. Immediately after this intense religious experience, he prayed with all his strength for those who had cruelly used him and persecuted him throughout his lifetime. Then he stood up at the meeting and testified about what he felt in his heart during his intense religious experience and how his heart was so strangely warmed by the outpouring of God's tremendous love for him. John Wesley was nearly thirty five at the time of his intense religious experience in that hall in Aldersgate Street, and he came to the full realization of why God had plucked him as a brand from out of the burning those many years ago. His teaching ministry would never be the same after his deep personal religious experience at Aldersgate.

In August 1738 Wesley visited various Moravian centers in Germany because of the affective influence that the Moravians exerted on him in Georgia, in the Fetter Lane Society, and in the Aldersgate group. He wanted to learn more about the Moravians. He returned in September, realizing that there were many Moravian viewpoints with which he could not agree. Wesley was, after all, a devoted Anglican High Churchman.

Constantly powered and continually sustained by his Aldersgate religious experience, Wesley spent the next fifty three years of his life wholeheartedly in the service of religious instruction and church administration.

A great deal of John Wesley's fame derives from his religious instruction ministry. It has been reliably estimated that in the years following his intense religious experience in Aldersgate Street, Wesley taught approximately 52,400 religion lessons (sermons) in the British Isles, to say nothing of the countless times he taught religion to individuals whom he met along the way. Wesley regarded the whole world as his parish. He tried to go wherever he believed God needed him the most urgently. Hence he tended toward giving religious instruction lessons in the open fields and lanes, town marketplaces, and industrial areas—any locale where he might assemble an audience of learners, and where piety and church attendance were low.

Unlike his colleague George Whitefield (1714–1770), Wesley did not teach in an impassioned, dramatic manner but rather quietly. All together, Wesley traveled about 250,000 miles on horseback and carriage in his post-Aldersgate religious instruction ministry.

Wesley's prodigious religious instruction activities were not confined to oral teaching. He also wrote extensively. He published his religious instruction lessons (*Sermons*), which remain highly influential down to the present day. Together with his brother Charles he wrote hymns (religious instruction lessons in song). He authored little textbooks on religion and other topics. He wrote books on history, philology, and medicine. He abridged Milton and compiled a dictionary. And he wrote his legendary *Journal*.

The avowed goal of Wesley's oral and written religious instruction activities was a deep and committed Christian lifestyle, one that he variously called holiness, perfect love, sanctification, and Christian perfection. An eminently practical religious educator, Wesley constantly stressed the absolute necessity of good works as flowing along with personal experiential faith. For him, the true Christian life is one of *devotio*, the consecration of the whole person to love of God and love of neighbor, to personal piety, and to the religiously imbued amelioration of social ills. He strongly urged his followers to receive the sacrament of the Eucharist every time they could, at least every Sunday and daily if possible—Christians have what Wesley himself termed "the duty of constant Communion." For Wesley, holiness is a method of living, a faith-full way of life. Thus he prescribed for his followers a methodical and disciplined way of living a personal, social, and ecclesiastical life unto holiness. It was this emphasis on Christian perfection as successfully achieved through disciplined method that earned Wesley's group the name Methodists. Wesley's strong adherence to corporate Christian discipline was partly a consequence of his interest in Roman Catholic religious orders, most notably the Jesuits.

John Wesley firmly believed that in order to be effective, the religious educator had to read a great deal. Thus he regarded it as his sacred duty to read books that he believed to be important for his religious instruction ministry. While on horseback traveling from place to place, Wesley read as he rode. In later years, an admirer bequeathed her carriage to Wesley, whereupon he transformed it into a little traveling library.

As a supremely practical man, Wesley realized that his efforts in religious instruction and church renewal could not be successful or long lasting if he engaged solely in oral and written religious instruction activities. Wesley clearly understood that organization and administration were essential in order to follow up, sustain, and enhance the herculean religious instruction efforts that he and his associates were making. When he was banned by local Anglican clergymen from preaching at the Fetter Lane Society and in many London churches, he boldly formed his own separate religious group at the Foundry in July of 1740. By 1743 he had established two more chapels in London alone. In the succeeding years he rapidly set up religious societies throughout the British Isles. All these religious societies were formed in such a way as to be directly under his control. Wesley organized the societies into "classes" and "bands", each with its own "leader" and "stewards." Over all the separate Methodist societies was the Conference, an annual governing council composed of key Methodist leaders. At the Conference important administrative and doctrinal issues were debated and decided, and also general religious instruction initiatives were selected.

Since his disastrous experience with Sophia Hopkey, Wesley did not seem to have given serious thought to getting married. His ascetical way of life imbued him with a strong valence against marriage. He viewed celibacy as "the more excellent way," to use his own words in imitation of Scripture. He was very much influenced by the Apostle Paul's practical observation that marriage prevents persons from devoting every fiber of their being to the Lord's service without reserve (1 Cor 7:32–35). Wesley further believed that the married state would divert money away from the funds he required to simultaneously support his itinerant religious instruction ministry and his numerous charitable causes. At one time he even published a short work recommending celibacy as highly beneficial to the spiritual life. But at a meeting of the Conference in London in 1748 his colleagues persuaded the forty-five year old Wesley that he could marry without either suffering loss to his soul or seriously eroding his religious instruction ministry. Very shortly thereafter, Wesley fell ill and was nursed back to health by Grace Murray in Newcastle at a special institution dedicated to taking care of "sick and worn-out preachers." Grace was a widow thirteen years younger than Wesley and a devout Methodist. She possessed the unusual combination of mystical tendencies and practical service in the Methodist organization—an ideal conjunction for Wesley. He became formally engaged to marry Grace not just because he fell in love with her but also and very importantly because he believed that she could be of signal assistance to him in his work as a religious educator. Not knowing the full circumstances of the situation, John's brother Charles secretly intervened and saw to it that Grace married John Bennett, one of John Wesley's preachers. Rejected and psychologically weakened by the Grace Murray episode, John fell into the clutches of Mary (Molly) Vazeille, a wealthy, middle-aged widow of a successful merchant. In February 1751 John fell on some ice and sprained his ankle. He was nursed by Molly at her home. Less than ten days later he and Molly were married. The very next day he taught a major religion lesson (on his knees because of his injured ankle).

The marriage proved to be yet another amorous disaster for John Wesley. At home Molly was a harridan, scolding John frequently. She steadfastly refused to accompany her husband on his many religious instruction trips throughout the British Isles. She grew extremely jealous because much of John's religious instruction work required him to be in close proximity to younger women. Early in 1771 Molly left her husband. In his *Journal* John wrote: *"Non eam reliqui; non dimisi; non revocabo."* ("I did not leave her; I did not send her away; I will not ask her to return.") There were a few temporary reconciliations, but none lasted. In the early autumn 1781, the waspish Molly Wesley, a constant thorn in the side of her husband, breathed her last. John did not learn of her death until several days after she was buried.

It has been observed that great men not infrequently have the misfortune to marry women who neither understand nor cooperate with their grand mission in life. In such cases the marriage is usually unhappy at worst and indifferent at best. Thus it was with John Wesley.

Even though Wesley endured an unhappy marriage that caused him much sorrow and grief, he remained staunchly opposed to divorce.

To his dying day Wesley thought of himself as a true and loyal priest of the Church of England. He saw his mission as that of a special messenger, a canonical priest extraordinary (*sacerdos extraordinarius*) raised up by the Holy Spirit to breathe warmth and life into the Anglican Church's ministry, a ministry often rendered ineffectual by the typically rationalistic and therefore lifeless work of so many of the canonically conventional clergy (*sacerdos ordinarius*). Wesley thought of the Methodism as an *ecclesiola in ecclesia*, a little church within the larger church, a concept that he had first encountered from the Moravians. For Wesley, Methodism was a kind of evangelical religious order within the Church of England, analogous to the separate religious orders within the Roman Catholic Church, all of which are part of and deeply loyal to the larger Roman Church. He wished Methodism to be a permanent reform movement within the Church of England, just as Roman Catholic religious orders often began as reform movements in that church. Ever the idealist, Wesley failed to realize the forthright experimentation that he pursued independently of Anglican ecclesiastical control would steadily and inevitably lead to a separation of Methodism from the Church of England. Wesley died a devout Anglican priest, the staunchly conformist leader of a distinctly nonconformist movement.

As he entered the last months of his life, the indomitable John Wesley was still working unrelentingly in his religious instruction efforts. On January 22, 1791, he wrote a friend: "I am half blind and half lame; but, by the help of God, I work on still." Despite these physical frailties, Wesley was still in remarkably good physical condition for a man of his age in the eighteenth century. At the beginning of February he began to work for three weeks from early morning till late at night distributing tickets to Methodist Society meetings and teaching religion to nearly two thousand people. Late that same month Wesley fell ill, and his friends knew instinctively that the end was not far off.

On March 1 Wesley's life began to ebb at a rapid and irreversible pace. Severely weakened, he sang in a feeble but love-filled voice at various times during the day the hymn "All Glory to God in the Sky," and, as much as he could, the hymn "I'll Praise My Maker

While I've Breath, and When my Voice is Lost in Death." He gave instructions for his burial. Even on his deathbed he was the religious educator: he asked those at his bedside to pray and praise. In the evening, after trying vainly to speak, he gathered all his personal forces and cried out, "The best of all is, God is with us."

When the dawn of March 2, 1791 slowly stretched its fingers in the eastern sky, John Wesley was already in the vestibule of death. His last word, spoken to those at his bedside, was "Farewell". A few minutes before ten in the morning, John Wesley, tireless religious educator and administrator, breathed his last. He was almost eighty-eight years old.

A friend who was present at Wesley's dying hours later declared: "A cloud of Divine presence rested on all."

Wesley's last will and testament reveals his vision of himself and his priorities. Usually persons begin writing an important document by stating their top priorities at the very outset. And typically persons conclude an important document by stating a top priority. This is especially true for a person like John Wesley, who was classically trained and thus was deeply aware of the basic elements of proper written composition. In the opening words of this will and testament he identifies himself only as a cleric in the Church of England and a Sometime Fellow of Lincoln College, Oxford. Thus Wesley's strength lay in the combination of that level of holiness rightfully expected of a member of the clergy and that level of learning rightfully expected of an academic. The very first thing that Wesley's will and testament mentions as inheritances to his heirs are all the books in his personal library. This clearly shows that for Wesley, all truly effective religious instruction efforts must be rooted not only in holiness but also in learning. For Wesley, learning is essential for a religious educator because learning illumines love, points out where love should and should not be directed. Conversely, love is crucial for a religious educator because learning without love is arid rationalism and ineffective ministry. Wesley's will and testament then goes on to list the many things to be given as bequests to different persons. The very last thing and thus culminating provision that Wesley's will and testament mentions is once again books. He bequeaths to each of those itinerant religious educators who still remain Methodists for at least six months after his demise the eight volumes of his sermons "as a little token of [his] love." In his final instructions from the grave, John Wesley once again links love and learning as the two indispensable characteristics of every authentic religious educator.

Up until the late 1730s John Wesley was a reasonably effective religious educator, though of course he did undergo some reverses. What was it that caused him to change from being merely an ordinarily successful religious educator into being an extraordinarily successful religious educator? What was it that caused him to change from being a religious educator who worked reasonably hard into a religious educator who worked incredibly hard? What was it that caused him to change from being a solidly dutiful religious educator into a perpetually enthusiastic religious educator? What was the fundamental source of his burning zeal, unflagging energy, vigorous persistence in overcoming all manner of hardships great and small? What was the font and wellspring of his unsurpassing love for the religious instruction ministry? The answer to all these questions, and indeed the key to Wesley's life and ministry, is the intense religious experience that he had on May 24, 1738 in the meeting of a religious society at Aldersgate Street. For devout Methodists, as well as for those Christians in other faith groups whose traditions are as all-embracing as the wide-open arms of Christ, Wesley's religious experience at Aldersgate is comparable to Paul's intense religious experience on the Damascus road and to Augustine's intense religious experience in the Milanese garden. For these three great religious educators, it was a profound religious experience that became the decisive wellspring and gyroscope for their personal lives and for their religious instruction apostolates.

Prior to his intense religious experience at Aldersgate, Wesley's personal and ministerial conviction was primarily intellectual. Aldersgate transformed intellectual conviction into a personal experience that inflamed his heart. In his intense religious experience at Aldersgate Wesley came into firsthand contact with the burning love of God for him, the love of God as lived, felt, and experienced in the depths of his mortal being. His Aldersgate religious experience was an existential synapse between God in his energizing and life-giving love on the one hand and Wesley in his frail but receptive human condition on the other hand. From the religious instruction perspective, Wesley remarked that in the months preceding Aldersgate he had been teaching religion but his heart was not in it. In the years before Aldersgate Wesley the religious educator, even at his best, had taught faith to others until they had it. But now, through Aldersgate, his own faith was sealed by God and confirmed by others.

In, through, and after Aldersgate, John Wesley's intense religious experience became him and he became his religious experience to such an extent that in all of Wesley's voluminous writings Aldersgate is only mentioned twice—once when he gave his account of it, and once years later. People typically do not find it necessary to explain to others the ground of their existence probably because this ground cannot be adequately explained.

From the religious instruction perspective, Wesley's intense religious experience at Aldersgate did not so much make him great as it made him useful. Aldersgate was absolutely essential in order for Wesley to achieve his enormous potential as a highly successful religious educator. Without his profound religious experience he probably would have been just another religious educator. For Wesley the purpose of faith is love, and love by its very nature seeks to dynamically spread itself—which is precisely the core of all religious instruction activity.

Wesley's deeply moving religious experience at Aldersgate did not arise out of nothing, however appealing a *deus ex nihilo* explanation might seem to those who regard religion as a kind of ultra magic. Aldersgate had definite antecedents, all of which favorably disposed Wesley to be both ready and receptive to a cataclysmic religious experience. Indeed there is a sense in which Aldersgate was almost inevitable (in the freewill sense of that term) because of Wesley's previous encounters with the divine. His deeply religious upbringing, his devoted work with the Holy Club, and his frequent reception of the Eucharist all acted as felicitous predispositions to Aldersgate. His reading of the Christian mystical writers, which increased in intensity with the passing of years, also disposed him to the personal encounter with God at Aldersgate. Wesley's earlier intense religious experience in 1725 almost surely acted as an especially strong disposer. His pre-1738 religious instruction work also played a significant predispositional role, since he worked for God as strongly as he could. Especially important as a disposer was his psychological openness to direct divine intervention in his life.

It is my own firm and central belief, a belief grounded in both my personal and vicarious experience, that we religious educators cannot totally and radically answer our call within a call until we have had an intense personal religious experience.

Intense religious experience will greatly assist us in making our call within our call absolutely and irrevocably central in our consciousness.

Intense religious experience will transform our teaching apostolate and will raise us up to a profoundly new realm of consciousness, both of which are essential if we are to completely optimize our religious instruction efforts.

Few things will prove more foundationally important for a truly successful religious instruction apostolate than intense religious experience. Our teaching ministry will never be the same after we have undergone an intense religious experience.

Intense religious experience in no way dispenses us from either possessing the requisite religious substantive content or being highly skilled in the art/science of teaching. What intense religious experience does for us religious educators is to break open the crust that often encases religious substantive content so that we can behold face-to-face what is really fundamental and important in Christian living. Once we have existentially encountered the essence of true religion, we will be able to center our teaching efforts on what really matters most in Christian living. We will then be able to deliberatively fashion instructional procedures that open the world of deep and true religion for learners. And we will even be able to fashion instructional procedures which have the power to facilitate intense religious experience, something that the empirical research has demonstrated to be possible.

Our religious instruction ministry will never be the same after we have had an intense religious experience.

After we have had an intense religious experience, a cloud of special divine presence will rest on our work and suffuse it.

Through intense religious experience, our own religious instruction efforts as pedagogically incarnated in competent teaching activity will be sealed by God, no matter what others may say and no matter how others may judge us.

In and through and by our undergoing intense religious experience, we are sacramented to the Lord in a special manner. The grace and divine energy that flow through us through intense religious experience can help us significantly to more deeply sacrament the already holy act of teaching.

Intense religious experience will be our gyroscope, always keeping us and our apostolate on course.

Intense religious experience will surely bring us closer to Jesus in brotherly love, a closeness we can share, as appropriate, with learners. History has shown repeatedly that nothing brings a person closer to God than intense religious experience.

Intense religious experience will also bond us closer to the historical Jesus who modeled and shared our religious instruction ministry.

Intense religious experience will serve as the chief energizing force in our religious instruction work. As a result of this kind of religious experience we will be able to press on with vigor and joy even when the instructional obstacles seem insurmountable.

Intense religious experience will bestow on us a perpetual enthusiasm for our work as religious educators, in accordance with the contours of our personality.

After we have had an intense religious experience, no sacrifice will be too great, no work too arduous, no hardship too difficult, and no task too menial in the wholehearted and successful accomplishment of our religious instruction apostolate.

Intense religious experience will sustain us through thick and thin. It will prevent burnout. It will be the warm life-giving flame deep within us that will keep us and our apostolate burning until the very end.

Though intense religious experience is so vitally important for bringing us closer to God, what is crucial from the religious instruction standpoint is that it brings our teaching efforts closer to God. For us as religious educators, what is central about intense religious experience is not that it makes us holy but that it makes us useful.

Have our hearts been "strangely warmed" by an intense religious experience of God? If not, why not? God is always ready to bestow an intense religious experience on us? Are we ready?

To what extent are we religious educators always existentially open to the explosion of the divine in our hearts through intense religious experience? To what degree have we crusted ourselves over with the impenetrable shell of ideology or doctrine or affective closedness, all of which render it extremely difficult for us to have an intense religious experience?

Do we strive to eschew psychological narrowness and actively seek psychological openness?

Do we religious educators earnestly and continually attempt to engage in activities that tend to dispose us to having an intense religious experience?

How many times a day do we consciously and intentionally draw close to God in prayer in our thoughts, affects, and overt actions? Do we receive the Eucharist often?

How often do we read the writings of the mystics—persons who have achieved the highest level of intense religious experience and who share their thoughts and feelings and actions with us?

It is axiomatic in life that the more persons value a reality the more these persons will seek after that reality and the more these persons will be open to receive that reality when they encounter it. To what extent do we religious educators deeply and truly value intense religious experience as crucially important to our personal lives and our professional lives?

Performance Objective: I will strive earnestly to make all religious instruction activities a personal experience for each learner because this kind of teaching tends to foster genuine religious experience in learners (and also in me).

9

The Journey

One of the most frequent, most enduring, and most compelling central themes running throughout much of the world's greatest literature in all eras and in all lands is that of the journey. The journeys depicted in world literature are carefully constructed allegories of the journey into oneself, a journey toward progressively deeper understanding (cognition), love (affect), and service (lifestyle). The fictional journeys portrayed in great literature have a universal quality about them in the sense that the main characters as well as the central thread of events speak to each of us in some way as we continue our own personal life journeys into ourselves.

Allegories such as the journey into oneself are composed by authors to serve an interrelated twin purpose, namely, instruction and entertainment. Because an allegory typically presents deeper spiritual themes in the guise of material representations, it often is an effective instructional device for many persons due to the natural human tendency to be attracted at least initially to the material form of reality.

Allegorical fiction is written or told because the authors believe that the deepest truths in all their rich and varied contextual existence often are described more accurately in allegory than in straightforward prose. Because a good allegory conveys more than one level of meaning simultaneously, it enables a person to discover that life can be understood, loved, and lived on several different planes.

A well-told allegory of life, especially the spiritual life, attempts to touch the religious ideal by renewing it in personal and world consciousness so that through the allegory deeper life-truths escape their parody and encrustation in dogma.

In what is possibly the world's first major piece of fiction, *Gilgamesh* (c.2400 B.C.–c.1200 B.C.), the story is told of the journey of an ancient Sumerian king in search of immortality and the ultimate meaning of life and death, a pilgrimage in which he travels throughout the land, and in the process comes to deep friendship and its subsequent loss, to a memorable forest passage, and to the river discovery and eventual loss of the plant of eternal youth. The *Odyssey* (c. 725 B.C.) is the story of the Greek hero Ulysses who, after the end of the Trojan War, journeys for ten long years through a great many hardships, perils, and adventures on the way home to his wife, son, and native land, and thus to himself. The *Aeneid* (30 B.C.–19 B.C. is the tale of the Trojan hero Aeneas who leaves the burning ruins of Troy and journeys through a wide variety of difficulties, adventures, and great love in order to fulfill his destiny by laying the foundation of what would become the great imperial city of Rome.

Medieval chivalric romances such as *Le Conte del Graal* (c. 1180) and *Le Morte d'Arthur* (c.1470) tell of the quest for the Holy Grail in which the knights Perceval and especially Galahad journey forth in search of the most sacred of all vessels and with it true and unsullied religion. The *Divine Comedy* (1307–1321) is the journey that Dante takes to the deepest regions of his soul by progressively experiencing the final realities of hell, purgatory, and heaven. *Everyman* (c. 1490-1498) recounts the journey of a representative human being who travels on the road that every person must take to death, and how he gradually comes to the illumination that his own gifts of fortune such as material goods and his own gifts of nature such as strength are all blown away at the grave like dry leaves, leaving only good works and the sacraments to secure redemption.

Modern literature is no less replete with grand allegories of the spiritual journey than are the majestic works of fiction written in the ancient and medieval worlds. *Don Quixote* (1605–1615) is the tale of a man who sallies forth on what initially is a chimerical adventure in the knight-errant style but whose maturing interaction with his traveling companion becomes an often unawared journey into the purpose of existence, the nature of reality and truth, the basic meaning of success and failure, and the inner sources of character. *Robinson Crusoe* (1719) is the story of a man shipwrecked for twenty-eight years on a seemingly deserted island where he is forced by complete isolation and an unfriendly environment to undertake an inner journey through which he finds himself and God initially through rebellion and punishment but finally through repentance and deliverance. *Moby Dick* (1851) recounts the voyage of a group of diverse men who set out to kill a gigantic white whale and in the process make the journey into themselves wherein they grapple with such basic perennial problems as the conflict between good and evil, the clash of free will and fate, and the struggle to find meaning and fulfillment in a harsh, inscrutable universe. *Siddhartha* (1922) tells of the spiritual journey of a young Hindu Brahmin who successively lives and subsequently rejects the life of a student first at home and then with the holy ascetics in the forest (knowledge), the life of erotic passion as the lover of an accomplished courtesan (sensuality), the life of a successful businessman (power), and finally comes to enlightenment from listening carefully to the river from which he learns the essential oneness of the universe, timelessness, and all-embracing love.

The spiritual journey is, of course, a central and permeational theme in that benchmark nonfictional literature which each major religion throughout the history of the world has regarded as inspired. For example, the Egyptian *Book of the Dead* (the proper name of which is *Book of Going Forth by Day*) (c.2400 B.C.–c.525 B.C. provides the magic formulas and rituals that were placed in or on the tombs of the deceased to protect, guide, and equip the dead person in that individual's journey to and during the afterlife. In both its immediate and ultimate meaning, the *Bible* (c.1250/900 B.C.–c.96 A.D.) is the story of the journey of a people to God and the journey of God to his people.

The ongoing journey of each person to God forms the living axis of all authentic religious instruction. Each learner is present in the religious instruction event as one called by God to journey unto him, whether the learner realizes this or not. And we religious educators have our own special call within a call, a vocation that forms the axis of our own journey unto God as actualized by helping others in their own spiritual journeys.

Sacraments are focused channels of grace given at key times in a person's journey through life: birth, puberty, vocation and career, times of eucharist and times of sin, and the close of life. As is the case with the sacraments of the Eucharist and Reconciliation, the sacrament of teaching is waiting and available throughout the person's journey. It is our sacred and awesome responsibility as religious educators to bring the sacrament of teaching into the lives of learners of all ages as they proceed through the journey of life.

To what extent do we religious educators have the courage and the foresight to teach religion as an exciting and never-ending adventure in human living, the greatest of all possible journeys?

To what degree do we religious educators have the vision to see and appreciate that our teaching activities make up the main road that God has called each of us to take on our own personal journey to the divine? Operationalizing this question somewhat, how frequently do we religious educators see our teaching activities as our own direct spiritual journey to God, a journey that takes place step by step on the long and winding road of concretely assisting learners week in and week out to know God, love God, and do godly actions?

How often do we religious educators help those whom we teach to see their religious learnings in the existential context of their own personal journey to God? Or do we teach religion in such a fashion that they see their religious learnings as a series of lifeless facts and isolated cognitive dogmas?

Do we religious educators do as much as we should to help those whom we teach to see their religious learnings not so much as the acquisition of outcomes fixed in themselves but more importantly as outcomes that are necessary and helpful steps on their own continuing personal journey to God?

To what extent do we religious educators help those whom we teach to see their religious learnings both as indicators of past progress on their journey to God and as helpful predictors of future general directions in this continuing pilgrimage?

To what degree do we religious educators consciously use those kinds of instructional procedures that singly and collectively take learners on a personal journey into themselves, a journey that might well involve going out of themselves in order to find themselves and God?

The religious instruction enterprise is one in which both learners and educators travel together on the journey to God. Are we paying sufficient attention to our own journey as we teach learners, remembering that the quality of our religious instruction efforts constitutes the most important factor in determining how well we make the journey?

Performance Objective: At the end of every week I will write an entry in my professional journal briefly chronicling what happened during the various religious instruction events of that week. The axis of this part of my journal will be the degree to which these events constituted a personal journey of religious faith and love on the part of the learners and me, as contrasted to a mere assemblage of facts. At the end of every month I will review my journal entries for the preceding month to ascertain the degree to which I have made progress in the task of transforming religious instruction activity into a continuously upward journey of religious faith and love.

10

Smokehouse

There are two primary and competing viewpoints on how a person becomes a true and authentic religious educator. The first of these viewpoints is that of lamination while the second is that of the smokehouse. Usually these contrasting viewpoints are not expressed openly and straightforwardly, but they are nonetheless present and operative in the actual making of a religious educator.

Central to the lamination viewpoint is the belief that religious instruction consciousness, knowledge, and skills are laminated on top of an individual's personality so that he thereby becomes a religious educator. In this conceptualization, an individual becomes a religious educator by superimposing and then firmly bonding a layer of requisite professional awareness and behavior on top of his everyday personality.

Basic to the smokehouse viewpoint is the belief that an individual's personality becomes thoroughly suffused by religious instruction consciousness, knowledge, and skills so that through this slow process she becomes a religious educator. In this conceptualization, a person becomes a religious educator by opening her entire self-system in such a long-lasting porous manner that her everyday personality is completely permeated, thoroughly colored, and entirely flavored by requisite professional awareness and behavior.

In smokehouse-style preparation and ongoing professional development, the whole self-system of the religious educator is completely suffused with religious instruction consciousness, knowledge, and skills so that the person becomes religious instruction activity. In lamination-style preparation and ongoing professional development, the self-system of the religious educator remains fundamentally untouched because religious instruction consciousness, knowledge, and skills are only bonded on top of rather than thoroughly interpenetrated with the religious educator's personality system.

In smokehouse-style preparation and ongoing professional development, the entire personality of the religious educator is changed by and transformed into religious instruction awareness and behavior. In lamination-style preparation and ongoing professional development, there is no basic personality change and transformation since religious instruction activity is an impermeable layer lying on top of the educator's personality.

In smokehouse-style preparation and ongoing professional development, the educator's self-system becomes so thoroughly blended with religious instruction consciousness and behavior that religious instruction activity can never be separated from the educator's overall personality. In lamination-style preparation and ongoing professional development, religious instruction activity is essentially distinct from the religious educator's personality because lamination is the superimposition of one stratum on top of another without ever intermingling with it.

In short, the smokehouse image suggests total suffusion, as when a red liquid is poured into a glass of clear water and then shaken. In marked contrast, the lamination image suggests a veneer, such as a marble-topped wooden table or a formica-covered kitchen counter.

In a smokehouse, the total penetration and suffusion of the food by the smoke means that the smoke and the food become one. In any kind of preservice and inservice growth that is authentic and true, the educator's own self-system becomes one with religious instruction activity: I in religious instruction activity and religious instruction activity in me. Through smokehouse-style preparation and ongoing professional development, religious instruction becomes not our work but our lifework, a lifework of our whole and entire self, a lifework which so thoroughly and completely inhabits our lives that at every waking moment we are acting as a religious educator manifestly or latently in one form or another.

The smokehouse image is rich with meaning and significance for the preparation and ongoing improvement of a religious educator. Let us briefly explore some of the more important characteristics of actual smokehouse operation and then meditatively connect these with our own preparation and ongoing professional development as religious educators.

Just as there are two primary fused contents in every religious instruction act, so also are there two primary meshed contents in every functioning smokehouse. The food in the working smokehouse is analogous to the substantive content in the religious instruction act. The smoking procedure is analysis to the structural content in the religious instruction act.

The food placed in the functioning smokehouse is not changed by the smoke swirling around it and through it. Pork does not become beef in the smoking process, for example. What happens to the food in the functioning smokehouse is that it is affected to a certain extent, depending on the type, quality, and characteristics of the food placed in the smokehouse. Smoking does not bestow some totally new flavor on the food but rather brings out some of its latent possibilities while at the same time flavoring it to a degree. All of this relates to our own preparation and ongoing professional development as religious educators. Our basic personality structure does not substantially change in smokehouse-style professional formation and development. What slowly changes is the way in which our basic personality structure is flavored and cured and colored and thrusted. In this gradual and pervasive change, we do not lose our personalities. Rather, we gain ourselves, we actualize ourselves in ways not otherwise possible. Smokehouse-style preparation and ongoing professional development bring out and flavor our personalities so that we can better love and serve the Lord in more productive religious instruction ministry.

Meat and fish typically taste better when smoked fresh as contrasted to being defrosted and then smoked. The fresher and the more natural the personalities that we religious educators put into the smokehouse of professional preparation and ongoing development, the more richly flavored and the more fully competent we will be in our religious instruction work.

Better taste results when meat and fish are smoked with their bones intact. Our religious instruction activities will be more distinctive, more broadly flavored, and more effective in reaching a wide variety of people when we place ourselves in the smokehouse of preparation and development with the bones of all our personal characteristics and idiosyncrasies intact. Much as the bones and meat interact with each other subtly but importantly during the smoking process, so too our own particular personal qualities interact with our generalized self-system in such a way that we religious educators come to possess the enhanced flavor typical of every well-smoked product plus that crucial individuality so necessary for the kind of religious instruction activity that is successful for others and fulfilling for ourselves.

When the skin is left on game and fish while it is being smoked, the result will be more moist and tender and thus more delectable. The skin protects and possibly lubricates the meat and fish during the smoking process. In our initial preparation and subsequent on-going development as religious educators, it is important for us to refrain from any attempt to remove the "outer" surface of our personalities in the erroneous belief that by so doing we will thereby expose our "inner" selves more fully to the beneficial effects of the smokehouse of professionalization. In actuality, we only are what we completely are, "inner" and "outer" together in dynamic concert. Each has a necessary and fundamental function in our growth as religious educators. Smoking only the skin of our personality and not the meat will result in an overcooked "outer" and an under-cooked or even an uncooked "inner." Removing the skin of our personalities and smoking only the meat will make the flesh dry and tough. We should strive to put our whole self-system in its entirety, "outer" as well as "inner," in the smokehouse of professionalization if we are to place the full repertoire of our personal gifts at the disposal of learners.

Although the nature and distinct characteristics of the food (substantive content) in the smokehouse are absolutely essential, the way in which the food is smoked (structural content) is equally essential in bringing about the final result. Let us now meditate on some of the major elements of the smoking process.

First and foremost, proper control of the structural (procedural) variables involved in the entire smokehouse operation is necessary to obtain a product of the desired quality. The most important of these variables include smokehouse construction, temperature, fuel, air flow, and humidity because each of these has a pronounced effect on the appearance, flavor, texture, juiciness, and smoke penetration of the final product. The meat or fish can be of the highest quality, but if smokehouse control is weak or absent, the result will be disappointing. We religious educators might possess the finest and holiest of personalities, but if the key variables in the smoking process of our initial and ongoing professionalization are not carefully controlled to produce the desired results, we will not achieve the fullness of our religious instruction potential.

To ensure satisfactory control, a smokehouse must be properly constructed. A good smokehouse is built of stone or brick rather than of wood so that it will not burn down. This type of construction also insulates a smokehouse from penetration from undesirable outside entities such as unwanted animals and insects. Although it is relatively airtight, nonetheless a smokehouse does have vents at the bottom to allow air to enter and vents at the top to let the excess smoke to escape. More often than not a smokehouse is tall and slender, which permits the smoke to optimally mingle with the air, swirl around the food, and eventually escape. We religious educators must do all in our power to make sure that the metaphorical smokehouse in which our initial preparation and continuing professional development take place is constructed in such a careful manner that we gain the great number of benefits accruing from the smoking process. This metaphorical smokehouse should be sufficiently fireproof that the flames of external pressures and internal frustrations will not cause burndown or burnout. The smokehouse of our professional preparation and ongoing development should be well insulated to keep in the flames of our zeal and the meat of our vocationed selfhood while at the same time keeping out the animals of distraction and the insects of gimmickry. Yet the smokehouse of our preparation and ongoing professional development ought not to be airtight because then the flame will go out, the smoke will cease, and the meat of our vocationed selfhood will decay. We need the proper number of entrance openings in our preparation and professional development in order to let in the requisite air to come in so as to keep the flame burning and the smoke swirling. We also need some strategically situated escape openings in order that the flame does not become so hot that the meat is improperly cooked and in order that the smoke does not become so dense as to inhibit the inflow of requisite oxygen which would cause the smoking process to stop.

The fuel source used in the smokehouse makes a significant difference in the resultant taste and flavor of the food. Wood is generally considered to be the finest fuel source for smoking food of all kinds. Hardwoods are typically superior to softwoods not only because softwoods emit sooty smoke and produce a dark product with a bitter taste but also because hardwoods give off a wide variety of wonderful aromas that impart distinct and delectable flavors to the smoked food. Different hardwoods produce different taste sensations and should be used discerningly according to the type of food being smoked and the kind of taste desired. Hickory produces a strong and piquant taste that is good for red meats as well as for big and small game; it usually is undesirable for fish. Mesquite gives rise to a strong and sweet taste that is good for big and small game; it is undesirable for lamb. Cherry wood provides a mild and fruity taste that is good for poultry, pork, and salmon; it is undesirable for swordfish. Applewood supplies a delicate and fruity taste that is good for turkey and pork; it is undesirable for swordfish,. The disadvantages of hardwood include the following: difficulty in obtaining the desired type, expense, and afterburn ashes which must be removed. In the metaphorical smokehouse of our initial preparation and continuing professional development as religious educators, we need to keep our fuel source very fresh and well stocked with the finest kind of the right material, no matter where it is located and how difficult it is to obtain. For religious educators, this fuel consists in reading first-class religious instruction books, pursuing graduate studies in those religious education programs that stress the nature and skills of teaching as well as the foundations of the field, attending premier religious education conferences at the national and international levels, improving teaching skills by repeatedly practicing pedagogical analysis and pedagogical control in the local Teacher Performance Center, participating in joint professional study groups and cooperative task groups with superior religious educators in our locality, and of course engaging in passive and active prayer. When and how we will use these necessary top-notch fuels depends on the different personality characteristics and professional requirements of each religious educator as well as the results we wish to achieve in the metaphorical smokehouse of preparation and never-ending professional development. These professional development fuels, like hardwoods, are relatively costly in terms of time and effort and difficulty, but they are essential if the inherent capabilities and manifold textures of our own personalities are to be richly enhanced and gorgeously flavored with the penetrating smoke of top-quality professional development fuels.

The flow rate and flow pattern of the smoke is an important feature of any truly effective smokehouse. The smoke should flow over and through the food not too slowly and not too quickly if the mouthwatering result is to occur. Flow pattern is also important because the smoke should swirl through the smokehouse in such a way that each part of the food becomes exposed to the proper amount of smoke. In the metaphorical smokehouse of our own professional preparation and ongoing development, it is vital that the smoke which emanates from the religious instruction fuel pass through our self-system at just the proper rate, not too slowly and not too rapidly. Only in this way can the rich smoke of professionalism thoroughly and modulatingly penetrate our personalities in such a complete fashion that we ourselves become inextricably fused with the deep transforming flavor of religious instruction consciousness and activity. It is also important that the flow pattern of the smoke of professionalism be carefully regulated so that it fully permeates every single dimension of our self-system without exception.

Preparing the food before it is placed in the smokehouse is quite helpful in bringing out the rich potential of the smoking process. Advance preparation of the food varies according to the type of food to be smoked and the kind of taste desired. Cheese and nuts entail only a small amount of preparation prior to being put into the smokehouse. The smoky flavor of fish and game can be distinctively enhanced by marinating them prior to smoking. The taste, juiciness, and tenderness of the final product is discernably affected by the composition of the marinade—the relative amounts of salt, water, herbs, spices, tabasco, and the like. Additionally, the length of time the food remains in the marinade prior to smoking exerts a decided impact on the final product. The food should be cured in the marinade so that it is soaked to that degree which will result in the desired taste to be achieved. Before we place ourselves in the metaphorical smokehouse of professional religious instruction preparation and ongoing development, it is not only helpful but usually imperative that we prepare ourselves sufficiently in advance so that the smokehouse experience can exert its wonderful religious instruction effects on our entire self-system. The nature, degree, and duration of these recurrent advance preparations depend on many factors, including our own personality structure, previous experiences, and desired results. The composition of the professional marinade in which our personalities are figuratively soaked, and also the length of time we remain in this marinade, should be carefully controlled so that they enhance in just the right degree the flavor and texture of our religious instruction consciousness and performance. An overly concentrated or unbalanced marinade, or an overly long immersion in the marinade, will result in masking the distinctiveness of our singular personalty. On the other hand, too weak a marinade, or too little soaking in the marinade, will fail to add the requisite flavor of professionalism to our self-system.

Once in the smokehouse, the carefully marinated food must remain for just the right length of time if the desired result is to ensue. If the food is left in the smokehouse for too long a time, it will become oversmoked. If the food is left in the smokehouse for too short a time, it will become undersmoked. Proper timing depends on a wide variety of factors including the type of food to be smoked, the characteristics of the particular food, the kind of fuel, and the desired result. So too it is with us religious educators in the metaphorical smokehouse of our professional preparation and ongoing inservice development. We must do whatever we can to ensure that the time spent in the smokehouse is just right, not too long and not too short. The proper time in the smokehouse will allow the savory smoke of professionalism to thoroughly infuse our entire self-system so that in this felicitous permeation process our own distinctive personalities can become completely suffused with professionalism. Too long a time in the smokehouse will cause the smoke to overpower and even cancel out the important subjective qualities which constitute our own special gift to the religious instruction task. Too short a time will not enable our personality to become sufficiently infused with the sweet smoke of professionalism with the result that we will become inadequately professionalized in our consciousness and in our performance.

It is essential that a smokehouse contain a pit or receptacle to catch the grease or other drippings that ooze from the food during the smoking process. If this is not done, the grease and other drippings will flow downward into the fire and cause deleterious flareups or fall to the floor and eventually result in a rancid odor or slippery surface. All this is analogous to the metaphorical smokehouse of our own religious instruction preparation and ongoing professional development. As the rich, transforming smoke of professionalism permeates every part of our self-system, we necessarily excrete those individual faults, misdirected energies, and other personality traits that are unsuitable for the successful accomplishment of the religious instruction task. This undesirable grease must be caught and discharged in order to minimize the possibility of flareups and malodors, both of which can significantly harm the process of our becoming truly professional and also hurt our own overall personality growth. In our personal spiritual life, confession/reconciliation for some individuals and balanced religious counseling for others serve as the washable pit or removable receptacle to catch the grease of our sins and character blemishes. In our professional life of initial preparation and ongoing inservice development as religious educators, we must find some useful concavity to catch and dispose of our unwanted smokehouse drippings. Such a concavity might include a close friend, a significant other, a group of superior religious educators in the area, a competent spiritual director, or the like.

Let us now meditate on some additional points that show how the smokehouse constitutes a particularly apt metaphor to guide and make probable the success of the long process of the religious educator's preservice preparation and ongoing inservice development.

The task of successfully smoking food to bring about a truly delectable result is not an easy one. In actuality, this task is rather difficult. This fact is even more true for the metaphorical smokehouse of the religious educator's preparation and continuing professional development than it is for smoking fish or game in an actual smokehouse. Other things being equal, we religious educators should not select tasks because they are easy but because they are difficult. Why? Because down deep we know full well in our personal life, our spiritual life, and our professional religious instruction life that the most worthwhile tasks typically involve considerable difficulty.

The process of smoking food takes time. Top-quality smoking is done very slowly; it simply cannot be rushed if the desired mouthwatering result of delicious flavor, fine texture, and lovely appearance is to ensue. A classic traditional smokehouse imparts a more pronounced and richer flavor to the food than is the case with the much quicker electric or gas artificial smokers because the food is left in the authentic smokehouse for a longer period of time than it is in the artificial contrivances. Slow smoking in the smokehouse allows the smoke to gently penetrate the food so that the taste of the food is optimally brought out rather than overpowered by the quick rush of smoke in an electric or gas smoking device. In an effort to speed up smoking time, kerosene or lighter fluid are sometimes used as starters in the traditional smokehouse. However, this procedure gives a decidedly unpleasant taste to the food; additionally, it can be quite dangerous. As in the case of an actual smokehouse, the process of thoroughly suffusing the religious educator's consciousness and performance with the enhancing smoke of professionalism is necessarily slow. It takes time, a long time, to truly think like a religious educator, feel like a religious educator, and act like a religious educator. Quick smoking, regardless of the reasons that motivate this procedure, simply does not produce the high quality result that comes from the slow smokehouse process of penetrating professionalism. Artificial quick starters, which use the kerosene of real or imagined personnel shortages, or the lighter fluid of disdain for the value of professional preparation usually have undesirable consequences: the religious educator's consciousness and performance will be forever flavored by the unpleasant odor of artificiality, and the seeming success of the educator's work will sooner or later go up in flames.

Cooking food in a smokehouse is a science and an art combined. It is a science because it is based on the scientific principles that govern the major elements in the smokehouse and their interaction—how the airflow, temperature, humidity, fuel source, amount of marination, size of the smokehouse, and the like affect a particular kind of food. Human knowledge of the scientific principles underlying effective smokehouse operation has improved over the passage of time. Smokehouse operation is also an art because successful smoking requires that the person in charge initially arrange, and during the smoking process frequently rearrange, the variables in the smokehouse so that the desired result occurs. The desired result itself is often different depending on the personal gustatory preferences of an individual. The fundamental operation of the metaphorical smokehouse of our initial and continuing religious instruction professional development is also a science and an art. It is a science because it rests firmly on those scientific principles governing effective ways of preparing and continually developing a finely tuned religious instruction consciousness, affects, and performance. Though still in its early childhood, the knowledge of these scientific principles has grown enormously since the latter part of the nineteenth century. Metaphorical smokehouse operation to produce the complete religious educator is also an art because the necessary variables during preparation and ongoing inservice development must initially be arranged and frequently rearranged during the process to bring about the final result. This result often varies depending on the personality characteristics of the religious educator, the religious instruction task for which the educator is being prepared or is now engaged, and the like.

The process of smoking meat and fish in a traditional smoke-house is slow, long, arduous, and exacting. But the rewards are well worth the effort. Probably the most obvious reward is that the flavor, aroma, and appearance of smoked food are significantly enhanced as compared to unsmoked food. By and large people prefer the taste and smell of smoked products. Therefore smoked food is more in demand and thus commands a higher price than the same product when not smoked. The same holds true for those religious educators who undergo smokehouse-style preparation and ongoing professional development. These religious educators generally are more highly respected, are in more demand, and receive greater spiritual and financial rewards because of their smokehouse-style preparation and ongoing professional development.

Another major benefit accruing from the long, slow, and exacting smokehouse process is preservation. Until the advent of refrigeration in the late 1870s, the entire smokehouse process, including marination, was a primary method used to preserve meats from spoiling. The classic smokehouse process preserves food longer than do electric or gas smoking methods because in the smoke-house the smoke penetrates the food more thoroughly and more completely than is the case with quick-smoking devices. Religious educators whose preparation and ongoing professional development take place in a metaphorical smokehouse are likewise more preserved from spoilage than those of their colleagues who went through a quick-smoking process or no smoking process at all. As the months and years of religious instruction activity roll by, quite a few religious educators become stale in the apostolate, grow weary, lose interest, have burnout. Although the metaphorical smokehouse process of preparation and ongoing development does not guarantee the prevention of such spoilage, nonetheless it does tend to inhibit or at least retard this decay and thus preserve the religious educator as a person and as a professional far more than is the case in quick-smoking preparation and development or no smoking at all.

To what extent are we religious educators willing to professionally prepare and then continually develop ourselves through the slow, long, arduous, and exacting smokehouse process? Or do we seriously compromise our call within a call by opting for some less rigorous and less satisfactory quick method?

To what degree does the smoke of religious instruction activity so thoroughly and deeply penetrate our everyday consciousness and activity that our personality takes on the flavor, texture, aroma, and appearance of religious instruction? If we are to bring out the sacramentality inherent in the religious instruction act, do we not have to let this sacramentality suffuse our very being?

What do we do in the concrete to always make sure that the smokehouse of our preparation and ongoing professional development is well constructed so that it is eminently capable of bringing about the desired result?

How often do we take great pains to see to it that the fuel source is of the highest quality?

Do we do as much as we can do to select the finest metaphorical herbs and spices and salts from which to make the marinade?

Do we habitually place our entire self in the smokehouse, or are there dimensions of our personality that we withhold?

To what degree do we make it a practice to carefully monitor our progress at every stage of the metaphorical smokehouse process of professionalization?

Performance Objective: Sometime this month I will telephone or write other area religious educators and arrange to come together to organize a first-class ongoing inservice professional development program for us or to improve the present program if one already exists. The goal of this inservice professional development program is to ensure that religious instruction activity thoroughly permeates every fibre of our being rather than being laminated on top of our personalities. I will work diligently to make sure that this inservice professional development program is well constructed and avoids superficiality or gimmickry. Together with my colleagues in this program, I will carefully select the ingredients of this professional development program, including regular reading of serious top-notch books specifically in the area of religious instruction, spiritual enrichment, common prayer experiences, professional fellowshiping, working in the local teacher performance center, and the like. Our group will strive to ensure that our inservice professional development is such that it proceeds slowly and surely in order that all of its aspects thoroughly penetrate the consciousness of every religious educator in our group. We will develop specific markers and checks to guarantee as far as possible that all the members place the totality of their personalties in the smokehouse of inservice professional development rather than just interpenetrate part of their selves. We will establish a formative evaluation system in order to periodically monitor how well we are doing in this regard. Our group will meet biweekly until we have devised an excellent workable professional development program which will significantly enhance the effectiveness of our religious instruction work through making our ministry completely permeate every dimension of our being.

11

State of Consciousness

Some years ago I was teaching a regular graduate-level course, "The American School in Crisis" at the University of Alabama at Birmingham. The course dealt with the many major crises impacting public schools in the United States, problems such as drugs, gangs, poor discipline, lack of adequate parental involvement, attention deficit disorder, teenage pregnancy, single parent homes, anti-intellectualism, low work ethic, inadequate funding, lazy and poorly prepared teachers, and so on.

The students in the course were all public and private schoolteachers pursuing their master's degree in one or another specialization in educational studies.

Because of the great number of widely diverse topics in a course such as this, and because I wanted the students to learn to base their own instructional procedures on solid research rather than on well-meaning but scientifically unverified hunches, I used the seminar technique. All the students were required to spend considerable time and effort doing careful research on a particular crisis of their choosing, to write an in-depth research paper on that crisis, and then to give an hour and a half interactive presentation to the other students offering the fruits of their research through a wide variety of instructional devices.

Week followed upon week, and before long it was time for the last student to present the results of her scholarly investigation to the other learners. Her presentation was as dreadful as her research. It lacked preparation, care, adequacy, work, and delivery. It was terrible in every way, especially when contrasted to the energetic and well-researched presentations made by her fellow students.

After the class session was over, I walked out of the room feeling quite dejected. A few steps out of the door, after everyone else had left, one student came up to me. He was an Evangelical Protestant minister and indeed could pass for any one of those ubiquitous beaming televangelists. His hair was immaculately blow dried. He wore a bright green jacket, thin striped shirt with a bright tie, tan polyester-blend trousers, rimless eyeglasses, and a perpetual smile.

"Good course, good course!" exclaimed the preacher in his eternally cheerful resonant voice. "I really learned a lot."

Still feeling downhearted, I responded in a discouraged tone of voice: "That last student certainly gave a dreadful performance. I wish she had worked harder."

"Oh," the preacher responded in an upbeat mood, "that's really not important. It was just so good that she was here!"

This brief incident highlights two significantly different states of consciousness in the religious helping professions. The Evangelical Protestant minister was living in and responding from an overall ministerial state of consciousness. In stark contrast, I was living in and responding from an educational consciousness.

In terms of how persons interpret an event, feel about it and act upon it, what is important is not only the bald facts in themselves or even the concrete circumstances of that event but far more crucially and significantly the state of consciousness into which persons incorporate the relevant facts and circumstances.

Consciousness in the sense I am using this term here is not just a way of looking at reality but even more a way of being in and being toward reality.

Ministerial consciousness is a broadly based, generalized, indistinct, and dispersive way of looking at reality and being toward reality. Some key characteristics of ministerial consciousness include an approach to persons and things primarily and proximately in terms of salvation, a totally acceptant and uncritical welcoming stance, a deliberately generalized and diffused desire to help others without much thought given to specific objectives and practices, and a concentration on the overall comprehensive goal with a concomitant tendency to disvalue the acquisition and constant sharpening of facilitational skills.

For its part, educational consciousness is a circumscribed, definite, convergent, and focused way of looking at and being toward reality. Some key characteristics of educational consciousness include an approach to persons and things primarily and proximately in terms of facilitation itself, a welcoming stance given in terms of present or future facilitational possibilities, a deliberately specific and highly focused desire to help others learn coupled with careful thought given to particularized objectives and practices, and a concentration on both comprehensive and intermediate goals with a concomitant tendency to highly value the acquisition and constant sharpening of facilitational skills.

Educational consciousness represents the deliberate fashioning of a more generalized and sometimes inchoate mode of helping into a highly focused, task-oriented, skill-permeated form of assisting others to live more enriched lives cognitively, affectively, and lifestylistically. Educational consciousness is a focusing and sharpening of ministerial consciousness so as to more effectively attain desired objectives.

Religious educators who operate out of an educational consciousness have an habitual awareness of any and every opportunity to facilitate learning outcomes. Their whole self-system is mobilized and is at the ready to facilitate learning. Their psychic antennae are finely tuned to even the slightest possibility of capitalizing on a teachable moment when one surfaces, or of creating a teachable moment when one does not presently exist. The whole existence of these religious educators is consciously and unconsciously oriented toward facilitation. This is the first thing that automatically springs to their minds, their hearts, and their conduct in any and every circumstance in which these religious educators find themselves.

To what extent do we religious educators operate out of a well-developed educational consciousness?

To what degree do we view everything we encounter in our lives not just "on the job" but throughout all our waking moments from the standpoint of facilitation of learning?

Can we honestly say that we are always prepared habitually, even in the least likely circumstance, to engage in facilitational behaviors?

Are we constantly at the ready to confect the sacrament of religious instruction to any kind of learner in any sort of situation?

Have we made every effort to have at our instant disposal a wide repertoire of successful facilitational procedures that we can instantly deploy when the teachable moment arises or when we wish to bring the teachable moment into existence?

We are faithful to our divine call within a call, and we are successful as religious educators, to the extent to which we operate out of an educational consciousness. Conversely, we lack faithfulness to our call within a call, and we will lack optimum success as religious educators, to the extent to which we do not operate out of a thoroughgoing educational consciousness.

Performance Objective: I will strive to develop a habitual instructional consciousness, one that always views things primarily in terms of facilitating religious outcomes. I will accomplish this objective by pausing after each religious instruction event in a formal or informal setting to reflect on whether there was even one incident which occurred during that event in which I failed to deal with the learner or with the situation primarily from a facilitational mode. I will then instantly resolve to make sure that in the next event I will approach everything from a facilitational axis. I will continue to do this every day until I have developed an instructional consciousness that is habitual and automatic.

12

Influence

When I was nearly nine years old, my parents sent me to a boys' boarding school named Coindre Hall located on the north shore of New York's Long Island. The school was operated by the Brothers of the Sacred Heart. These holy and virile men lived and worked and taught and prayed in close communion with the boys day in and day out. The Brothers of the Sacred Heart exerted an extremely powerful personal, intellectual, and religious influence on my life, and I will always be grateful to them. The five years I spent there were among the happiest in my life. Coindre Hall then as now has a special and shining place in my heart.

I was the first boy who showed up the first Sunday of the first year of Coindre Hall's existence. Having never seen the building before, I was overwhelmed by what I beheld. Though originally built as a extremely large mansion for a wealthy man named John McKesson Brown, it was in fact so beautiful, so magnificent, and so spacious that it truly was a castle not only in the sight of a wide-eyed eight year old boy but in the sight of any world traveler. Sitting grandly on a gently sloping hill surrounded by woods and fields and overlooking picturesque Huntington Harbor, Coindre Hall was an ideal place for a young boy to grow up amidst beauty, nature, and holiness. Study and work, prayer and play, religion and life were exquisitely intertwined during my stay in those first five years of Coindre Hall's existence.

It was in one of my classes at Coindre Hall that I heard the illustration I am now going to recount. I do not remember if I heard it in religion class or in some other class. Coindre Hall was not one of those Catholic schools whose religiosity consists primarily in a cross on top of the building, a religion class, a crucifix in the classrooms, some statues standing silently in the corridors, and little else in the way of religion. Coindre Hall was a school in which religion truly permeated the entire curriculum, in which religion was integrated—not dragged in artificially by the heels but appropriately and naturally integrated—into everything we learned inside and outside the classroom.

"When we die and go to heaven or hell," the brother told us, "it will be for all eternity. Do you know what eternity is, boys?"

The boys thought for a bit. Then one of us raised his hand and replied, "Eternity is a very long time." Another boy was more effusive, "Eternity is a very, very, very long time."

"In one way you are right", responded the brother. "But you know, none of us really has a true idea of eternity because none of us has personally experienced eternity. We have experienced time, and we even have experienced what we imagine is a long time, but we have never experienced eternity. Unless we personally experience something, we really don't understand truly what that thing is. We can only know it indirectly. So let me give you an illustration that will indirectly give us a very faint glimpse of how long eternity really is."

"Let's imagine," the brother told us boys, "that this huge building, this immense Coindre Hall, is composed not of walls and rooms but is really just one enormous solid block of granite. Now granite is one of the hardest of all rocks, and so takes a very long time to wear away, even just a little."

"Let's pretend that a great dry spell came over all the earth and that rain never ever fell again except for one small drop once every million years. And let's pretend that this single drop of rain fell right on the solid granite Coindre Hall. When Coindre Hall will have been completely eroded by the solitary raindrop falling just once every million years, eternity will have just begun."

For me, this example was a powerful illustration, which probably accounts for the fact that I have remembered it all these years. The brother's depiction of eternity shows us religious educators a great deal about the nature, importance, and duration of our religious instruction activity.

When we interact with a person, part of what we are and what we do remains with that person not only for the rest of the individual's life on earth but for all eternity. This fact is true whether we or the other person recognizes it or not.

Henry Adams was right when he wrote that teachers affect eternity; they can never tell where their influence stops.

The kind and quality of the religion we teach remains with the learner for all eternity. The religious cognitions, attitudes, values, love, and lifestyle we teach to learners continues with them throughout their lives and throughout all eternity.

Now this is real influence. This is powerful influence. This is lasting influence. This is influence that is hard to match.

But this truly awesome influence of the religious educator automatically brings with it the equally awesome responsibility to work with all our minds, with all our hearts, with all our energies, and with all our skills to make sure that every religious instruction event is the best it can be.

Our call within a call as religious educators perforce demands that while we are preparing, enacting, and evaluating the religious instruction event, we always keep in mind the ultimate teleological goal of the event. Thus we always have to rigorously ask ourselves the haunting question: What is the relationship between the here-and-now religious instruction event and eternity? Put more specifically, what are the consequences of our preparation, enaction, and evaluation for the eternal welfare of the learner—and ourselves?

To what extent is religious instruction always alive and awake in our consciousness during all our waking moments?

To what degree are we constantly at the ready to facilitate religious outcomes in season and out?

How frequently are we professionally primed to facilitate religious outcomes at all times and in all places ranging from a chance meeting to a religious instruction event in a formal setting?

How carefully do we prepare our lessons?

How often do we take exquisite care to perform the religious instruction act with consummate skill, whether this act is carried out in a formal or informal environment?

Do we continually and rigorously evaluate our pedagogical moves during the teaching event?

Do we spend at least one hour a day engaging in that kind of high-level professional reading necessary to expand our vision of education and improve our tactics of teaching?

Performance Objective: I will carry in my wallet or purse a sturdy small card with the word INFLUENCE nicely printed on it in large letters. I will place this card in such a position that each time I open my wallet or purse I will see it. Whenever I see this card, I will pause for a brief moment and bring to renewed awareness the fact that everything I do in the religious instruction event will influence the learner not only then but for all eternity as well.

13

Leadership

Precisely at 1400 hours (2 P.M.) on October 6, 1973, the Syrians from the north and the Egyptians from the south launched a massive, coordinated surprise attack on the state of Israel. This exact time and date was selected by the Arabs for three very important military reasons: the tides in the Suez Canal were particularly favorable for the Egyptian invasion forces, the moonlight was beneficial to the Egyptians and Syrians that night, and all of Israel was at a standstill because this was the afternoon of Yom Kippur, the holiest day in the Jewish religious calendar when many Jews were in the synagogue, and the Israeli military defensive forces were not in a state of immediate readiness. This date also fell within the Islamic holy month of Ramadan. Hence the coordinated military strike against the state of Israel had added religious significance for the Arabs.

To the north of Israel, the Syrians invaded the Golan Heights, which the Israelis had seized during the Six Day War of June 1967. In the south, the Egyptians smashed across the Suez Canal and poured into the Israeli-occupied Sinai desert.

Despite stiff Israeli resistance, the invading Egyptian military forces won victory after victory in a short space of time. On October 8 in the Sinai the state of Israel suffered the worst military defeat in its history. The next day, however, the Israeli lines began to hold to the extent that the Egyptian forces failed to make any more significant territorial gains for the remainder of the war.

On Sunday morning, October 14, Egyptian armored vehicles launched a massive attack between 0600 and 0800 hours (6 A.M.–

8 A.M.). Thus began one of the largest tank battles in the entire history of modern warfare, with some 2,000 tanks locked in fierce combat along the Sinai front. When the smoke of battle had cleared, the Israelis had won a decisive victory: 264 destroyed Egyptian tanks lay strewn over the desert sands and the attacking Egyptians suffered more than 1,000 casualties. This monumental struggle of the tanks proved to be the turning point of the war on the southern front.

On October 22 at 1852 hours (6:52 P.M.) Suez Canal time, a cease-fire between Israel and Egypt went into effect. Because some fighting took place after that time, a second cease-fire was signed two days later. On November 11 Egypt and Israel signed a formal ceasefire agreement, which ended the war on the southern front. Skilled military analysts as well as astute political observers believe that the Yom Kippur/Ramadan war in its own way set the stage for Egyptian president Anwar Sadat's historic 1977 visit to Jerusalem, Egypt's subsequent recognition of the state of Israel, and eventually the Arab-Israeli peace agreements of the 1990s.

Like many Americans at the time, I closely followed the Yom Kippur/Ramadan War in the newspapers, magazines, and electronic media. Television coverage of the hostilities was splendid and provided such a high degree of concreteness, immediacy, and detail that it seemed to viewers like me that we were right in the midst of the battles along with the troops and tanks and planes.

I vividly remember watching an extended television news program that was broadcast around the time of the first and second cease-fires in the Egyptian phase of the Yom Kippur/Ramadan War. A seasoned television reporter was standing alongside a dusty Israeli tank that which was squatting in the desert sands and surrounded at various distances by other Israeli armored vehicles. The top lid of the tank opened and out came an Israeli tank commander up to waist level. The uniform of this rugged-looking man was covered with dust and grime, and it seemed as if sand was mixed in with his hair.

After exchanging some preliminary questions with the tank commander, the television reporter asked, "Why was it that, after being completely surprised by the Egyptian invasion of the Sinai and having lost your initial battles in the desert, the Israeli infantry and armored troops finally prevailed?"

"Let me tell you what I think," said the earnest, battle-hardened Israeli tank commander. He looked out over the vast expanse of desert as he spoke. "Even though this war was short, it was difficult and hard fought. And don't let anyone back in your country or in the rest of the world underrate the Egyptians. They had first-class tanks, missiles, and other weaponry. Their generals were very good. In fact their commander-in-chief, General [Ahmed] Ismael, is as fine a supreme military leader as there is in the world today. One of our Israeli generals compares him to the great Field Marshal [Mikhail] Kutusov, whose dogged military strategy led to the eventual defeat of Napoleon in Russia. And don't think for a moment that the Egyptian troops were ill prepared or cowardly. They were well-trained, especially their crack troops. And they fought valiantly."

"Well," responded the television news reporter, "if the Egyptians had first-class weaponry, fine generals, and good troops, why did Israel win the war?"

"That's easy. Throughout the whole history of warfare, it is always the human factor that is ultimately decisive. Let me give you an example from this war. Our Israeli officers know their troops very well. This is especially true of the junior officers who are right up there with the troops at the forward battlelines. I have heard reports that when spotting an enemy emplacement, the Egyptian lieutenants would say, "Men, there is an enemy position over there that is very important for us to take. I want you to go forward now and capture that position!" The Israeli lieutenants, on the other hand, would say, "Men, there's an enemy position over there that is very important for us to capture right now. Let's go! Follow me!""

All of us religious educators are automatically leaders by the very fact that we are religious educators. Our call within a call demands that we be instructional leaders. It is through effective instructional leadership that we and those under our care participate grace-fully in the sacrament of teaching. We should always bear in mind that the key role, the central definition, the all-encompassing task of the religious educator is to so structure the teaching situation that learning will take place as a result. This is what instructional leadership is all about. There are, of course, other kinds of leadership tasks in religious education, such as director of religious education in the local church, or central office religious education administrator. But even these persons have instructional leadership as their primary all-consuming task, albeit on a different level and in a different way.

What is our own leadership style with learners? Do we tell them, "Learn this or that. I will watch you as you engage in the learning task." Or do we say to learners, "This is what has to be learned. Follow me as I do it with you." Or, "This is what has to be learned I have done it already. Follow the way I did it."

What is our leadership style with volunteer religious educators or with others who are under our authority? Do we tell them, "This is how you should teach. Try this procedure and I will watch you as you do it." Or do we say: "This is how things should be done. This is how we should teach. Follow me as I do it with you until you get it perfect."

The technical instructional term for follow-me leadership is modeling. Intentional modeling is an instructional procedure in which the religious educator deliberatively engages in a particular cognitive, affective, or lifestyle behavior that the educator wishes the learner to acquire. When done skillfully, modeling is one of the most potent of all instructional procedures, especially in the lifestyle domain. While modeling has its limitations, especially when it is regarded as producing results automatically or when it is used indiscriminately, this instructional procedure can nonetheless be highly effective.

To what extent do we religious educators intentionally model cognitive, affective, and lifestyle religious behaviors to learners of all ages, circumstances, and environments? To the teachers under our care? To the clergy with whom we work? Is our leadership that of telling or that of doing?

Performance Objective: Whenever I ask a full-time or volunteer religious educator to undertake a new religious instructional initiative, I will not just talk to that religious educator about that initiative. I will also make sure that I myself first become competent in that particular initiative and then concretely model it in a real-life instructional situation for the benefit of the other religious educator.

14

At Work Always

Whatever else it was, the twentieth century was the age of science. And it was theoretical physics that became the ultimate foundation, principal cutting edge, and crowning achievement of the age of science. The breakthroughs made in theoretical physics were overwhelming, and their extensions into the practical world were as profound as they were far-reaching.

The period from 1900 to 1930 was the golden age of theoretical physics not only in the twentieth century but quite possibly in the entire history of the world. These were exciting and exhilarating years. In 1900 Max Planck proposed his quantum theory. From 1905 to 1916 Albert Einstein gave the world his special and general theory of relativity. In 1913 Niels Bohr propounded his theory of atomic structure. In 1927 Werner Heisenberg offered the uncertainty principle. And in the same year Niels Bohr advanced his complementarity principle. All of these great scientists won the Nobel Prize.

The two giants of this golden age were Bohr and Einstein. Some have made the argument that of the two, Bohr was the greater and the more influential. Einstein proposed one overall foundational way of looking at reality; Bohr advanced two ways. Einstein for most of his life worked primarily by himself in relative seclusion; Bohr was very much an educator who at an early age founded and became the yeasting force in the enormously influential Copenhagen Institute for Theoretical Physics. Einstein remained an ultraspecialist; Bohr interrelated theoretical physics in an organic fashion to all of life and human welfare. Einstein, a Jew, verbally decried Hitler's persecution of the Jews and fled Germany to the safety of the United States very shortly after Hitler rose to power when the Jews were not yet officially and openly persecuted by the Nazis. Bohr, a Gentile, concretely did the opposite about the horrible Nazi situation at considerable risk to his own life. And, of course, in what was one of the most foundational and exciting debates in the whole history of theoretical physics, the 1920 Solvay Conference, Bohr decisively bested Einstein and in the process confirmed the validity and cardinal role of quantum mechanics in the field of theoretical physics. Bohr, even more than Einstein, transformed the century.

The 1920s were, in the words of the great American physicist J. Robert Oppenheimer, an "heroic time" for theoretical physics. This heroic time, wrote Oppenheimer, "was not the doing of any one man; it involved the collaboration of scores of scientists from many different lands, though from first to last the deep creative and critical spirit of Niels Bohr guided, restrained, deepened, and finally transmuted he enterprise. It was a period of patient work in the laboratory, of experiments and daring action, of many false starts and many untenable conjectures, of debate, criticism and brilliant mathematical improvisation."

Bohr's preeminent position among twentieth-century physicists stems from a unique combination of several factors, each of which just by itself would qualify a person to occupy a privileged place in the pantheon of great scientists. He had an uncanny intuition that brought him immediately to the essential features of the physical phenomena he was examining. He also had an extraordinary ability to trace at one glance the widest implications of these phenomena. Furthermore, he was never content at a superficial or even a relatively deep analysis of physical phenomena; rather, he had an almost irresistable urge to search out the most profound dimensions of the problems presented by these phenomena. In a fruitful permutation of the pre-twentieth century view that physics is a branch of natural philosophy, he constantly probed into the epistemological foundations and extensions of physical phenomena. And finally, he continually sought to actively interface physics at every level with knowledge and action. In a word, Niels Bohr was the complete scientist.

Bohr's ideal of science was to spend day after day, week after week, month after month, year after year in the arduous and sometimes excruciating struggle to order his concepts in humble submission to the lessons that he and his associates learned from nature and from Nature. As Léon Rosenfeld testified, no twentieth-century scientist ever lived up to this ideal of the scientist with more devotion than Niels Bohr.

In accord with the scientific ideal as uncompromising service to the truth no matter what that truth might reveal or where that truth might lead, Bohr was very open in all respects. He worked very hard to come to that truth. Toward this end he assembled around him many of the most important international physicists of the day, men who would not only help him broaden the implications of his work but would also challenge him on this point or that, often intensely and sharply.

He worked just as hard disseminating the truth as he did to finding it in the first place. He labored days and weeks over each word and phrase of his published papers and international lectures, composing and then repeatedly reworking what he had written so that the end result expressed his position with utmost accuracy.

Niels Bohr was born in Copenhagen in 1885. His father was Christian Bohr, a famous university professor of physiology who read Goethe, Shakespeare and other great authors aloud to his children. Christian Bohr's home was a gathering place for a constantly expanding circle of intellectuals who discussed a wide variety of topics in a gracious setting. One of the regular guests was Harald Höffding, an important philosopher. Niels and his younger brother Harald were sometimes allowed to sit in quietly on the discussions. The intersection of philosophy with theoretical physics that characterized Niels Bohr's work probably began with his childhood contact with Höffding.

Christian Bohr actively encouraged his sons to participate vigorously in sports during their school days. Both Niels and Harald were excellent soccer players with the Akademisk Boldklub (university soccer club). Though Niels narrowly failed to qualify for the Danish national soccer team in the 1908 Olympic Games, Harald did qualify. The Danes went on to win the silver medal, due significantly to Harald's brilliant play at halfback. After graduating from the university, Harald became a celebrated mathematician.

After receiving his doctorate from the University of Copenhagen in 1911, Niels Bohr went to England. He worked first with J. J. Thomson, the discoverer of the electron, and then with Ernest Rutherford, who did pioneer studies in radiation and atomic structure and who had a major and continuing influence on Bohr. In 1913 Bohr propounded his famous atomic theory, a key discovery that departed in a seminal manner from classical physics and paved the way for a host of later major advances in the field.

In 1916 Bohr became Professor of Theoretical Physics at the University of Copenhagen. A year later he approached the appropriate officials to establish an Institute of Theoretical Physics. After a great deal of lobbying and fund raising, a new building was constructed and the Institute was inaugurated in 1921 with its founder Bohr as director. Bohr remained active in the Institute for its entire existence, administering, inviting, initiating, innovating, animating, encouraging, and exhorting.

Almost immediately the Institute became the dominant force in international physics because it was both a research and an educational center—the educational activities being a natural arm and extension of its research function. Much of the Institute's truly enormous impact stemmed from its international character. Over six hundred scientists from nearly forty countries lived and worked alongside each other for varying periods of time in an environment completely devoted to research and its dissemination. The Institute was deliberately far removed from political tensions and animosities. The discussions among its members blended physics with philosophy, art, and literature—and virtually no politics. It was the pursuit of pure science as Bohr understood it that united this diverse group of scientists.

In the 1930s and beyond, while still continuing his research at the Institute, Bohr was almost inevitably drawn into the turbulent outside world of political activity. Detesting Hitler and his persecution of innocent persons, Bohr was instrumental in persuading key

Italian and German scientists to defect to the United States. At considerable risk to his own life, he arranged for Danish Jews to flee the country. He worked heroically against the Nazis and fled Denmark under hair-raising circumstances at the very last moment, just as the Nazis were about to arrest him. On several occasions he met with Winston Churchill and Franklin Roosevelt to discuss the sharing of atomic secrets. Bohr was an adviser in residence to the Manhattan Project, which developed the atomic bomb. After the war he argued in Washington, D.C. and around the world on behalf of international control of atomic weapons, and became one of the world's most ardent champions of the peaceful use of atomic energy. In recognition of these efforts, he was given the very first Atoms for Peace Award, a very prestigious honor. He actively pursued research in theoretical physics until his death in 1962. In his lifetime he received more prizes, awards, medals, and honors than any other scientist of the twentieth century.

From the onset of his professional career right up until his death, Bohr was such a tireless worker that his colleagues, including the younger ones, frequently could not keep up with him. His ideal of a professional, his ideal of a scientist, was to be at work always, not only in his laboratory but also at home talking with his wife, playing with his children, going boating, and skiing. Ruminating on his work in environments quite different from those of the laboratory sometimes enabled him to significantly reconceptualize and reconfigure the problem with which he was struggling in the laboratory in such a way as to gain fresh new insights that might not have come to him had he worked on these problems only in the laboratory.

Even with his strong constitution, great enthusiasm, and vast amount of energy, there were times when the heavy stress of constant work proved too much for Niels Bohr not only in terms of his health but also in terms of the ongoing creativity of his work. One such time occurred toward the end of February 1927, with momentous results for the world.

In late 1926 and the beginning of 1927 Bohr, together with Heisenberg, was working heart and soul at the Institute on a seemingly insuperable problem of truly alarming proportions. If left unanswered, this enormous problem would seriously undermine theoretical physics in general and quantum mechanics in particular. Simply stated, the problem was this: When subjected even to the most careful scientific observation and experiment, certain physical phenomena sometimes exhibit two mutually exclusive and even contradictory states. For example, light reveals itself sometimes as being composed of particles, at other times of waves. But if light is composed of particles, it cannot be composed of waves. On the other hand, if light is composed of waves, it cannot be composed of particles. Both cannot be correct at one and the same time because each seemingly excludes the other.

By the middle of February 1927 Bohr had reached the point of physical and mental exhaustion wrestling with this excruciating problem. He decided to get away to a completely different environment so that he could not only relax but even more importantly work on this wrenching problem in an atmosphere that left him more or less undisturbed. Accompanied by his beloved wife, Margarethe, Bohr left for two weeks of skiing in the mountains north of Oslo. As he maneuvered down the slopes amidst the spectacular clean beauty of the snowy mountains with the bracing air slapping his face and the light bouncing off the trees and mountainsides and mountaintops in so many different hues, the blockages that he had encountered at the Institute became layered away and he arrived at a truly momentous and breakthrough solution to the seemingly insuperable problem that had been haunting him for so long.

On the first morning of his return to Copenhagen, Bohr raced excitedly down the steps of his home, across the graveled drive, and bounded up the stairs of the Institute looking for Heisenberg. Then he revealed his discovery. The young German, who had himself working long and hard on what was to become the uncertainty principle, listened, disputed, nuanced, expanded, affirmed.

During the next two months Bohr and Heisenberg worked together constantly and relentlessly at the Institute. Occasionally they would go for a walk to further hammer out all the dimensions of the solution. Only when Margarethe would drag them away for meals would they briefly interrupt their incessant joint work. They also made sure that Wolfgang Pauli, whom Bohr called "the conscience of physics" because of his superb and withering critique of every new proposal, was involved because if anyone could find weaknesses in what they were working on, it was Pauli. By spring-time, when the flowers blossomed and the trees bloomed in Copen-hagen, the great principle was ready. J. Robert Oppenheimer called it "the inauguration of a new phase in the evolution of human thinking." John Wheeler, another eminent physicist, termed it "the most revolutionary scientific concept of the century." Heisenberg gave the term "uncertainty principle" to his own crucial aspect of the overall comprehensive solution. Bohr called his dimension the complementary principle.

The groundbreaking complementarity principle holds that vali-dated contradictory explanations of an atomic phenomenon are both true at the same time. Far from being mutually exclusive, these validated contradictory explanations are necessary if human-ity is to gain a complete and thus truly accurate view of the atomic phenomena. Each separate aspect, even when contradictory, is a necessary complement to the other. The complementarity principle is not a philosophical superstructure imposed on atomic reality; rather, it is logically contained in quantum mechanics itself, since quantum mechanics necessarily includes human study of the atomic world. Scientific study relies on careful human observation. The very conditions of observation themselves circumscribe, limit, and influence the particular aspect of the atomic phenomenon that is found and described. Hence complementarity is absolutely nec-essary for a full and true understanding of atomic phenomena be-cause complementarity enables science to join the fruits of obser-vations made from differing vantage points. This complementarity, this inclusivity, this reconciling of dualistic polarities all fit in nicely in with Bohr's overall philosophical view of the basic unity and harmony in all the universe.

Ultimately, the complementarity principle was and still remains a new and extremely important philosophical theory of knowledge, an integrative epistemology.

From 1927 until his death in 1962 Bohr spent a great deal of time endeavoring to show that the complementarity principle is applicable not only to atomic physics but to all areas of living and nonliving reality, as, for example, subject versus object in psychology, or physicochemical mechanism versus teleological function in biology.

To be faithful to our call within a call, we religious educators must be at work always. Jesus the religious educator was faithful to his call, and hence he was at work at all times and in all places.

To be as successful as we can be, we must be at religious instruction work always.

To be as sacramental as our call within a call requires, we must be at our religious instruction work always, even when not formally "on the job."

Are we at work always, no matter where we are, whether teaching learners, relaxing with friends, attending church, playing with our children?

Are we always thinking and feeling and acting to the appropriate degree like religious educators, or is religious instruction work just an outer stratum of our lives that we can peel off as soon as we leave the formally designated religious instruction job site?

If we religious educators are not at work at all times and in all places, how can we be truly open to incorporate those important insights that every different kind of environment can offer us? If we are not at work always, how can we make those fructifying connections between our religious instruction activity and other milieux?

Do we religious educators work tirelessly day and night until we arrive at the solution of an important religious instruction problem with which we are confronted? Or do we work halfheartedly on the problem at the formally-designated job site and not at all while at home or during leisure activities?

To what extent do we constantly wrestle in season and out with daily religious instruction problems such as how to teach more effectively, how to incorporate research more fruitfully into our work, how to place our teaching practice directly within the overall context of theory so that we can be more successful? Or are we content just to remain in the same old rut, the same tired. familiar routine?

Do we religious educators continually strive to reconceptualize and reconfigure the instructional problems that face us so that in the end we will arrive at a creative and workable solution? Or do we just unquestioningly accept like sheep the directions of this textbook series or that workshop leader?

Do we get away from our religious instruction activities from time to time because we just want to get away, or because we are becoming tired of religious instruction activity, or because we want to be at work only forty hours a week? Or do we get away so that in addition to getting away, we can come to new vantage points and gain fresh vigor for our religious instruction activity?

To what degree do we isolate ourselves from viewpoints that differ or even oppose ours? Conversely, to what extent do we frequently strive to work with those religious educators and others who have perspectives that go counter to our own? How secure are we in the face of the possibility that other viewpoints might well complement or even replace ours? To what extent are we afraid to open ourselves to collaborate honestly with others whose outlook contradicts ours?

Are we our religious instruction work? Simultaneously, is our religious instruction work us? To be at work always means that in every respect we are our religious instruction work and that our religious instruction work in every respect is us.

Performance Objective: Before going on vacation or to a party, I will bring to mind a particular major religious instructional problem that I need to solve. During the vacation or the party I will keep this important problem somewhere in the active regions of my mind—not in a way that ruins or even diminishes my enjoyment but in a manner that will ensure that wherever I am I will be always working for the Lord in the fulfillment of my call within a call as a religious educator.

15

Desire

Throughout the entire last quarter of the twentieth century, Béla Karolyi surely was the most famous and most successful gymnastics coach in the world. In one eleven-year period alone, his athletes won seven Olympic gold medals and fifteen world championships. Mike Jacki, executive director of the U.S. Gymnastics Federation. stated that the one factor in the last quarter of the twentieth century that exerted the greatest effect on U.S. gymnastics, overwhelmingly, was the presence of Béla Karolyi. His enormous success in vitalizing woman's gymnastics in the United States was not restricted to national and international competition. His fame and success were an important factor in hastening the explosion of interest in woman's gymnastics in the United States. By the turn of the century, there were almost 5,000 private gymnastics clubs and perhaps an additional 90,000 school, college, and recreational gymnastics programs throughout the county.

By the year 1995 Karolyi's students had won 169 medals (84 gold, 46 silver, 39 bronze) in world class and international competitive gymnastics tournaments. This is a feat unparalleled in the history of international gymnastics. As of 1998, he is the only active gymnastics coach to have developed medal winners at six consecutive Olympic Games. He has been the personal coach of most of the major female gymnasts in the final quarter of the twentieth century, including such world-class luminaries as Nadia Comaneci, Emilia Eberle, Mary Lou Retton, Julianne McNamara, Dianne Durham, Kristie Phillips, Phoebe Mills, Betty Okino,

Dominique Moceanu, Svetlana Bouginskaia, Kim Zmeskal, and Kerri Strug.

Béla Karolyi was born in Romania on September 13, 1942, in Cluj, a small coal-mining town in Transylvania, a distinct geographical and cultural region of Romania that was part of Hungary from the eleventh century until the end of World War I. His grandfather had been the town's first schoolteacher. He also formed his own opera and theater troupe to culturally enrich the life of the miners. Béla's father was a civil engineer. In high school Béla was an outstanding athlete setting several national records in the hammer throw and playing as a member of Romania's national handball team that won the world championship. At age eighteen, while attending the five-year University of Physical Education, he flunked the practical physical examination in gymnastics. Always a person positively challenged by failure, Karolyi took a long, hard look at himself. He was shocked at what he found. To be sure, he was large and strong—but not in real command of his body. For example, he could not even perform the simple physical maneuver of turning upside down on the rings used in gymnastics. When he tried, the blood flowed into his head and he was unable to breathe. He came to realize how little he could manage his body and how little he knew about his personal abilities. After a period of intense introspection, Karolyi decided to change in order to significantly better himself. He went on to major in gymnastics. Later he matriculated in the Institute for Physical Education at the University of Bucharest where he subsequently attained a master's degree in physical education.

While attending the university, Béla fell in love with Marta Eross, another gymnast. After graduation in 1963, they got married. Bela got a job teaching gymnastics in Cluj, while Marta took similar job in a nearby village. Béla and Marta were highly successful. From their rickety school training halls, Béla's and Marta's gymnastic teams won competition after competition and began to be a dominant force in school gymnastics throughout Romania. In 1968, at the direct request of the Romanian Ministry of Education, Béla and Marta were invited to establish and direct a special state-sponsored gymnastics school. As the site for this new boarding school, complete with various buildings and a fine staff of teachers and coaches, the Karolyis chose Onesti, a middle-class town near the Russian border on the opposite side of Romania from Transylvania.

Béla was firmly convinced that the key to producing outstanding gymnasts is to begin intensive training when a child is very young. Therefore, he and Marta scoured Onesti and the outlying regions to observe kindergartners and first-graders at play. Out of a pool of about 25,000 children, Béla and Marta selected the most promising for concentrated training at his new school compound. It was not long before the Karolyi school at Onesti began to dominate Romanian women's gymnastics. As a result of his enormous success, Béla Karolyi was named to be head coach of the Romanian national gymnastics team.

At the Montreal Olympics in 1976, one of Béla's discoveries and students, Nadia Comaneci, stunned the entire world by attaining the first perfect score ever awarded in Olympic history. Indeed, the Karolyi-educated Comaneci went on to gain seven perfect scores in the 1976 Olympics, an unprecedented feat. She also was the youngest Olympic champion in the Games of 1976. Béla's strong, superbly coached Romanian team ended many years of Soviet domination of woman's gymnastics. Since the late 1940s, the Soviet Union had poured hundreds of millions of rubles into a gymnastics-making machine with the finest teachers in the finest facilities and using the same basic training techniques. One man, Béla Karolyi, working in an outlying province of a poor small country and developing his own training procedures, had toppled the seemingly invincible Soviet woman's gymnastics empire.

The Soviet government felt humiliated in the eyes of the entire world by the outstanding performance of the Karolyi-trained Romanian women gymnasts in the 1976 Olympics. Soon after, the Soviets put a great deal of pressure on its subservient satellite Romania. As a result, the Romanian government cut funding for Karolyi's training facility. It ordered Nadia Comaneci transferred to another gym, this one in Bucharest. Government bureaucrats hassled Karolyi in a variety of ways. They followed him everywhere. They forced him and his female gymnasts to travel around the country making speeches about how the Communist system

and its manifestations was the chief factor responsible for the outstanding success of the Romanian woman's gymnastics team.
Karolyi balked at these demands to make frequent speeches, stating
that they disrupted the rigorous and demanding training procedures
which the girls had to undergo if they were to be outstanding gymnasts. Thereupon the government labeled Karolyi as controversial
and hassled him all the more. His ongoing battles with the government authorities reached their worst point at an international competition held in Moscow in 1980. At the end of the gymnastics
competition, the judges from the Soviet Union and its servile satellite Poland scored the incomparable Nadia Comaneci just low
enough (after 28 minutes of "deliberation") to cost Romania the
victory—by five thousandths of a point. The volatile Karolyi grew
very angry, waving his arms and pounding the table with his fist to
signify his extreme displeasure over the patently unfair ruling. This
public display of disagreement with the Soviet judge enabled the
Romanian government to ratchet up its official designation of
Karolyi from "controversial" to the much worse label of "politically disapproved behavior." Thenceforth security guards were sent
to accompany the Romanian woman's gymnastics team whenever
it went on tour outside the Communist bloc of nations. For the Romanian government, this was the beginning of the end for Béla. For
Béla, it was also the beginning of the end—but not in the way in
which the Romanian Communist Party apparatchiks had imagined.

In late March 1981, the Romanian woman's gymnastics team
was on tour in New York City. The entourage included security
agents from the Romanian secret police who posed, somewhat
clumsily and transparently, as masseurs, chauffeurs, and journalists. The security agents accompanied the team to prevent defec-
tions to the West and to hold press conferences during which they
took pains to emphasize that Communist ideology was chiefly responsible for producing the outstanding Romanian female gymnasts. The night before the team's airplane was scheduled to leave
for Romania, Béla and Marta, together with Géza Pozsar, the
team's incomparable choreographer, stayed up debating whether or
not to defect. They were caught in a cruel dilemma. They feared
that if they returned to Romania they would suffer reprisals. On the

other hand, they feared that if they defected to the West the Romanian government would take punitive actions against their daughter Andrea and other relatives. Finally, at six o'clock in the morning, they decided to defect. They packed their suitcases. At seven o'clock Béla confided in Nadia Comaneci about the decision to defect. Nadia kept the secret. At 8:30, three and a half hours before the plane was schedule to leave, Béla assembled his beloved gymnasts together and bade them good-bye. Then the Karolyis and Pozsar disappeared into the crowded streets of New York. Béla was thirty-nine years old and spoke no English.

The evening of their defection they turned on the television in the apartment of Béla's widowed aunt who lived in Manhattan. The defectors stared at the television set in disbelief. President Ronald Reagan had been shot that same day. Béla wondered what kind of a life they were getting in to in the United States. The following morning they went to the immigration office and encountered employees who were as rude, as lazy, and as disinterested in the long lines of applicants as were the bureaucrats in Communist countries. Béla was really disheartened.

An acquaintance named Les Sasvari, then vice president of the U. S. Gymnastics Federation, heard of the Karolyis' defection to the West. Himself an expatriate coach from Hungary, Sasvari empathized with Béla's desperate situation. He suggested that the defectors go to California where the opportunities for gymnastics coaches were better than those in New York. With their last dollars the defectors flew to Los Angeles; there Béla visited all the gyms in the city but none wanted his services. He finally found work as a part-time longshoreman on the docks of Los Angeles. He and Marta lived in one of the cheapest, dirtiest, most run-down motels near the docks in an area frequented by drug dealers and users, prostitutes, drunks, and brawling sailors. To supplement his income as a longshoreman Béla took jobs cleaning the smelly bars and sweeping the filthy floors of seedy restaurants on the waterfront. Sometimes he ate from the leftovers in the restaurants. At other times his main meal was a pretzel purchased from a street vendor. He and Marta spent all their spare time watching the children's television program *Sesame Street* in order to learn English.

Two months after his arrival in Los Angeles Béla got in touch with Paul Ziert, a gymnastics coach at the University of Oklahoma. Ziert was one of the few American gymnastics coaches whom Béla had known from international competition. Ziert was able to get Béla a job in a summer gymnastics camp in Oklahoma and later a position as assistant coach at the university's physical education department. Ziert also gave Béla some additional coaching work in his private gymnastics club. Béla and Marta were saddened by what they found. "All the kids wanted to do was to have fun," said Béla. "They didn't want to have any responsibilities. Just fun. They had no desire to feel proud of achieving something."

In September of that same year the Romanian government allowed the Karolyis' seven-year old daughter to immigrate to America. Now the Karolyis were free to begin their new life in earnest. In February 1982, with the help of some investors, the Karolyis started their own gym in Houston, Texas. Béla and his faithful partner Marta tacked posters on trees and telephone poles all over the city announcing the establishment of the Karolyi gym. Twenty-four students signed up. It was not too long after that Béla's students began to win championships. First it was the Texas Class I title. Then for the first time someone from the Houston area won the vault championship in the nationals. Word spread quickly throughout Texas and the entire country that the coach of Nadia Comaneci had established a training facility in the United States. Many potentially premier female gymnasts flocked to the new gym. Within a couple of years Karolyi's training facility enrolled six hundred students. Béla purchased a fifty-acre ranch, established a 20,000 square-foot gymnasium, and added dormitories, tennis courts, and a swimming pool for his girls. He has cattle, horses, and a seemingly endless gaggle of dogs. After his smashing success in the 1984 Olympics, he received advance royalties of $350,000 to coauthor a book. He had become the most famous and most successful coach of female gymnasts in the world.

Béla Karolyi's rapid and enormous success in American women's gymnastics caused a great many of the other American gymnastic coaches to be jealous of him and bitter about his spectacular triumphs. Just two years after he began his own gym, one of his students, Mary Lou Retton, became the first American woman ever to win an Olympic gold medal in All-Around Gymnastics. In that same Olympics, another of Béla's students, Julianne McNamara, won the gold medal in the uneven parallel bars competition. To the chagrin of the other coaches, Karolyi had quickly gained the reputation of turning merely talented girls into phenomenally successful world-class champions—girls like Phoebe Mills, Chelle Stack, Rhonda Faehn, and Brandy Johnson, to name just a few. Other coaches were embarrassed when some of their prize athletes deserted their gyms and enrolled in Béla's training facility. These coaches deeply resented Béla's media-star status and his charisma. It was Béla, not they, who attracted the preponderance of media attention, who was the most quoted, who was most admired by the public, and who attracted the best young girls to his gym. More of Béla's students competed in the Olympics than those of any of the other American coaches. Above all, the other coaches were furious that Béla did not "play the game," preferring instead to do things his own way.

Many of the other coaches retaliated against Béla in two ways. First, they frequently used racist remarks about him. They likened the Transylvanian-born Karolyi to Dracula, sucking blood from his athletes and journalists alike. One rival coach cracked: "Karolyi is almost an animated cartoon character. You could dress him up like a vampire." Another told reporters: "When you deal with Karolyi, you are stroking a puppy dog who is really a werewolf". Other coaches frequently poked fun of his heavy accent, saying that it was reminiscent of dark doings in murky Transylvanian castles. One rival went as far as asserting that "Karolyi is a Communist who has used capitalism to the ultimate," especially with reporters and the public.

The second form of retaliation was far more insidious. Whenever possible they did everything in their power to prevent Béla from coaching in the Olympics, even though the American national team had more members from his gym than from any other training facility. In the 1984 Olympics in Los Angeles, he was passed over for coach and even for assistant coach. Béla was reduced to using an equipment handler's pass to get on the floor of Pauley Pavilion to guide Mary Lou Retton and Julianne McNamara to their championship performances. In the 1988 Summer Olympic Games in Seoul, Don Peters, the designated coach of the American female gymnastics team and head of a rival gym, declined to name Béla an assistant coach. Karolyi then refused to go to Seoul in any capacity. When four of Béla's students made the team while none of Peters' students qualified, Peters quit and the U. S. Gymnastics Federation named Karolyi as coach. The federation also changed its long-standing rule so that any coach with an athlete on a national team is automatically named to the overall squad. Many coaches complained to the Federation. Mike Jacki, then head of the Federation, countered: "Some coaches say we bend the rules for Béla. We don't. Other coaches complain about him, but they should realize he helped make it possible for *all* of them to be with their athletes on the competition floor. Many coaches telephone me and tell me that I have to get rid of Karolyi. I support Béla. He's a winner and I think he's got a tremendous amount to offer us. Sure, there are times when I get upset with him. But there are times I get upset with other coaches as well. I don't know if some of these coaches disregard the fact that Béla consistently produces great female gymnasts. He is too good to not have him be a part of things."

Béla's long-time friend Paul Ziert accurately assesses the problem which many other coaches have with Karolyi: "He is a brilliant coach. And he represents absolute commitment to gymnastics. Maybe that is what is so threatening."

One writer put it this way: "Béla's peers do not like him. His peers resent him. His peers wish they were him."

Not every women's gymnastics coach is jealous and envious of Karolyi. For example, Steve Nunno, the second most important and successful coach of American female gymnasts, studied briefly under Béla before starting his own gymnastics program. Nunno wanted to see how Karolyi consistently produced winners so that when he formed his own gym he too could produce winning female gymnasts. "A lot of U.S. coaches fought Béla and didn't like him," Nunno once said. "I decided to study him and see how he does it. I found out. He works harder than anyone else. He works more hours, pushes his athletes harder, and asks them to do more than they think they can. The reason why I am so successful is because I and my gymnasts work as hard as Béla and his girls."

For his part, Béla just brushes away the criticism directed at him by many of the other coaches. He contends that the other coaches are jealous of him because he poses a direct challenge to what he calls "their safe and sweet mediocrity." He believes that he has consistently shown other coaches that it is necessary for a successful coach to push hard and sacrifice much in order to achieve something special. "All I have to offer is my own honest hard work, which I invest in the kids." In his self-assured manner, Béla would to say to rival coaches: "Guys, go out and produce. Beat me. Then I will be no one. It's time to pick the coach based on the performance of his athletes. To misuse resources because others are jealous is dumb. That's not what made the United States great."

Karolyi's athletes pay a very high price for their outstanding success. Indeed, Béla's female gymnasts are trained longer, harder, and more intensely than athletes in virtually any other sport. Their daily practice routine would make a professional football player woozy. But it is precisely Karolyi's relentlessly demanding training style that has made his athletes so phenomenally and consistently successful. For eight hours a day six days a week the girls go to the mat again and again until they perfect a routine. Mary Lou Retton once said: "When you get to a meet, it is a big relief because you only have to do a routine once."

The standards that Béla sets for his girls (and for himself) are extremely high. Every single move, every single combination of moves, every single routine must be repeated over and over and over again until performed perfectly. The mother of one of Karolyi's young gymnasts once told a sports reporter: "He doesn't want good; he wants a [perfect score of] 10."

This constant all-out effort and endless repetition during training not only perfects the gymnast's physical skills; it also builds her confidence. When she enters a meet, she knows she is better prepared than her opponents. And she also knows that she has repeated the routine so often and to such a high degree of skill that performing the routine during a meet is, in one sense, just another repetition.

Karolyi, the relentless taskmaster, works as hard as his athletes—and they know it. During the long punishing daily training sessions with their merciless intensity, he darts nervously from girl to girl telling each one: "Go for it—*hard!*" Often he personally demonstrates a move, putting his whole heart and soul into physically illustrating how a move should be executed. His eyes seem to be everywhere on the training floor. He misses nothing.

He never relaxes when in the training hall or at a meet. And he does not permit his athletes to relax during training sessions or during competition. "Relaxing when you should be working," he says, "is the worst thing that can happen to anyone who wishes to be truly successful."

Some would-be Olympic champions begin their training at Béla's gym as young as two years of age. "You need a minimum of eight years of training to become a world-class gymnast," he says. "If you start at eight, you're already sixteen. That's already almost too old. Female gymnastics is a young girl's sport. So we start out with two- and three-year olds. The program is designed to give them more and more information about gymnastic skills. We try to build strength, flexibility, self-confidence, regardless of what kind of athletic activity they do later, whether or not it's gymnastics. The training that we give on the gym floor will feed into all other aspects of a girl's life."

Such a demanding, long-lasting program as Karolyi's requires not only a high level of desire from the young girls; it also requires a great deal of desire on the part of parents. Parents, especially mothers, are encouraged to come to the training hall and watch their daughters work out in Béla's gym. There is a special observation section in the gym. Parents, and anyone else, are strictly forbidden to walk onto the sacrosanct training floor. The floor where Karolyi teaches and the girls learn is a holy place, sort of a Transylvanian *dōjō*.

In the training gym as well as during meets, Karolyi is a master motivator. "Béla knows how to motivate and inspire," said one of his best gymnasts. "That's why we athletes are willing to pay the high price he continuously exacts from us. And that's why we are so devoted to him."

Karolyi regards motivation by the coach as an essential part of effective training and successful competition. He motivates by constantly encouraging his gymnasts to work very hard, to strive always to outdo their best performance. He does not hesitate to criticize the performance of his girls during training. Sometimes this criticism is relatively mild: "What are you do- o-o-o-ing?" he will chide in his heavy Transylvanian accent. At other times he will sharply chastise the performance of one of his girls: "Is no good. You're like a dead dog. Do it right this time!" But as a master motivator, Béla also has a reward system, which he uses judiciously and only when it is merited. Occasionally he emits a low, rolling "Go-o-o-o-d" when a gymnast has executed a good move. When a girl has performed a particularly fine move, he pats her on the head. The reward that Béla's girls most covet both in training and in competition is his famous bear hug. He gives a bear hug only when one of his gymnasts has performed a perfect move, a 10. To his gymnasts, a bear hug from Béla is almost the equivalent of an Olympic gold medal.

Karolyi's training procedures are built around his firm conviction that adequate gymnastic performance, and especially outstanding performance, is a combination of the physical and the psychological, of bodily skills and internal desire. Béla's teaching procedures are all orchestrated in such a way as to build up his gymnasts both physically and psychologically. "This is the natural way of doing things", he likes to say. "Everything I learned about training gymnasts I first learned in the school of life." He is uncharacteristically modest about his coaching procedures: "I have developed a few very efficient techniques and the methodology to teach them. But eventually it just became a matter of continual development of the basic skills. We were always going further, further, further. Polishing moves. Perfecting one skill makes possible a new one. We would introduce a turn, a twist, an additional movement, and suddenly the girl had a new skill." And when the girls had either gained new skills or developed a higher level of performance in the old ones, they were by that very success internally motivated to work even harder to excel. Their psyches became open to new technical possibilities. It is the girls' burning desire to excel that ultimately is the engine which enables these female gymnasts to productively mobilize their physical skills in such a way as to excel.

Yet with all of this, Béla is firmly convinced that mutual respect between coach and gymnast, between teacher and learner, is crucial for success. In his view, a coach can work long and hard with an athlete, but unless there is reciprocal respect there will be no long-range success. "There is no successful one-way program," Béla likes to say. "It takes years to develop a relationship between a gymnast and a coach. If this relationship worsens or disappears, I suggest a breakup."

The glue that binds the deep professional relationship between Karolyi and those whom he lovingly calls "my leetle ones" is an unquenchable blazing desire to excel beyond the levels of what most persons think is possible. An especially vivid and dramatic illustration of this desire-fueled relationship between Karolyi and one of his "leetle ones" occurred at the 1996 Olympic Games held in Atlanta, Georgia.

The powerful Russia team, which had won gold medals in female gymnastics at many past Olympics, were favored by the experts to once again win the team first prize. The Romanians and the Americans were regarded as close contenders. The team event consisted of a series of different kinds of bundled competitions calling forth different kinds of skills from the gymnasts.

In the compulsories, the American female gymnasts finished a close second to the Russians. In the uneven parallel bars the Americans turned in six nearly flawless performances. Then in the balance beam event, the Americans gave a strong performance. After this the American team held their own in the floor exercises. At the end of these four competitions, the Americans were slightly ahead of the Russians for the team gold medal. The only event that remained in order for the American female gymnastics team to bring home the first-ever team gold medal was the vault. Individual American female gymnasts, notably those coached by Béla Karolyi, had won gold medals in previous Olympics, but the Americans had never won a team gold medal. The pressure was on the American women to turn in an excellent performance in the vault.

In each team event, six gymnasts compete but only the scores of five of them count. The performance of the lowest-scoring gymnast is eliminated. In the vault, the first four Americans did very well, and it was projected that they would maintain their razor-thin lead over the Russians, who had not yet competed in the vault. The fifth American was Dominque Moceanu, one of the brightest stars of the American female gymnastic team. In the vault, each competitor is given two attempts, each of which is given a separate score. The higher of the two scores is the one that counts toward the overall team scorer; the lower score is discarded. To the shock of everyone, the fourteen-year old Moceanu turned in a terrible performance on both attempts in the vault, falling and landing on her rear end. The higher of Moceanu's two scores was a 9.20. If the sixth and final member of the American team did not score very well and thus eradicate Moceanu's poor score, the team would not win the gold medal.

The sixth member of the American team was a relatively unheralded eighteen-year old girl named Kerri Strug. She had earned the all-important "anchor position" as the final gymnast in the vault by virtue of the fact that she had placed first in this event in the U.S. tryouts for the Olympic Games. Strug had wanted to be a gymnast since she was a very young girl. She tried various gyms for training but was not satisfied until at the age of twelve she decided to move to Houston to train with Béla Karolyi. "If I wanted to go to the Olympics, I knew I needed to make a change in gyms. Béla knows how to win." In high school Strug was a straight-A student who graduated a year earlier than normal. As a gymnast in Karolyi's gym, she was always in the shadow of Kim Zmeskal and Dominique Moceanu.

Of all her Olympic teammates in that summer of 1996, Strug was the one who was the most sensitive psychologically and the most sensitive to pain physically. Because of her sensitivity, Béla always treated her more gingerly than the other girls in his gym. He called Strug "Baby" not only because she was the baby of her family but because he felt he had to treat her a bit less astringently in his highly demanding training sessions. She was never touted by the media as one of Béla's fearless little girls with the heart of a lion.

She was the quiet, dependable understudy in Karolyi's gym. In short, of all the members of the 1996 American Olympic female gymnastics team, Kerri Strug was probably the least likely to attain great fame.

And now, all of a sudden, the team gold medal hopes for the American female gymnasts hung on the performance of Baby, of Kerri Strug. Greatness, or at least the opportunity of greatness, was thrust upon her by dint of the weak performance of the otherwise superb Dominique Moceanu. The pressure was enormous. But so was the opportunity.

On the first of the two vault attempts allotted to her, the diminutive 4-foot-8-inch Strug charged down the runway, made her vault, and landed badly, severely twisting her ankle in the process. She thought she had broken her leg. Her score was a woeful 9.162. She was on the floor writhing in pain. She thought she had broken her ankle because of the pain and because she heard her ankle pop when her foot landed on the floor. But she also knew that with a score as bad as this, there was no way that the American team would beat the powerful Russian team.

By the international rules of international gymnastics, Strug had only thirty seconds to decide if she would try the vault for a second time. If she had been a basketball player, a trainer would have rushed onto the court to test the severely injured ankle, and there would have been a delay of five minutes or so. If she were a tennis player in a competitive match, she would have had a full ten minutes to make a decision about whether or not to continue, as the great German tennis star Boris Becker had done the month before at Wimbleton. But Kerri Strug was a gymnast, and thirty seconds was all she had to make the greatest decision of her life.

She quickly glanced over at her teammates. She could hear every one of them pleading with her to make one more try in order to win the gold medal for the team. She then looked over to her personal coach Béla Karolyi who, together with Steve Nunno, was positioned outside the barrier because Béla's wife Marta and Mary Lee Tracy were the official head coaches for the 1996 American female gymnastics team.

Karolyi called out to her: "We need at least a 9.6 to win the gold."

"I can't feel my leg," Strug told Béla excitedly. "I can't feel it. I think I've broken it."

"We've got to go one more time," Béla responded. "Shake it out."

"Do I have to do this again?" Strug asked, suffering from great physical pain.

"Can you, can you?," Béla wanted to know.

"I don't know yet," responded Strug.

"You can do it, you can do it, you can do it," exhorted Béla the master motivator over and over again. He was appealing to that all-important high level of desire that he knew Kerri Strug possessed. He looked right into Kerri Strug's eyes. At that moment the two partners, coach and athlete, bonded as they had never bonded before. Unquenchable desire was the bond.

Strug went within herself to tap into the vast reservoir of her great desire. She knew that the team gold medal rested on her performance because this was the last team event for the Americans. But she also knew that she was badly hurt and in great pain. She remembered that her perfectionist father, a heart surgeon, was always fond of telling her to put everything into whatever she does, to spare no effort. She recalled what her father said once to a friend of hers: "Kerri is totally self-motivated, has great desire, and wants to be perfect all the time." She thought of the great physical pain she was enduring. She also realized that even the slightest list in her stride on the second vault attempt would cut into the perfect rhythm she needed and thus would destroy the possibility of a high score in the vault. Surely her great pain made the attainment of the necessary rhythm all but impossible. She was well aware that she would be doing a Yurchenko 1½, a gymnastic move which has a start score of 10.0—the highest degree of difficulty in the vault. Almost anyone would have to say that with her debilitating injury and the great pain she was in, it was foolhardy to make a second vault.

The clock was ticking. Her thirty seconds were almost up. She looked at Béla. "I will do it! I will! I will!" Her great desire had won out over the pain and over the specter of impossibility.

As Strug returned to begin her second vault, her limp became increasingly more pronounced. "She's badly hurt," said NBC television play-by-play announcer John Tesh excitedly. "She has turned an ankle or something worse."

As she was about to begin her race toward the vault, Kerri Strug winced in pain. She bit her lip. She said a brief prayer: "O Lord, help me to do it." Then, fueled by intense desire and little else, she raced down the runway and headlong into the Yurchenko 1½, a roundoff flic-flac into a backward 1½ salto with a 1½ turn. She soared above the horse with magnificently clean, tight turns. She nailed her landing perfectly, coming down on both feet. Exhibiting that high level of courage that is born only of desire, she then raised her severely injured left foot in the air just long enough to satisfy the rules of gymnastics competition. Her face was contorted with pain. She then crumpled to the floor in physical agony and called for help.

Very shortly afterward the judges announced her score. The crowd of 32,620 in the Georgia Dome went wild. Béla was delirious with joy. In her second vault, Kerri Strug had scored a superb 9.837. The Americans had won its first-ever team Olympic gold medal in female gymnastics. The United States had a team score of 389.225, followed closely by the Russians with 388.404, and then by the Romanians with 388.246.

The medics came over right away to attend to the injured Kerri Strug. They put on a temporary cast to protect her injured ankle and two torn ligaments. Unable to walk to the podium to receive the team gold medal with her victorious teammates, Béla Karolyi carried her to join her teammates for the medal ceremony. After the ceremony was over, Béla carried Kerri, Olympic gold medal around her neck and tears of combined pain and joy in her eyes, around the stadium as a concrete symbol of great Olympic bravery brought on by enormous desire—a living triumph of desire over overwhelming adversity. Anyone looking at this photo can readily see in Béla's eyes as he looks at Kerri an enormous admiration for this young girl, a girl in whom desire triumphed. Here was a timeless Olympic moment. The photograph of Béla Karolyi carrying the bemedaled yet suffering Kerri Strug, her left leg in a temporary cast, is probably the most famous picture in the whole history of gymnastics, and one of the leading pictures in any sport in the 1990s.

After the triumphal walk, Strug was placed on a movable stretcher and wheeled off to the nearby Crawford Long Hospital for Xrays. As she lay waiting on the stretcher waiting, Béla kissed her gently on her forehead. "It's OK, Baby. It's all right." He then walked away. He had done his job. The rest of the glory that night belonged to Kerri Strug.

Later that evening Kerri returned to the Georgia Dome Media Center for a news conference. She entered the room on crutches, her foot encased in a special boot that circulated cold water around the ankle so as to reduce the swelling. She expressed mixed emotions to the throng of reporters gathered there. She said that she was glad to have been able to help the team win the gold medal but was sad that her injury might prevent her from participating in the all-around competition. "I've waited and wanted and trained so very hard to compete in the all-arounds, and now my injury might have taken this away from me," she told the reporters. She was not satisfied with having contributed so greatly to the American team victory against seemingly insuperable physical odds. Her desire had not abated. She had earnestly wanted to achieve both her goals: the team gold medal and the all-around individual gold medal.

Daniel Carr, the U.S. team physician for the 1996 Olympics, said that Strug's ankle would take a minimum of three weeks to heal and that to compete any more until the healing was complete would do much further damage. But Strug, desire still ablaze, continued to take physiotherapy and to work on her routines in whatever ways she could in the very far-fetched hope that she would be ready to compete in the all-arounds, which were held six days after her magnificent performance in the team competition. Minutes before the all-arounds were to begin, Béla told Kerri that the doctor had said, "No go." "Kerri did not take it well," Béla said later. "She believed she could do it."

Some of Béla's jealous critics inside and outside the gymnastics world accused him of telling Kerri that she had to make the second vault in the team competition. Strug has repeatedly and emphatically

denied this accusation. She has always insisted that the final decision to vault a second time was hers and hers alone. "I'm eighteen
years old now. I can make my own choices", Strug has frequently
said. And she vigorously defends Béla. "He is a tough coach. If he
wasn't so successful, he wouldn't get criticism. It's not right how
everyone tries to find fault with him."

Olympic champions typically become champions because they
take very much to heart the official Olympic credo: "*Citius, altius,
fortius*" (faster, higher, braver). This credo underscores the absolute
necessity of desire—no matter how fast one runs, one must burn
with desire to try and run faster the next time, vault higher the next
time, be braver the next time. What makes an Olympic champion,
what makes every winner to be a winner, is the minimization of
past achievements and a concomitant blazing desire to do better in
each succeeding attempt.

Béla Karolyi strongly believes that in the final analysis, the one
quality that is most fundamental for the success or failure of a gymnast is desire. "Every kid who enters my gym program wants to be
a Nadia Comaneci or a Mary Lou Retton. But basically, when
you're talking about a kid who is possibly going to become a good
gymnast, you're talking about two types. The first have athletic
ability. That's easy to test. But psychological ability is ultimately
even more important, and that's much harder to test. It's hidden. I
watch for it. And I continuously try to build it up." A burning desire
is vital for success and lies at the very base of outstanding success.
Only a burning desire will push a gymnast to work beyond the
limit, to push herself to standards she never before thought possible. Only a burning desire will enable a gymnast to strive to do better than her best. Only a burning desire will energize a gymnast
never to settle for anything less than a perfect performance. Only a
burning desire will drive a gymnast to repeat a move or a routine
over and over and over again until she does it right. Only a burning
desire will motivate a gymnast never to give up regardless of how
unpromising or even hopeless a situation appears to be. Only a
burning desire will equip a gymnast to have the blazing level of intensity that is necessary to prevail.

"It takes a long time to discover whether a gymnast has the burning desire to excel, to win", Béla observes. "If a gymnast doesn't have this all-consuming desire to do better than her best, it's been a waste of time. So you try to find out as fast as you can."

Karolyi contends that whereas a girl who comes to his gym might have the requisite burning desire, it is up to the coach to bring it out, to make it come to full flower. "This is not something we introduce for half an hour. It is built up through a long period of time," Béla notes. "I look in the eyes of our gymnasts. I see the level of desire in the eyes."

If the good God were to look into the eyes of us religious educators, how brightly would he find the flames of desire? To what extent would our eyes be aglow with religious instruction desire?

How high is our level of desire to give up everything, to sacrifice all, for the sake of the religious instruction apostolate? Our call within a call does not automatically bestow upon us a burning desire to do everything in our religious instruction apostolate as perfectly and as sacramentally as it can be done. Rather, our call within a call brings with it the responsibility to gain this burning desire at the earliest possible moment and to be inflamed by this desire for the rest of our lives.

Is our desire all-consuming? If not, why not?

To what extent do we desire complete and absolute commitment to the towering demands and daily grinding exigencies of the religious instruction apostolate?

To what degree do we truly desire always to excel at every single thing we do in our religious instruction apostolate?

Do we really and truly desire to do better than the very best at all times and in all circumstances as religious educators?

Is our desire such that it propels us to do things perfectly, no matter what the cost to us personally? Or is our desire weak and tepid?

Does our desire motivate us to prepare perfectly, to enact perfectly, to follow up perfectly as we engage in our religious instruction apostolate? Or is our desire only a romantic notion in our mind rather than a propulsion to do nitty-gritty things such as to enact the religious instruction act as perfectly as possible, and then some?

To what extent does our desire impel us to sharpen our skills by regularly reading first-class books in the field of religious instruction?

Do the coals of our religious instruction desire burn brightly all day? Can we actually feel the red-hot fire of desire within our hearts?

How frequently does our desire flag so that we relax or take it easy when we should be working at open throttle in the religious instruction apostolate?

To what extent is our desire so powerful that we never give up, no matter what situation confronts us as religious educators?

Do we habitually desire never to settle for anything less than the very best as we engage in the day-to-day activities of our religious instruction apostolate?

How often does our desire wane or melt in the face of opposition or resentment?

Is our desire so powerful that it enables us to conquer whatever jealousy others might have of us and the religious instruction work we are doing?

Do we try always to fan the flames of our desire so that our desire burns ceaselessly at the maximum level?

To what extent do we have that very high level of desire that is necessary if we are to be outstanding religious educators?

If we do not have a continuously high level of burning desire to do everything it takes to be an outstanding religious educator, are we worthy of the religious instruction apostolate?

Performance Objective: Whenever some important religious instruction task proves especially difficult or when I am stressed out by the exhausting rigors of the educational ministry, I will inflame the level of my apostolic desire by repeating to myself over and over again: "I *will* accomplish this task! I *will* accomplish it!"

16

Care

It is a sad fact of life that the more we use a thing of significant value, the less valuable we perceive that thing to be. The value of the thing does not change with frequent use. What changes is our perception of its value. We take so many valuable things for granted largely because we use them all the time: air, water, sunshine, rain, fire, a comfortable home, church services, electricity, clothes—and words.

Words arise out of personal and group experience. Words are not natural. They are invented because of a basic need to place one or another form of human experience into a cognitive symbolic form for the purpose of communication. The power and richness of any word is directly proportional to the depth and range of the experience to which that word points. This is precisely where etymology comes in. Etymology traces the development of a word from its earliest recorded occurrence in the language where it was found and then charts its subsequent transmission from the ancestral language to its cognate languages. Etymology reveals the original experience or set of experiences that lies at the base of a word and that the word was initially intended to codify in a cognitive fashion.

In our rationalistic contemporary era, people are often blind to the power and range of the words they use because they are frequently unaware of the pervasive experiential base and source of these words. One highly practical function of etymology is to help us recover the original experience which a word symbolically encapsulates so that we can use this experiential base to give us important insights into and helpful guidance on the conduct of human affairs.

A word frequently used in the field of religious instruction is care. A glimpse into the etymology of the English word care will help religious educators unlock the powerful experiential basis of this word and assist us to significantly enhance the effectiveness of the caring dimension of our overall teaching activity.

The English word "care" has its origins in the Latin *cura*. This Latin word passed into Old French, where it became *cure*. From there it found its way into English and came forth as care.

The Latin word *cura* has two basic meanings. The first of these, and the more usual, is care. The second meaning, also essential, is cure.

In its first meaning as care, the word *cura* was used by ancient Latin writers in a wide variety or organically intertwined ways. The core of the interrelated meanings of *cura* centers around taking for and taking care of a person, object, or activity. Flowing from this core meaning, Latin writers also used the word *cura* in a variety of other senses, all of which were implicitly contained in the core meaning of *cura* as taking care of and taking care for. Thus *cura* means paying serious attention to a person, object, or activity to ensure that it is properly taken care of. *Cura* means taking charge of and often engaging in supervision to see that a person, object, or activity is properly cared for (the Latin *curator* and its direct English derivative have this denotation). *Cura* means taking pains and going to considerable trouble to make sure that a person, object, or activity, receives the requisite care. *Cura* means concern and solicitude to ensure that a person, object, or activity is properly cared for. *Cura* means anxiety and worry in the sense of being deeply concerned that the care which is given will be genuinely helpful to a person, object, or activity. Finally, *cura* means sorrow and grief at the possibility that the care that is given might not be successful.

The Latin word *cura* also means cure. This meaning is intrinsically related to the denotation of *cura* as care because taking care of and for a person itself tends to bring about a cure of whatever ails that individual. Latin writers used *cura* to mean medical care of a sick person leading to a successful cure. *Cura* means medical treatment of an illness or a disease (hence the Latin *curabilis,* which means both medical treatment and curable). *Cura* also means healing. Of especial interest to religious educators is that *cura* was occasionally used by Latin writers to mean spiritual cure. This meaning was taken up not just in Old French but also in modern French where the Gallic word *cure* means, among other things, the cure of souls, and the word *curé* means the pastor of a French church, the person who has care of souls and who works to bring about spiritual cure. (In English, the word "curate" means a member of the parish clergy, especially an associate pastor, who cares for souls and with God's help cures souls through competent care.)

To discharge one's duties with care as well as to care for others in a human way is a direct and very potent key factor in curing the physical, cognitive, affective, and lifestyle deficiencies in others. This very important fact was dramatically demonstrated in a celebrated empirical research study conducted by René Spitz with babies born to unwed mothers. This study examined two groups of babies through the first year of life. The babies in group A were cared for by their own mothers or by caring mother substitutes. These babies received at least the minimum level of satisfactory medical attention; they also received a great deal of warm loving personal care by the mother or mother substitute. The babies in group B were attended to by trained nurses in accordance with high professional medical standards and in an objectively clinical, detached manner. To be sure, the babies in group B received superior medical treatment (in the objectively clinical sense of that term) than the babies in group A. At the end of the study, group A babies had made normal developmental progress, while group B babies were tragic on all counts, Of the ninety-one babies in group B, thirty-one died (despite elaborate medical precautions). The rest were apathetic and had regressed in intelligence; only five could walk unaided. Spitz concluded that personal care constituted the primary variable that caused the dramatic differences between the two groups. Specifically, the babies in group A received much more personal care more frequently and with more affectivity than did the babies in group B.

Spitz reported that his conclusions were similar to related European and American empirical research studies of infants who received fine clinical medical attention but did not receive a goodly degree of personal care (such as is the case with infants who grow up in an institution rather than at home with their parents). These European and American empirical research studies found that practically without exception these infants developed subsequent psychiatric disturbances and became asocial, delinquent, feeble-minded, psychotic, or problem children.

As a result of these and other research studies, medical practitioners came to realize that personal caring is not something that lies outside of their medical practice with patients but rather is a central dimension of their work their patients. In other words, care is a key ingredient in effecting physical cure.

Clergy have also begun to recognize that care plays a central role in bringing about the cure of the spiritual ills and deficiencies of those with whom they work in a wide variety of formal and informal environments.

In all the helping professions, ranging from the medical arts to religious instruction, care is not something outside of or in addition to clinical competence. On the contrary, care is a necessary and intrinsic part of competence.

It should be emphasized that care does not mean some kind of fuzzily warm or generally well-meaning kind of attention to a person. Such a mentality belongs more properly to the category of a feel-good kind of self-indulgence and a sloppy form of sentimentality than it does to genuine care. In its authentic form, care is that concrete embodiment of love and concern and devotion that takes great pains to ensure that one's caring actions are done with requisite proficiency, with carefulness that everything is done properly, with vigilant attention to details, and with unhesitatingly going the extra mile when called for by the situation. What fundamentally distinguishes care from wholly objective clinical practice is that care is done out of personal love and concern and devotion, a love and concern and devotion that are evident to the person receiving the care. It is this love and concern and devotion combined with proficiency and carefulness and attention to details and going the extra mile that bring about the cure. Love and concern and devotion are not enough to effect the cure. Nor is proficiency or carefulness or attention to details or going the extra mile of themselve sufficient to bring about the cure.

As religious educators, we are sublimely blessed by God's call within a call to teach religion to persons of all ages and in all sorts of milieux. To teach religion is essentially to bring about a cognitive, affective, or lifestyle cure for something that is lacking in others. This lack might be intellectual, such as insufficient knowledge or understanding of the doctrinal elements of Christianity. This lack might be affective, such as attitudes, values, or love that are not representative of the highest Christian principles. This lack might be lifestyle, such as actions that are unsatisfactory when measured by Christian standards of conduct. It is incumbent on us religious educators to make sure that care for learners is a central and necessary element in bringing about an effective and long-lasting cure for those whom we teach.

An age-old axiom in sacramental theology is that a sacrament gives what it signifies. One of the most important things that every sacrament signifies, and therefore gives, is cure because a sacrament is quintessentially a caring act of God. So too it is with the sacrament of teaching: It has the power to cure what ails learners in their cognitions, affects, and lifestyle.

To what extent to we religious educators infuse all of our teaching activities with care—care not in the sense of some fuzzy, warm feeling of wanting to help the learners but care in the sense of concretely doing the best to ensure that those for whom we care instructionally will indeed learn to the optimum degree?

Are we truly devoted to learners by doing everything it takes in large and small matters to help them learn?

To what degree do we see care as a necessary part of our instructional competence? How often do we avoid the anguish involved in competence by saying that all we have to do is care for learners in a warm, fuzzy manner?

Do we really and truly realize that by inserting care into the overall framework of instructional competence we will thereby help bring about a cure for whatever cognitive, affective, or lifestyle deficiency ails learners? Do we realize that the process of cure by care will sometimes hurt the learner initially, like cauterizing a wound?

To what extent are we scrupulously careful in preparing, executing, and evaluating our religious instruction activities? To what degree are we careful, care-full, full of care to do things in the best manner possible? If we are not careful, care-full, full of care, how can we justify our existence as a religious educator, a person called by God to care mightily for human beings?

Do we make every effort to ensure that mature, self-sacrificing love, care, and concern for learners swirl through our instructional activities?

To what extent do we pay serious attention to each learner—his needs, her interests, his problems, her concerns? To what degree do we pay serious attention to structuring each element in the teaching situation with great care to all the details?

Do we religious educators take consummate pains to see to it always that each learner receives the best possible instructional care? How often do we go to considerable trouble to make sure that all the conditions are as optimum as possible to bring about the desired learning outcome? Do we sometimes shrink, if even only a little, from the continual sacrifices we are called on to make in order to truly care for each learner instructionally?

To what extent do our religious instruction behaviors communicate to learners that we really care for them deeply, devotedly, warmly, and as persons?

Do we have affective concern and solicitude for each learner in the sense that we are eager to attend to all those many pedagogical details that optimize our instructional efforts?

How frequently do we worry that the instructional care we give learners might not be sufficient? How often do we experience sorrow and grief at the thought that the instructional care we provide to learners might not be as successful as we or they wish?

Performance Objective: In the next seven days I will select in my mind one learner who regularly seems to be experiencing an especially noteworthy cognitive, affective, or lifestyle difficulty either in the religious instructional event or in life generally. During the ensuing weeks I will treat that person in an especially caring manner by incorporating an extra degree of overtly warm, caring behaviors into the existing repertoire of competent instructional procedures that I customarily use with that individual. Once my heightened caring behaviors have borne instructional fruit—which might take a great deal of time—I will select in my mind another learner who seems to be experiencing considerable difficulty. I will then repeat the caring process with that person.

17

Perseverance

In the north of Sweden near the Arctic Circle where each fallen snowflake seems to cast its own separate shadow in the low winter light, and every flower seems to dazzle the heavens in the high summer light, there once lived a Lutheran pastor of a small country church. He was a very devout man who was much loved by his parishioners and greatly respected by his brother pastors in the region.

One year it happened that the parish received a benefaction which was given on condition that some sort of decoration be added to the church. The benefaction stipulated that the decoration be pastoral in the sense that it would tend to lead a person who saw it to renounce sin and embrace virtue.

The pastor decided to use the money from the benefaction to hire a skilled artist to paint in dramatic fashion on the wall of the church the inescapably dire consequences which befall a person who deals with the devil. The pastor was an avid and expert chess player, and so it was natural that he would commission a fresco using a chess match as a metaphor of what always happens when a person plays with the devil.

The fresco was completed several months after it was begun. It depicted an innocent-looking boy about ten years of age playing chess with the devil. The boy represented all of humanity. His face and posture reflected sadness and dejection. Seated on the opposite side of the table was the devil with a triumphant, smirky smile on his face. One look at the fresco showed unmistakably that the devil had the boy decisively in check.

The pastor had worked closely with the painter to ensure that there was no way the boy could escape the devil's check.

News of this unusual church fresco traveled far and wide throughout Scandinavia and indeed throughout much of Europe. Stirred by curiosity and challenge, chess experts from all over the Continent came to the little country church to see if they could figure out how the boy—who, after all, represented themselves—could escape the devil's check. All failed in their attempts, and they went home learning the lesson that the fresco was teaching: If you deal with the devil you will certainly lose.

Then one day when the sun reached its zenith in the summer sky, an internationally famous chess grand master arrived at the church door. He had journeyed all the way from central Europe to examine the famous fresco. He carefully studied it and after an hour concluded that there was no apparent way to escape the devil's check. But the grand master did not give up and go home. For seven days and seven nights he studied the fresco without interruption, summoning all his vast experience gained from the championship chess matches in which he had played and from his thorough knowledge of all the important matches that had taken place in the history of championship chess. All his waking moments were spent in the church scrutinizing the fresco. He had all his meals brought to him in the church. He even spent his nights sleeping in front of the fresco.

On the morning of the eighth day the grand master figured a way out of the devil's check. He challenged the pastor to continue the match. The grand master played the boy's pieces while the pastor played the devil's pieces. After some hours, the game ended with the boy, in the person of the grand master, winning the match.

Our call within a call as a religious educator requires us never to give up in any here-and-now or long-term instructional situation but to examine the event carefully and steadfastly until a solution reveals itself.

To what extent are we religious educators willing, even eager, to steadfastly persevere with a difficult instructional or administrative problem until it is solved? Is not one prime characteristic of a sacrament—including the sacrament of teaching—that it never gives up trying, no matter how unfavorable are the odds?

Do we religious educators give up too easily when confronted with a difficult teaching problem? Or do we persist until the problem is successfully resolved?

If, after working with one or another learner for a long time without success, do we tend to give up on that person? Or, instead, do we try even harder to bring about the desired learning outcome?

Successful perseverance, as contrasted to unsuccessful perseverance, often demands creative approaches to problems. Creative approaches enable us to solve problems or difficulties that initially appear to be unsolvable. Sometimes these creative solutions jump out at us. More often, however, these solutions come about by dint of long, hard, grinding work on our part.

Our call within a call dictates that we religious educators ought never to give up on a difficult instructional case but press forward relentlessly to help all learners come to an understanding, a love, and a lifestyle that is patterned after that of Jesus.

Performance Objective: The next time I come up against a seemingly insuperable religious instruction problem of major consequence, I will not dismiss the problem as unsolvable. Rather, I will stay with that important problem unceasingly and creatively until I have resolved it, even if this takes a long time and a great deal of effort.

18

Being Used

There were many persons in the nineteenth century who were more powerful and more prominent than Bernadette Soubirous, but few who were more holy.

She was born in January 1844 in the mountain village of Lourdes, nestled amidst the Pyrenees in southwestern France. Her parents were religiously devout and financially impoverished.

Bernadette was sickly for almost all of her life. When she was six years old, she began to suffer from the severe asthma that remained with her until her death. When she was twelve, she contracted cholera. Because of Bernadette's poor health, her illiterate parents did not send her to school. She ardently wished to receive First Eucharist. To prepare herself for the reception of this greatest of all sacraments, she attended some catechism classes. Both the priest who taught these classes and also the woman who took care of Bernadette and taught her at home found her to be somewhat on the intellectually dull side, or at least intellectually simple.

The morning of February 11, 1858, broke cold and damp in Lourdes, with a veil of mist shrouding the mountains and even invading the village itself. Around eleven o'clock, when the mist had lifted, Bernadette and two of her girlfriends went to gather firewood. They eventually came to a place where Bernadette had never been before, a wild and uninhabited site called Massabielle right by a canal flowing from the Gave River. Set into the rocky hill of Massabielle was a large cave. To the right of the cave was a spacious oval recess, or grotto. Very soon after arriving at Massabielle, Bernadette received an apparition of Mary, the mother of God. All in all, Bernadette received eighteen apparitions from February 11 to July 18, 1858. She was met with constant disbelief and frequent scolding from the pastor of her parish church, and with heavy-handed opposition from the police and other civil authorities.

To shield her from the crowds, the press, and the civil authorities during the period of the apparitions, Bernadette was sent as a day student to a local school operated by the Sisters of Charity and Christian Instruction. Later she became a boarding student there. In July 1866 she entered the motherhouse and convent of this congregation of women religious in the city of Nevers in order to become a nun.

Bernadette's years in the convent were her hidden life. She was cut off from Lourdes and the pilgrimages. She had little contact with the outside world. First as a novice and then as a professed nun, she lived what most persons then and now would regard as a humdrum and extremely routine existence with little or no stimulation from the outside world.

Life in the convent was filled with intense pain in body and soul for Bernadette. She suffered very much from a wide variety of physical ailments, including severe asthma, tuberculosis, a large tumor on the knee, and vomiting blood. Her mental and emotional sufferings were even greater, due to the cold and cruel treatment that she was forced to endure relentlessly from her religious superiors and occasionally from the other nuns.

Throughout her life after the apparitions, she repeated over and over again: "Pray for me, a sinner."

In the spring of 1879 Bernadette died in the convent at Nevers and was buried on the feast of the Ascension in the Chapel of St. Joseph. She died as she had lived, expiring immediately after she had recited the words of the Hail Mary, "pray for us sinners."

It was Bernadette's last Hail Mary on earth.

Thirty years after her death, Bernadette's body was publicly exhumed as part of the ecclesiastical process of beatification. The corpse was found incorrupt. The flesh had retained its original whiteness. There was no odor or trace of decay. However, the clothing and the rosary with which she was buried were disintegrating. The scientists who examined the corpse affirmed that there were no chemicals, no embalming fluids, and no preservatives of any kind in the dead body.

To the present day, Lourdes has remained the most popular pilgrimage site in the Western world. Millions of people have journeyed to Lourdes to be physically healed of serious illnesses by drinking or bathing in the waters that flow from the miraculous spring about which Mary told Bernadette and whose many amazing cures have been authenticated by scientists of various religious faiths and none at all.

When I was eighteen years old, I traveled with my mother to Lourdes as part of a summer grand tour of Europe that she gave me as a religious and cultural present. My experience at Lourdes was one of the highlights of my life; it still remains deep in my heart. Lourdes is a very special place. Participation in religious events at the grotto and in the evening candlelight procession in the mall in front of the church, as well as just walking around the sacred precincts of the shrine, are precious moments that are truly unforgettable.

A well-known incident in the life of Bernadette happened one Sunday in 1876. From the day she entered the convent, she was forbidden by her superiors to discuss her apparitions at Lourdes with the other nuns. Notwithstanding, some nuns occasionally tried to trick Bernadette into talking about the apparitions. On that particular Sunday, one nun showed Bernadette a photograph of the grotto of Massabielle. The nun watched Bernadette's face intently to see her reaction. Bernadette looked at the photograph and quickly turned away, saying: "I am like a broom in the corner of a room. The Blessed Mother used me as a broom to do some work for her. When the job was completed, I was put back in the corner. That is my task on earth."

Being a broom means being a person who is used by others in one way or another. Being a broom means having others take advantage of us. A prime axis of Bernadette's vocation was to be used by God as a broom for his sake and for the sake of others.

Religious educators sometimes complain about being used. But do we realize that being used by God to teach persons to become more religious is one of the main features of our call within a call?

Sometimes we religious educators gripe about members of the clergy using us to do the religious instruction work that they themselves should be properly doing. Sometimes we grouse that religious education administrators are using us by taking advantage of us in various ways. Sometimes we grumble that our learners are using us by placing unreasonable demands on us or by asking us to work hard during the instructional act while they take it easy.

If we think about it, being used by people and by God is a requirement of all religious educators if we are going to teach individuals and groups to grow religiously.

And if we continue to think about it, being used by others is part and parcel of the sacrament of teaching. Is not a sacrament basically a reality whose primary purpose is to be used for the sanctification of others?

A broom is valuable only to the extent to which it is used. The mission of a broom is to be used. The more a broom is used, the better it fulfills its role as a broom. The unused broom is unfit to be a broom and should be discarded.

So we religious educators should rejoice in being used. We should rejoice in the fact that God has seen fit to use us as his religious educators, a call within a call not given to many persons in this world.

Jesus the religious educator was used by persons all the time. Being used was at the heart of his mission as religious educator. Can it be any different for us, whose central mission in life is to carry on the religious instruction work of Jesus in our time? Every religious educator basically is a broom whom God is using to teach learners how to come closer to him.

How eagerly do we embrace the God-given opportunity of being used for the better accomplishment of desired religious instruction objectives?

Performance Objective: Whenever I believe that a religious instruction superior, colleague, or learner is using me, I will quickly ascertain whether my being used by that person actually advances one or another worthwhile religious instruction goal. If either my reflection or my gut feeling shows me that I am being used for that individual's ego aggrandizement, then I will refuse to be used. But on the other hand, if my reflection or my gut feeling reveals that my being used actually furthers significant religious instruction goals, I will not complain about being used. Rather, I will thank God and will rejoice that he is giving me the wonderful grace of being used for his religious instruction service. I will then fully and gladly cooperate in being used for the Lord's religious instruction ministry.

19

Talking Versus Doing

Of all the glories of religion in the twentieth century, she was surely the most glorious.

Of all the shining stars of religion in the twentieth century, she surely shone the brightest.

Her name was Teresa and she spent most of her ministry for Christ in the slums of Calcutta.

She was born Agnes Gonxha Bojaxhiu in Skopje in the Macedonian region of what was then Serbia on August 26, 1910. (In the Albanian language, Gonxha means "flower bud".) Her Albanian parents were deeply religious. Nikola ("Kole") Bojaxhiu, the father, a politically active man, was a prosperous merchant who frequently traveled throughout Europe on business. A stern but loving parent, Kole took a keen interest in his children's lessons, urging them to always work hard. He fed the poor at his own table and set a living example of service to the community. He liked to tell his three children: "Never accept a mouthful unless it is shared with others."

When Agnes was eight years old, her father died. Her mother Dranafile ("Drana") did not possess the commercial skills to keep her deceased husband's business going, and so she supported the family by using her needlework talents to make and sell fine handcrafted embroidery. Though the family was no longer wealthy, Drana continued Kole's charitable ways, giving food and assistance to the poor, the old, and the infirm. Later in life Agnes would recall: "Many of the poor in and around Skopje knew our house and none left it empty-handed. We had guests at our table every day. At first I used to ask: 'Who are they?' Mother would answer: 'Some are relatives, but all of them are our people.'" Agnes interpreted the phrase "our people" to mean the poor, who are always God's special people.

Before and after Kole's death, the Bojaxhiu family was happy and cohesive. They sang songs together and prayed daily. The family made annual pilgrimages to the famous Balkan shrine of Our Lady of Cernagore, situated at Letnice in an especially beautiful setting in the mountains of Montenegro. For a month and a half each summer Agnes and her older sister Aga were allowed to stay in Letnice to gain physical refreshment as well as spiritual nourishment. Her annual pilgrimages to the shrine in Letnice exerted a powerful impact on her life.

At the age of twelve Agnes Gonxha Bojaxhiu received a call from God to enter the religious life. Over the next six years Agnes examined herself frequently to discern the validity, contours, and direction of her call.

In 1924 Franjo Jambrenkovič arrived in Skopje as associate pastor in the Bojaxhiu's parish church. His religious education work there was to have a profound effect on young Agnes. He organized a sodality (a youth religious club dedicated to Mary the mother of God), one for boys and the other for girls. Agnes joined the sodality and became an active member, participating in a wide variety of religious activities of a charitable and educational nature. Jambrenkovič was deeply interested in the missions. He would read to the parishioners and to the sodality letters and articles written by Croatian and Slovenian missionaries to Calcutta. He would also tell them inspiring stories of the missions in Bengal.

As a young girl Agnes was frequently sick and often confined to bed. There she developed a love of reading. Throughout her childhood and adolescence she was an avid reader.

Agnes had always wanted to become a teacher. Thanks to the religious instruction efforts of Franjo Jambrenkovič, she also felt drawn to the missionary life. When she was eighteen she consulted with Jambrenkovič about her vocation to be a sister. The priest suggested that she join the Loreto Sisters, an Irish congregation whose specific apostolate combined Agnes's lifework desires of being both a teacher and a missionary to India.

Throughout her life Agnes consistently declared that her specific vocation in life, though coming directly to her from God himself, was nourished and influenced by two confluent forces: the pervasive religious instruction atmosphere of her family and the focused religious instruction efforts of Franjo Jambrenkovič.

When she turned eighteen, Agnes told her mother that she had definitely decided to enter the convent and become a missionary to India. Though she was a very devout Catholic, Drana originally opposed Agnes's decision because she knew that by becoming a missionary sister Agnes not only would be relinquishing all her chances for marriage and a family but also would be leaving her country and family and friends to toil for the rest of her life in a strange faraway land. In the end, Drana gave Agnes her blessing and told her: "My daughter, if you begin something, begin it with your whole heart. Otherwise, don't begin it at all." Throughout her life, Agnes kept her mother's religious instruction words burning bright in her heart.

In September 1928 Agnes left Skopje and traveled by rail and ship to the relatively austere Loreto Motherhouse in the Rathfarnham suburb of Dublin. There she formally entered the congregation of the Loreto Sisters as a postulant, a word derived from Latin that means "a person requesting admission." While in Rathfarnham, Agnes learned English as well as the rudiments of life as a Loreto Sister.

In early December Agnes sailed for India to begin a two-year novitiate, a period in which a candidate for the sisterhood undergoes an intense period of spiritual formation and religious instruction necessary to enable her to live a consecrated life as a full-fledged sister. The novitiate of the Loreto Sisters was located in Darjeeling, a lovely town in the west part of Bengal. Situated in the Himalaya Mountains at an altitude of about 7,500 feet, Darjeeling was the summer capital of the British in the days of the Raj. Surrounded by visually delicious tea plantations and commanding a magnificent view of snow-clad Mount Kangchenjunga (28,168 feet) on a clear day, Darjeeling is even today a popular hill station and vacation resort for both well-to-do Indians and prosperous tourists from countries around the world.

After some months of additional preparation, Agnes formally became a novice in May 1929. Upon becoming novice, she took the religious habit, a special distinguishing garb routinely worn by all sisters in those days. (The use of the habit by sisters, brothers, and priests of the *regula* dates back to the saintly Pachomius [294–346] who introduced cenobitical monasticism in Egypt. See Eph 4:24.) In accordance with a practice that can be traced back at least to sixth-century monasticism, Agnes relinquished her first name and took a new name. The purpose of the name change was threefold: to cut oneself off as completely as possible from former worldly identification (Col 3:9–10), to put on the new person in the total dedication of self to Jesus (Rom 13:12–14; 2 Cor 5:17), and to model one's behavior as a religious on the life of the saint whose name the novice had adopted (Heb 13:7). Agnes took Teresa as her new name after the French saint Thérèse of Lisieux (1873–1897). Agnes felt that Thérèse constituted an admirable role model on two accounts. First, Agnes was a missionary (Thérèse had just been declared patroness of the missions by Pius XI). Second, Agnes's career of teaching school in a missionary land would necessarily be a simple and unexciting life. (Thérèse's spirituality centered around "the little way" of perfection through simple ordinary things of life and childlike trust.)

Most of Teresa's time in the novitiate was spent in the age-old traditional manner prescribed for the education of novices, namely, spiritual exercises, liturgy, religious instruction, and mortification. Additionally, Teresa labored in a nearby charity hospital helping the nurses in a variety of ways. Before beginning her daily work in the hospital, Teresa would spend a little time meditating in front of a picture that hung on the wall of the hospital pharmacy. In this picture, Jesus the Redeemer is shown surrounded by a crowd of sick persons. In these faces one could read the pathos and anguish of human existence. After her brief meditation, Teresa would open the door to a little gallery crowded with sick, starving, unhappy people. Many had walked hours just to get treated. Some people had open sores on their ears, legs, and feet. Others were full of bumps and cavities due to their many ulcers. Babies were suffering from numerous boils. Writing of these times, Teresa remarked: "All their eyes are fixed on me with indescribable hope. Mothers hand me their sick babies, just as the people in the picture do. My heart beats with joy. I pray that I can keep up your work, O Jesus!"

Two years later Agnes Gonxha Bojaxhiu, now known as Sister Teresa, took her first vows of poverty, chastity, and obedience as a Loreto Sister. She had become a professed sister. On May 24, 1937, she took her final—and permanent—vows. It was the feast of Our Lady Help of Christians. Teresa thought that this was a fitting day for her to take her final vows in a missionary congregation.

When Teresa had taken her first vows, she was sent to Calcutta to teach in two separate adjoining high schools. The first of these, St. Mary's High School, was operated by the Loreto Sisters for the daughters of wealthy Europeans who could afford the tuition plus room and board. The second high school, distinct from St. Mary's, was run by a diocesan congregation of Indian sisters for the daughters of prosperous Bengali families where the girls could be taught in their native language. Both schools enrolled a significant number of orphans and scholarship students from poor families. Teresa was to remain there for seventeen years, eventually becoming principal.

These two adjacent schools were located in Calcutta's Entally district, an ugly section of the city consisting of slums and filthy factories. The Loreto Sisters had purchased this property from the money given to them in a generous bequest made by a friendly Protestant gentleman. Behind high walls in this squalid neighborhood lay the beautiful grounds, carefully tended gardens, and a well-kept convent and set of school buildings.

Though she lived in a sealed-off island of tranquility surrounded by human degradation of every sort, Teresa nonetheless had frequent contact with the starving and the destitute of Calcutta. Together with girls from the sodality of both high schools, she regularly comforted patients in the Nilratan Sackar hospital, worked with the poor in the filthy Motijhil slum, and did other kinds of religious education tasks. When the school day was finished at Entaly, Teresa taught in St. Teresa's parish school. This school was located in another area of the city, and to reach it she had to walk through slums teeming with the starving, the sick, and the dying. On Sundays she visited the slums working there to the utmost of her abilities. People washed in dirty water running in the gutters. Dead bodies were often piled up on the sides of the streets waiting to be carted off by sanitation workers and dumped who knows where. The stench was almost unbearable. Above the noise and chaos of the slums rose the plaintive wails of sick and dying children.

On September 10, 1946, a day which later was to be celebrated annually by the Missionaries of Charity and Co-Workers as Inspiration Day, Teresa was on a train from Calcutta to Darjeeling where she and other Loreto Sisters made their annual retreat, a time for spiritual renewal, spiritual recentering, and spiritual reenergizing. While riding on that crowded train amidst the noise and the jostling, Teresa underwent an intense religious experience that changed the direction of her life. She later conveyed to a journalist the message contained in her intense religious experience. As she spoke of her experience, her face radiated gladness and shone with serenity and a deep sense of inner security: "I was sure that this was the voice of God. I was certain that he was calling me. The message was clear: I must leave the convent to help the poor by going to live among them. This was an order, a task. To fail it would be to break the faith. I knew where I had to be. I understood what I needed to do, but I did not know how to go about it."

Teresa never liked to talk with others about her intense religious experience. She once confided that "the call to God to be a Missionary of Charity is the hidden treasure for me, for which I have sold all to purchase." Another time she was asked if her intense religious experience came in the form of a vision, an inspiration, or what. Did she hear a voice, or something like as voice? Given the circumstances of a long train ride amidst the din and smells and jostling of many persons in close quarters while she was tired, how could she be sure that her intense religious experience was authentic: Could it have been an illusion brought about by fatigue and insufficient oxygen? Teresa responded: "The form of the call is not important. It is something between God and me. What is important is that God calls each one in a different way. There is no merit on our part. The important thing is to respond to the call."

After finishing her retreat at Darjeeling, Teresa returned home to the Loreto convent in Entally. She now had her call within a call to serve the poorest of the poor. But she did not know how to operationalize this call. In her mind, in her heart, and in her prayers she returned again and again to the words she heard from a missionary in India when she was a young girl living in Skopje: "Each person has a road to follow that is his own, and he must follow that road." Teresa prayed with all her heart for God to show her how to walk this road. She knew that the good God who gave her the call within a call would not desert her.

She knew also that the road would not be easy. History clearly shows that every great work of God has almost always had to pass through difficulties and misunderstandings, especially in the beginning and especially among those in the same household of faith. The response to the call within a call invariably requires dogged and steadfast perseverance on the part of the person receiving the call.

In the spirit of obedience Teresa asked Ferdinand Perier, the archbishop of Calcutta, to grant her permission to start a new diocesan congregation of sisters devoted solely to what she called "the poorest of the poor." The archbishop denied her request on three grounds: there was already an Indian congregation of sisters (the Daughters of St. Ann) working with the poor, the Vatican was not in favor of starting new congregations of religious women because there were too many of these groups, and the great political unrest at the time in India pitting Hindus against Muslims made it quite dangerous for Christian missionaries to be working in the slums.

After some further reflection, and impressed with Teresa's single-mindedness, the archbishop proposed that she join forces with the Daughters of St. Ann who were already working with the very poor throughout India, especially on the outskirts of the cities. Teresa declined the archbishop's offer because after each day of working with the destitute and suffering, the Daughters of St. Ann would retreat to the quiet and seclusion of their own convent cut off from the twenty-four-hour-a-day misery of the poor. Teresa's call within a call was to live twenty-four hours a day amid the poorest of the poor where these persons lived, suffered, and died.

Undaunted, Teresa prayed and prayed and prayed that the archbishop would change his mind. Scrupulously following canon law, she also wrote to the mother general of the Loreto Sisters in Ireland requesting that she be allowed to apply to the Vatican for an indult of exclaustration, which would allow her to reside as a religious sister outside her convent "in order to spend herself in the service of the poor and the needs in the slums of Calcutta, and to gather around her some companions ready to undertake the same work." In February 1948 Gertrude Kennedy, the Loreto mother general in Ireland, gave permission to Teresa. Now she was ready to ask the Vatican for an indult of exclaustration. Her petition to Rome was handled in the customary way, namely, through the Holy See's nunciature in Delhi. However, to Teresa's great distress, Perier now insisted that Teresa seek from Rome secularization and not exclaustration. Secularization meant that she would be no longer a woman religious and hence would not be able to found or direct a religious congregation such as the Missionaries of Charity. Perier put forth his views not only to Teresa but also in a separate letter that accompanied Teresa's request to the Vatican via the nunciature.

But God had plans that were at sharp variance with the desires of the archbishop of Delhi. It was not until 1971 that Teresa found out about the pivotal role in her case played by Luigi Raimundi, the apostolic nuncio to Delhi in 1948. Raimundi, who believed in Teresa, decided on his own initiative that as apostolic nuncio he possessed the necessary authority to grant the indult; thus it was not necessary to send Teresa's petition to Rome along with Perier's letter. Raimundi realized that if Teresa's request, accompanied as it was by Perier's missive, was forwarded to the Vatican, it would have been dealt with as just one letter among the hundreds of letters that arrive at Rome every day from all over the world and that Rome would have decreed secularization as Perier had requested. Raimundi believed, and rightly so, that he understood Teresa and the situation in Calcutta far more intimately and therefore more accurately than did Vatican bureaucrats, well-meaning though they were.

Raimundi did his work well. Thanks to his intervention, which was not known to anyone else at the time, the Vatican put its formal stamp of approval on Raimundi's action and sent Teresa the official indult of exclaustration. On August 7, 1948, she received the indult. She was now free to follow her own special road, her call within a call.

Nine days later, on August 16, 1948, Teresa left St. Mary's. She took off the habit of the Loreto Sisters and put on a cheap, simple white sari and open sandals on her feet. Leaving behind the comfort and security of her convent, she quietly stepped out into the street to spread "the fragrance of joy" over what Rudyard Kipling had once referred to as "the big Calcutta stink." She had only five rupees (less than a dollar) in her pocket.

On many occasions throughout her life Teresa said that "to leave Loreto was my greatest sacrifice, the most difficult thing I have ever done. It was much more difficult than to leave my family and country to enter religious life. Loreto, my spiritual training, my work, meant everything to me." But Teresa realized that when God calls, every tie must necessarily be broken, every ego attachment must be severed.

Always the effective religious educator, Teresa was deeply aware that her own zeal and dedication were not enough. She also needed technical competence if she was going to be successful in ministering to the needs of the destitute, suffering, and dying. So she set out for the city of Patna, where for several months she intensively studied nursing with the Medical Mission Sisters. The foundress and mother general of this congregation was Anna Dengal, a licensed surgeon as well as a wise and seasoned missionary. Dengal and Teresa clicked for a variety of reasons, not the least of which was that Dengal had herself struggled to obtain permission from the Holy See for her sisters to practice surgery and midwifery in the hospitals in which the sisters worked. Over the months Teresa poured out her heart to Dengal, telling the older sister of her plans and hopes. One day Teresa told Dengal that as far as possible the members of her future congregation would lead the lives of the poor whom they served. Teresa was firm in her conviction that the sisters of her order would not only live and dress as the poorest of the poor but also would eat only salt and rice, the humblest of Bengali diets. Dengal admonished Teresa: "If you want your sisters to get sick and die along with the poor, then give them only salt and rice to eat. Do you want your sisters to help the poor and the sick, or do you want them to die along with poor? Do you want your young sisters to perish, or do you want them to be healthy and strong so that they can labor effectively for Christ?" Teresa regarded this as one of the best bits of religious instruction she ever received. She realized that the key issue was not what the sisters ate but rather the relation of what they ate to the success of their apostolate to the poorest of the poor. The goals of the apostolate are primary, and all other things are secondary. So Teresa decided that all members of her future congregation would eat whatever they required to do an effective job in their apostolate. They would eat no more but no less than was necessary for them to work successfully.

From her years as a professional religious educator and geography teacher at St. Mary's, Teresa knew the instructional value of concrete symbols. Of themselves symbols can teach. And when combined with other instructional activities, symbols tend to increase the pedagogical potency of these activities. If she was to be optimally successful in her religious education work with the poorest of the poor, she would have to show these persons in symbol as well as in deed that she is existentially close to them. Thus in 1948, the year in which she began her new apostolate, she became a citizen of India. She stipulated that members of her future congregation should wear the same costume as the poorest of the poor—a cheap cotton sari costing in those days about a dollar, rough underwear, a rope cincture around the waist, and inexpensive but serviceable open sandals. The sari is decorated only with a crucifix pinned to the left shoulder, symbolizing the suffering that Jesus underwent for all human beings, and blue trim symbolizing the consecration of the congregation to Mary the Mother of God. No sister is allowed more than two saris, three white undergarments which cover her from the neck to the ankles, one bucket for washing, and a very thin mattress on which to sleep. A sister's entire collection of worldly goods can be rolled neatly in the mattress and tied tightly by a rope. There are no suitcases whatever. Their belongings are intentionally very meager so that the sisters can pack and be ready to move to another site within ten minutes. The sisters live in common dormitories without privacy, like the poor whom they serve. They eat the food of the people, using what is cheapest.

"Our rigorous poverty is our safeguard," Teresa liked to say. "We do not want to do what other religious congregations have done throughout history and begin serving the poor only to end up unconsciously serving the rich. In order to understand and help those who have nothing, we must live like them. The only difference is that these people are poor by birth, and we are poor by choice."

In addition to the regular three vows of poverty, chastity, and obedience, which are taken by members of every religious institute, the sisters in Teresa's congregation take a fourth vow: "to offer wholehearted free service to the poorest of the poor." This particular vow is unique to Teresa's group. Its observance by the sisters constitutes a binding promise to attempt to return in some small measure the limitless love of God by lovingly serving him in the least of humanity, ministering egolessly to those with whom Jesus most closely identifies—the poorest of the poor.

When she returned from Patna to Calcutta, Teresa did what she knew best: she taught. She began her new apostolate in a small hut in the fetid Motijhil slum very near her old convent in Entally. She assembled five local children and in the open air taught them to read, write, and keep themselves clean. When school was dismissed for the day, and also on weekends, she spent her time visiting the poorest of the poor wherever they might be, on the streets, in the gutters, in their wretched hovels. At first they distrusted her. They asked themselves: "Who is this woman? Why is she here? What is she doing? What is she up to? What does she really want?" But gradually they came to understand and became convinced. She was there because she loved them. Everything she did exuded her wholehearted unconditional love for them: caressing their sick babies, comforting them in their anguish, cleaning their filthy hovels, washing their clothes. It was obvious to all of the poorest of the poor that Teresa accepted them as they were, with all her heart, without any motive of personal gain or advantage.

It was not long before Teresa's heroic work began to attract followers. The first of these was Subhasini Das, a former student of Teresa's at St. Mary's School and the daughter of a wealthy Bengali family. By autumn 1950 the number of followers had grown to twelve. Most of them, like Subashini Das, had been Teresa's students at St. Mary's. The Vatican formally approved Teresa's request to establish a new diocesan congregation of sisters, since the group now had the required minimum of ten members. The name of the new congregation was Missionaries of Charity denoting that the prime purpose of group is to share God's joyous and bountiful love with the poorest of the poor. Sister Teresa now became Mother Teresa, the mother general of the congregation. Subashini Das took the name Sister Agnes as a loving tribute to Teresa's baptismal name.

The Vatican decree of recognition of the Missionaries of Charity read:

"To fulfil our mission of compassion and love
                    to the poorest of the poor we go:
    seeking out in towns and villages all over the world,
                    even amidst squalid surroundings,
        the poorest, the abandoned, the sick, the infirm, the lepers,
    the dying, the desperate, the lost, the outcasts
                            —taking care of them
                            —rendering help to them
                            —visiting them assiduously
                            —living Christ's love for them, and
        —awakening their response to his great love."

The hut in the Motijhil slum where Teresa began her apostolate to the poorest of the poor soon proved to be too small to accommodate the growing number of sickly, impoverished children who sought her help. She let it be known that she desperately needed to find a house to serve as a refuge for starving little children so that they could have a roof over their head, a decent meal, and a place to stretch out their legs if even for only a few moments. At the direct suggestion of his eight-year-old daughter, Michael Gomes, a prosperous Bengali Catholic resident of Calcutta who had earlier worked with Teresa in the Legion of Mary, offered Teresa the top floor of his spacious three-story home at 14 Creek Street for use in her religious education apostolate. The burgeoning Missionaries of Charity soon outgrew their quarters at 14 Creek Street. Through the help of a priest friend, a wealthy Muslim who had earlier been educated by the Jesuits, sold his large compound to the Missionaries of Charity for less than the price of the land on which the connected houses of the compound were built. To this day, 54a Lower Circular Road, now somewhat expanded, has remained the motherhouse and professional preparation center of the Missionaries of Charity.

In 1952 Teresa saw an elderly woman dying on the steps of a hospital. The woman was too weak even to brush away the insects that were biting her, the ants that were crawling all over her body, and the rats that were starting to gnaw at her feet. Teresa demanded—and received—from public officials a rundown building that she converted into the Home for the Dying Destitutes. She called it Nirmal Hriday because it was opened on the Feast of the Immaculate Heart of Mary. In English, Nirmal Hriday means Place of the Pure Heart.

Many babies in Calcutta were abandoned and left for die by parents too poor or too ill to feed them. Often these infants were placed in rubbish dumps or in the gutter by their impoverished and dejected parents. In 1955 Teresa opened Shishu Bhavan, a home for abandoned babies. Soon public officials began to send unwanted babies from all over Calcutta to Shishu Bhavan.

Leprosy, a devastating and highly infectious disease that eats away at a person's flesh, is one of the most feared of all illnesses throughout the world. The mere sight of a leper, especially in the advanced stages of this disease, is revulsive to most people. In the mid-1950s Calcutta had an estimated 50,000 lepers. Teresa found it very difficult to establish a home to take care of lepers because the neighbors would drive her away with sticks and stones, since they were frightened to have lepers live near them. In 1957 a Methodist minister offered Teresa some land at the outskirts of Calcutta for the purpose of establishing a leper village. There the Missionaries of Charity bathe the lepers, tend to their wounds, and give them spiritual comfort. Under the sign at the entrance to the leper village, now known as Titigarh, are the words: "Touch a leper with your compassion."

In 1964 Pope Paul VI visited India. He traveled around in a Lincoln Continental, then one of the expensive and most prestigious automobiles in the world. The Lincoln had been donated to the pope by the University of Notre Dame in Indiana. When Paul VI left India, he gave the car to Teresa at the Eucharistic Congress in Bombay in order that it should be placed at the disposal of what the pope described as her "universal mission of love." Teresa organized a raffle with the pope's automobile as the first prize. The raffle raised 460,000 rupees, five times what the car was worth. A non-Christian won the luxury automobile. Teresa gave all proceeds to the poor. With the money, she started a leper colony in West Bengal.

The following year the Missionaries of Charity was designated as a papal congregation under the direct protection and support of the Vatican. This meant that the Missionaries of Charity were canonically free to expand their apostolate outside of India. Teresa and her religious congregation had come a long way since that August day in 1948 when she stepped out of the carefully tended confines of St. Mary's School and into the stinking streets of a chaotic Calcutta slum.

By the end of the twentieth century about 5,000 sari-clad Missionaries of Charity were working in over 130 countries of the world, from Italy to Tanzania, from Venezuela to Australia, from Northern Ireland to Yemen, from Lebanon to Ethiopia, from the United States to Peru, from England to Haiti, from Germany to Kenya, from Belgium to Brazil—everywhere spreading love and hope and joy and teaching and healing. Teresa's absolute devotion to the poorest of the poor was recognized even by leaders of Communist countries who were militant and uncompromising atheists. In both the Soviet Union and Fidel Castro's Cuba, for example, she was granted official permission to open up houses for the poorest of the poor.

On the walls of every convent chapel of the Missionaries of Charity all over the world are written in the local language and in large letters the words of Jesus: "I thirst." This is an intentional religious instruction reminder of the central mission of each of the sisters and of how these women do in fact become deeply united to Christ in their work with the poorest of the poor.

In an era when most religious congregations of Catholic women were experiencing a sharp drop in vocations and were struggling to survive, Teresa's Missionaries of Charity were attracting a great many novices from throughout the world. This fact strongly suggests that quite a few potential sisters are more interested in a vocation centered around totally sacrificial red-hot religion than in a vocation that is oriented to a softer and less demanding form of service.

The religious education apostolate of Teresa and her sisters is not to make converts to Catholicism in return for shelter and help. The religious education mission of Teresa and her Missionaries of Charity is, as Teresa herself remarks, "to help a Hindu become a better Hindu, a Muslim a better Muslim, a Catholic a better Catholic," and so forth. Thus the Missionaries of Charity minister equally to persons of all religious traditions. The sisters never ever ask the religious affiliation of a beggar picked up from the streets, of a leper rejected by his family, of a dying woman refused admission to a hospital. Everyone who can be treated is fed, washed, and given a clean place to rest. Those who are beyond treatment are afforded the opportunity to die with dignity and according to the rituals of their faith; for Hindus, water from the Ganges on their lips; for Muslims, readings from the Koran; for Protestants, passages from the Bible; for the occasional Catholic, the last rites of the Church. For Teresa and her companions, every death should be a beautiful death, a beautiful experience.

Throughout her career, Teresa never asked for money. She always lived by the conviction that if she and the other Missionaries of Charity did God's will egolessly by serving the poorest of the poor, then God would somehow provide for the apostolate's physical and fiscal needs. When persons would ask how they could help the Missionaries of Charity, she never suggested a monetary donation; instead she asked them to do "something beautiful for God."

Over the years a torrent of major national and international prizes cascaded on Teresa. A mention of just a few of these will provide a glimpse into the inestimable esteem in which she was held throughout the world. She was the first recipient of the Templeton Prize for Progress in Religion. She was also the first recipient of the Albert Schweitzer International Prize in recognition of her "reverence for life." She also was the first recipient of the John XXIII Peace Prize. In Italy she received the Ambrogino d'Oro Award, and some years later the Balzan International Prize. In India, she received the highest award the government can bestow, the Bhjarat Ratrna (Jewel of India). From that country she also received the Jawaharlal Nehru Award for International Understanding, and some years later the Rajiv Gandhi Award. When she reached her seventieth birthday, her face appeared on Indian postage stamps, an unheard-of honor not only for a Roman Catholic sister but for a person born outside of India. In the United States, she received the Congressional Gold Medal in recognition for her humanitarian service around the world. At the presentation of this award the House of Representatives observed a rare moment of silence in her honor. When, at the White House, Ronald Reagan gave her the nation's highest civilian award, the Medal of Freedom, he joked that she might be the first recipient to take the medal and melt it down to donate money for the poor. In 1996 she was made an honorary citizen of the United States. Teresa made it a point to accept each and every prize in the name of the poorest of the poor. All prize money was immediately given to feed the hungry, heal the sick, and spread love and hope and joy to all who need it.

The most famous honor she received was the Nobel Prize for Peace in 1979 because "poverty and distress also constitute a threat to world peace." (Teresa of Calcutta had long said that "works of love are works of peace.") As is customary, the presentation of this award was made in the Aula Magna (Great Hall) of the University of Oslo. In the presence of King Olaf of Norway and many other

famous world dignitaries all decked out in their finest and most elegant formal attire was a small stooped lady dressed in the now familiar cheap white cotton sari with a blue border and a crucifix
pinned on her left shoulder. Just before commencing her acceptance speech prepared only with the sign of cross, she called upon
the audience to recite with her the Prayer of St. Francis of Assisi, *il
Poverello*. In the name of peace and in the desire for peace all those
present—Catholics, Eastern Orthodox, Anglicans, Lutherans,
Methodists, Baptists, members of all manner of Christian and non-
Christian faith groups, agnostics, atheists, and persons who had
long since forgotten how to pray or had never wanted to pray—
joined with her in those beautiful words: "Lord, make me
an instrument of your peace. Where there is hatred, let me sow
love . . . "

Teresa concluded her extemporaneous address by remarking: "If
we could only remember that God loves us, and we have an opportunity to love others as he loves us, not in big things, but in small
things with great love, then Norway becomes a nest of love."

Her rapt audience had never before experienced anything like
her.

At the informal reception which at her request replaced the ceremonial banquet customarily given in honor of the recipient of the
Nobel Peace Prize, Teresa stood to greet everyone. As was her custom at events such as this, she took as her only refreshment a glass
of water. Someone asked Teresa to see her Nobel medal. Teresa
could not remember what she had done with it. A few of her friends
scoured the hall in search of it. Finally the medal was found among
the coats deposited on a shelf at the entrance to the hall. Worldly
honors meant little to her. All-giving personal sacrifice for the
poorest of the poor was the all-consuming center and axis of her
interests.

From Oslo Teresa wrote her Co-Workers (laypersons from all
walks of life who work for periods of time with the Missionaries of
Charity) a beautiful letter in which she observed: "Today the poor
are hungry for bread and rice—and for love and the living word of
God." She was, as always, a religious educator first and foremost.

Teresa of Calcutta was easily the most famous and surely the most beloved woman of the last third of the twentieth century. She was so highly esteemed, in fact, that when she appeared on the same public platform as a pope or a prime minister or a president, it was the pope or prime minister or president who stood in her shadow. Some astute observers have noted that the knees of eminent world dignitaries seemed to buckle when they were in the presence of Teresa of Calcutta.

She disliked celebrity and regarded it as a great burden. But she accepted international acclaim as the necessary price she had to pay in order to expand her missionary work to the poorest of the poor.

Even saints or persons clearly on the way to sainthood have their adversaries. So it was with Teresa of Calcutta. Chief among Teresa's foes were some Latin American Catholic liberation theologians and their followers, some North American Christian social activists, and quite a few core feminists. These Latin American Catholic liberation theologians, coming as they did from a fundamentally neo-Marxist perspective, lashed out at Teresa for not attacking organized exploitation, class warfare, and injustice. Teresa never responded directly to their criticisms, but she often remarked that her own particular call within a call was to feed and comfort the poorest of the poor. In her view, other persons, especially the Christian laity, might have received a call from God to ameliorate unjust social structures.

North American social activists from various Christian faith groups also bitterly attacked Mother Teresa and her work. Thus, for example Jack Jennings, a Presbyterian (PCUSA) campus minister, roundly castigated Teresa's lack of interest in changing the systemic social system that he claimed give direct rise to the human tragedies with which she dealt. He sharply faulted Teresa for having what he termed "no element of prophetic criticism in her work." Two Catholic nuns also sharply attacked Teresa. Camille D'Arienzo, a member of the Sisters of Mercy, and Mary Loyola Engel, a former superior general of the Congregation of the Infant Jesus, verbally flogged Teresa accusing her of personifying what they believed was a hopelessly outmoded pre-Second Vatican

Council view of faith that did not frontally address systemic social evils. D'Arienzo further opined that Teresa was being used as a role model for what D'Arienzo believed to be outmoded docility to ecclesiastical authorities. Some other American sisters, albeit less vocally, criticized Teresa as implicitly rejecting the lifestyle and self-image of the highly activist "new nun" eager to reform society systemically, openly, and on all fronts. While never addressing these critiques directly, Teresa sometimes observed that before persons can go out and change social structures they have to be fed and taken out of total destitution. Dying people, the poorest of the poor, have to be taken care of right here and right now. She believed that given her call within a call, the most prophetic thing she could do was to minister egolessly to the poorest of the poor.

Some of the most blistering and unabashedly vitriolic attacks on Teresa of Calcutta came from feminists. They bitterly lashed out at Teresa for condemning abortion. They berated her for failing to center her attention on what they contended were male-dominated oppressive forces in society. Some feminists unequivocally rejected her support of traditional marriage because in their view traditional marriage is intrinsically oppressive to women. One of Teresa's most implacable feminist foes was convent-educated Germaine Greer, who wrote that "Mother Teresa is a religious imperialist . . . She is not ministering to the poor of Calcutta for their sake, but for the sake of her Catholic God." Greer contended that because of her religiously imperialistic mentality, Teresa "ultimately does more evil than good." Greer was particularly incensed by an incident that happened when she was being flown first class to collect an award from the Kennedy Foundation for services to humanity. Teresa was also being flown first class on that very flight to receive the same award. Greer was furious that Teresa did not even sip a drop of champagne or eat even the tiniest bit of caviar, or in fact consume any of the fine food served, but instead sat, with her head bowed (probably in prayer) and her body motionless in her seat. Especially galling to Greer was that the flight attendants knelt to speak reverentially to this tiny nun all the while virtually ignoring Greer and the other first-class passengers.

For her part, Teresa was too busy helping the dying, the lepers, and the acutely suffering to pay attention to the blistering critiques sometimes directed at her and her apostolate. But she often would say that her call within a call dictated not that she lead a revolution against systemic societal injustices but that she lead "a revolution of love" by reaching out, like Jesus, to one tormented body at a time. As to abortion, Teresa was, as always, uncompromising in her total advocacy of love and in her reverence for life in all its forms. "Any country that accepts abortion is not teaching people to love, but to use violence to get what they want," she told the U.S. Congress.

When Teresa grew to advanced age, she pushed herself just as hard on behalf of the poorest of the poor as she did when she was younger. She was no typical religious administrator, shutting herself in her office. She was in the gutters with the poor every day, except when she had to travel to other countries to briefly inaugurate or visit some Missionaries of Charity home. Even on her trips, she made it a point to go out to the slums in whatever place she was visiting to personally render assistance to the poorest of the poor there.

Sooner or later Teresa's tireless work was bound to exact its toll on her health. In 1983, when she was seventy-three years old, she had her first heart attack while visiting John Paul II in Rome. In 1988 suffered another heart attack, and the following year had yet another heart attack which almost proved fatal. At that point she was outfitted with a pacemaker. In April 1990 at the insistence of her physicians she announced her intention to resign as superior general of the Missionaries of Charity for reasons of failing health. A representative group of sisters was chosen to elect her successor. On September 8, 1990, Teresa was reelected with only one dissenting vote—her own. As a result, she withdrew her resignation request. The following year she suffered pneumonia in Tijuana, Mexico, which led to congestive heart failure. She was then placed in a hospital in nearby La Jolla, California. In May 1994 she was bitten by a rabid dog as she lovingly stooped to pet it in the slums just outside the motherhouse in Calcutta. In May of 1995 she broke three ribs in a fall. Three months later she was hospitalized for

malaria in New Delhi. In September she underwent surgery in Calcutta to remove a clogged blood vessel. In April 1996 she fell and
broke a collarbone. In August of that year she was again in a
Calcutta hospital, this time from malarial fever and failure of the
left heart ventricle. All of this led to a lung infection and intensified
heart problems. On November 22 she was readmitted to the hospital with chest pains and breathing difficulties.

Each time she was hospitalized she chafed to leave before she
should have in order to get back to personally helping the poorest
of the poor in the slums. When her physicians and hospital staff repeatedly told her that she had to cut down her work, her reply was
always the same: "There is so much work to be done."

Rapidly advancing age plus persistent ill health brought on by
unremitting overwork suggested that it would not be long until
Teresa would pass from this world. She once was asked if she
feared death. "No," she replied, "I see it all the time."

On Friday, September 5, 1997, death finally came to the Saint of
the Gutters. She died in her convent in Calcutta, right in the middle
of the slums. The cause of death was cardiac arrest. She was
eighty-seven years old.

Shortly after she expired, the Missionaries of Charity tolled a
huge metal bell mournfully. Word of Teresa's death spread rapidly
through the slums. Soon about 4,000 persons gathered in the warm
monsoon rain. Inside the motherhouse her body was dressed and
laid on a bed of ice. One by one the nuns filed passed the coffin,
touching her bare feet in the traditional Indian gesture of respect.

Knowing that many other people would want to view the body,
the Missionaries of Charity placed Teresa's body in the motherhouse chapel and allowed visitors to file in to pay their last respects. Her tiny body was surrounded with flowers and quietly
praying nuns.

Soon it became obvious that the chapel was far too small to hold
the many mourners who wanted to say a final good-bye to Teresa.
So the Indian government decided to hold the wake and the funeral
ceremonies in a large local sports arena, Calcutta's Netaji Indoor
Stadium. In a move unprecedented for a non-Hindu, the Indian
government also gave her an official state funeral.

In the stadium her body was laid out in an open casket, bare feet toward the altar. Her corpse, outfitted in the simple habit worn by the Missionaries of Charity, was elevated on a catafalque for everyone to see. Wreaths and bouquets of white roses, all gifts from admirers of one sort or another, were scattered around the floor of the stadium. Directly in front of her body were steps leading to a hastily improvised high altar. A huge banner covering the entire front of the altar proclaimed in very large letters one of Teresa's favorite sayings: Works of love are works of peace. Behind the altar was an enormous crucifix, signifying that the mainspring of Teresa's entire life, the mainspring of all Christianity, is total all-giving sacrifice done with and for love.

The music during the funeral Mass was deliberately chosen to avoid Gregorian Chant or Beethoven or any other Western form of music. Rather, a choir from the Missionaries of Charity sang in Hindi and Bengali, accompanied by native Indian instruments. The eulogy the funeral Mass was delivered by Angelo Sodano, a cardinal and the Vatican's secretary of state whom Rome sent to Calcutta expressly for that purpose. Far more eloquent than Sodano's eulogy or the mitered presence of the ten archbishops was an event that occurred at the Offertory procession. The gifts to the altar were brought by the lame and the halt—including, among others, an orphaned girl who had been found in the streets, a person suffering from leprosy, and a physically handicapped boy. This is exactly what Teresa would have liked. After the Mass was concluded, official representatives of India's other non-Christian religions—Hindu, Muslim, Sikh, Buddhist, and Parsi—stepped forward to offer blessings from their own traditions. These acts were completely in accord with Teresa's open stance toward religious pluralism. Following these multifaith blessings, dignitaries from countries around the world came to Teresa's coffin to offer condolences on behalf of their countries—persons such as Sonia Gandhi, the widow of India's former prime minister, the queen of Jordan, the queen of Spain, the queen of Belgium, the president of Italy, the president of Ghana, to mention just a few. Hillary Rodham Clinton, wife of the American president, paid her last respects on behalf of the people of the United States.

In an extraordinary show of respect for Teresa, the Indian government arranged to have her body transported from the Netaji Indoor Stadium back to the motherhouse, where she was to be buried in the same ceremonial carriage that in 1948 carried the dead body of Mohandas Gandhi and in 1964 bore the corpse of the nation's first prime minister, Jawaharlal Nehru. Hundreds of thousands of persons watched as Teresa's funeral cortege slowly wended it way through the streets. People showered flower petals from the rooftops onto her coffin. At one point the surging crowd broke through the bamboo barricades to touch Teresa's hands, which enfolded a rosary. Soldiers quickly moved in to form a human barrier around her dead body. Many other persons present at the funeral procession bowed with folded hands as her coffin passed by, quietly murmuring the age-old Hindu prayer of farewell: "*Shanti, Shanti*" ("Peace, Peace"—in this case, "Goodbye, Mother, go in peace").

She was buried in a simple ceremony in the motherhouse. Her final resting place is a long, narrow room that once served as the convent's dining room. The room faces the street. The tomb itself is a rectangular cement box about three feet high with a Bible verse etched on a white marble marker: "Love one another as I have loved you." She lived much of her life in the squalid slums, died amidst the slums, and now lies in her grave in a room in the slums facing the street teeming with the poorest of the poor.

The death and funeral of Teresa of Calcutta made front page news in newspapers all over the globe. The world went into mourning at her passing. Religious and political leaders from many countries rushed to express their condolences. John Paul II said that the loss affected him very deeply. Billy Graham, then the preeminent figure in American Protestantism, fondly recalled a time he had spent with Teresa years before in Calcutta: "When she walked into the room to greet me," Graham said, "I felt that I was, indeed, meeting a saint." Coretta Scott King, widow and partner of assassinated American civil rights leader said: "Our world has lost the most celebrated saint of our times." Bill Clinton, the American president at the time, remembered her as "an incredible person". The U.S. House of Representatives observed a moment of silence in her honor. In India, the loss was especially palpable. Outside Calcutta's holiest Hindu temple, where every morning blood sacrifices are made to a stone and gold statue of Kali, devotees paused before a life-sized figure of Teresa to pray and make obeisance. "We think of Mother not as a Christian but simply as the Mother," said Samir Banerjee, a Brahmin priest from the temple. "She was just the mother of us all." (To the world, she was called Mother Teresa; to the people in India, she was called simply "the Mother.")

Undeniably, Teresa of Calcutta was the globe's most unassailable religious personage.

Many inspiring stories about Mother Teresa have been widely circulated. One of my favorites is about an important conference on hunger and homelessness that was held in a major city. Some of the world's greatest political, economic, and social experts were invited to participate. Teresa of Calcutta was also asked to come.

Speaker after learned speaker gave eloquent analyses of the problems of hunger and homelessness, and often offered their own penetrating insights on how to alleviate these two great scourges of humanity.

At the conclusion of the conference a magnificent banquet was held to celebrate the great success of the conference. At the banquet the attendees one by one stood up and publicly shared their appreciative testimonies about how much they had learned about hunger and homelessness as a result of what they had heard at the conference.

Toward the end of the banquet, the attendees looked around for Teresa of Calcutta to find out her opinion of the conference. They searched and searched for her. No one could find her among the banquet guests.

It was only later that the attendees learned that while they were feasting on a superb gourmet dinner in splendid surroundings and enjoying the warm fellowship with one another, Teresa was in the streets of the city ministering to the hungry and homeless.

We religious educators like to say that our call within a call is central to our lives. To what extent do we just talk the call as opposed to living it fully and purely in everyday action?

To what degree do we religious educators simply talk about our religious instruction ministry as over against actually doing all the hard nitty-gritty work necessary to ensure the success of this apostolate?

A sacrament performs. A sacrament does. This is why a sacrament is efficacious. What specifically can we religious educators do in our everyday apostolate to make our teaching action oriented?

To what extent is our religious instruction ministry more talk than work?

How often do we spend time in attempting to impress others, especially those in authority, about how successful we are in the religious instruction apostolate when we could be spending this time working in the vineyard?

How many times do we propose grand ideas about religious instruction and then give to others the implementation of the difficult and unglamorous aspects of these grand ideas?

To what extent do we religious educators palm off the actual daily nitty-gritty work to others so as to avoid doing it ourselves— ostensibly in the name of delegation or shared authority?

Religious instruction is an action field suffused with theory and supported by empirical research. To what degree do we religious educators simply talk about our religious instruction ministry as contrasted to actually doing all the hard work of consciously grounding our apostolate in adequate theory and proven empirical research data? To what degree do we engage in mindless action? Conversely, to what degree do we religious educators engage in idle speculation or building castles in the air so as to avoid the hard work of concrete action?

To what extent are we religious educators overly preoccupied with planning to the detriment of actually working in the concrete aspects of the apostolate? Planning is absolutely essential to successful religious instruction ministry, but some religious educators spend more time than is necessary in planning so that they can thereby avoid doing the concrete, less glamorous, nitty-gritty tasks of implementing the plans.

How many times do we religious educators take time out to engage in idle chatter with our colleagues, friends, or acquaintances when we could be spending this time working with those who need us?

How frequently do we religious educators spend time with others congratulating ourselves on this or that religious instruction accomplishment when we could be devoting this time to the unending everyday requirements of the apostolate?

Does not the total dedication of Teresa of Calcutta to her apostolate shame each and every one of us religious educators? What are we religious educators going to do to lessen this shame? Right here. Right now. In the concrete.

Performance Objective: Whenever I come up with an important new idea on how to improve one or another aspect of my religious instruction activity, I will make sure that I do not just talk about it to my colleagues. Instead, I will develop a specific plan on how to actually transform my idea into concrete action. After I have put my plan into concrete action, I will give periodic attention to this activity until such a time as it has regularly produced the desired religious instruction results.

20

Sacrifice

I write my books and articles in what I call the *auctorium*, a small book-lined teakwood room in my house which I designed especially for engaging in scholarly writing. My computer sits on a desk right in front of a large three-paneled window that faces out on a pastoral landscape of trees in the foreground and rolling hills in the distance. On top of this window, between its outer frame and the ceiling, there hangs a lovely carved image of the head of the suffering Jesus. I purchased this moving olivewood carving near the Church of the Holy Sepulcher in Jerusalem when I lived there in the Old City for two weeks on a personal/professional pilgrimage in the mid 1990's. When I am wrestling hard in the *auctorium* with a particular concept or agonizing about the precise choice of words, my gaze sometimes floats up above the computer monitor to the pastoral view from the window and finally rests on the olivewood carving of the suffering Jesus. Meditating ever so briefly on that image, I appreciate once again that one of the most important attributes of Jesus was his never-ending sacrifice as he went about doing his twin tasks of redemption and religious education. Jesus sacrificed himself throughout his life so that persons could be redeemed and be well educated religiously. Effective and exact scholarly writing is very hard and demands from me and from others who do it a high measure of sacrifice. Throwing myself affectively into that olivewood carving of the suffering Jesus, I offer to Jesus the sacrifice entailed in my writing at that moment and at all other moments, in the realization that sacrifice is one of the most important and essential things I can do as a religious educationist in service of the Lord.

Sacrifice is a central and vivifying element in virtually every religion, including Christianity. Therefore, sacrifice should be a central and pervasive force in our work as religious educators. More than most other factors, it is sacrifice that sacraments our religious instruction work.

The English word "sacrifice" comes directly from the Latin *sacrificium*. This Latin word, in turn, is a derivative combination of two Latin root words. The first of these root words is the adjective *sacer* (masculine), *sacra* (feminine), *sacrum* (neuter). This Latin word means holy, sacred, consecrated, sanctified, hallowed. The second of the two Latin root words is *ficium*, the unstressed form of the verb *facere*, "to make, to do."

Thus we see through the eyes of etymology that there are two inextricably related core meanings of sacrifice. The first of these basic meanings is that of making an act or a thing holy, making it sacred, consecrating it, sanctifying it, hallowing it. The second core meaning of sacrifice is that of doing a holy act.

In its original and still fundamental meaning, sacrifice is essentially a holy act, an act which sanctifies that which is done. So inherently sacred is the act of sacrifice that even when an unbeliever makes a sacrifice, this act becomes a holy deed by virtue of the fact that it is a sacrifice.

Sacrifice of itself transforms and elevates a commonplace deed into a holy act, a sacred thing. Sacrifice is not just a door to the realm of the holy. More than this, the holy inhabits sacrifice.

Sacrifice is basically religious because it places an act or a thing into the realm of the holy. Sacrifice essentially consists of a gift that a person advertently or inadvertently offers to God, the source and being of the realm of the holy.

Virtually all religions yesterday and today recognize that allegiance and service to God consist not only in uttering words but far more importantly in giving to God something that is precious. In making a sacrifice, individuals deny themselves something of personal value as a way of achieving a greater good. For religious persons, sacrifice is a royal road to pleasing God, to venerating God, to accomplishing God's will. The degree of a person's sincerity, commitment, and religiosity is typically measured by the degree of self-denial which that individual makes for God. True sacrifice always involves surrender and renunciation.

Sacrifice brings redemption. Sacrifice is redemption. This redemptive core of sacrifice helps explain why most religions throughout history have attached such great importance to sacrifice. Religions that have stood the test of time have always emphasized that their members should live a life of sacrifice in order to be pleasing to God. And most religions in widely diverse eras and climes have made ritual sacrifice the energizing center of their worship service. Indeed, the worship rites and rituals of most religions are fundamentally a shape and solemnization of sacrifice. In ancient religions this ritual/worship sacrifice took the form of a sacrificial animal and in some cases a human sacrifice—objects of significant value to the members of that religion. In Christianity this ritual/worship sacrifice takes the form of the supreme sacrifice of Jesus himself, the sole sacrificial victim worthy of God, the sacrificial victim whose sacrifice unto death on Calvary is existentially renewed in the lives of all persons making their own individual sacrifices as well as in an extraordinarily unique incarnational manner during Eucharistic worship services throughout the world.

Sacrifice involves immolation of self to a greater or lesser extent. When persons make a sacrifice, they die to their own egos and egoistic desires. A great sacrifice means a great degree of death to ego, while a smaller sacrifice means lesser death to ego. It is this immolation of ego in the act of sacrifice that significantly contributes to the reality of sacrifice as a holy act. Just as the entire life of Jesus, most notably his passion, was a sacrificial immolation, so also persons who make sacrifices put the immolation of their own egos into a chalice held lovingly in their hands raised high in adoration and service to God.

Expiation is actualized in sacrifice. One major explanation for the success that typically flows from sacrifice is its expiational character. Because it is expiational, sacrifice sanctifies the one making the sacrifice and hallows the object of personal value which is being sacrificed. Hence sacrifice makes it possible for

God's grace to flow in special abundance both to the one making the sacrifice and to the sacrificial deed. Put in human performance terms, the act of sacrifice tends to help the person making the sacrifice to be more effective in that activity in which the sacrifice is being made. Furthermore, the act of sacrifice tends to directly enhance the success of the sacrificial deed.

Why did we become a religious educator? What causes us to remain a religious educator? Did we choose to become a religious educator because we thought it would be fun or at least enjoyable? Did we become a religious educator to feel good, to feel a sense of accomplishment for the church? Did we become a religious educator because we thought it would be a beneficial change of scene from another kind of job? Did we become a religious educator out of a sense of duty to God? Did we become a religious educator to significantly influence the lives of learners?

If we became a religious educator for any of these or kindred reasons but at the same time lacked a concomitantly strong sense of sacrifice, then we either did not receive from God the call within a call to be a religious educator or we responded very tepidly to this call. The call within a call means that the authentic religious educator is one whose entire life is one long continuous sacrifice to help learners in every way possible to know, love, and serve God. A religious educator is one who is called to be a sacrificial victim so that others might learn. The rest is wrapping paper.

To what extent is our life as a religious educator one unending sacrifice on behalf of facilitating learning?

We religious educators say we love God and want to do his will in the religious instruction arena. But these are empty words, a breath upon the fleeting wind if we fail to embrace the many large and small sacrifices that are part and parcel of the religious instruction apostolate.

If we think we have sacrificed enough as religious educators in following our call within a call, then we can be absolutely certain that we have not sacrificed enough.

There are many kinds of sacrifices that we religious educators are called on to make on behalf of facilitating learning. Time is one kind of sacrifice. Being away from our families and friends is another form of sacrifice. Rigorous attention to the unglamorous dimensions of the teaching process is another type of sacrifice. Maintaining a high energy level even when we are tired and weary is yet another variety of sacrifice. Working with clergy, colleagues, and parishioners who do not adequately appreciate our efforts is another form of sacrifice. Giving up a better-paying job to enter the religious instruction apostolate represents another type of sacrifice.

Though sacrifices come in many shapes and various forms, there is one thing common to them all, namely, suffering, surrendering something precious, dying to ego. It is these sacrificial rigors and hardships that redeem our instructional efforts and transform the everyday activities of teaching into a holy act. Sacrifice brings with it redemption, elevating even the most menial aspects of our religious instruction activities into the sphere of the holy.

The altar of our sacred sacrifice, the table of our ego immolation, the locus where our sacrament of teaching is confected, is the environment in which we teach, whether this environment be a formal or an informal one. The sacrificial act is the preparation, enaction, and evaluation of the religious instruction event. It is on the altar of our sacred sacrifice in giving everything we have to successfully facilitate the acquisition of desired learning outcomes that our religious instruction apostolate is sacramented. It is on this sacrificial altar that the sacrament of our teaching is consecrated and confected.

Our unending sacrifice is played out in all those things that are involved in getting everything just right in order that optimal learning outcomes will result from our instructional activities. It is a sacrifice for us to carefully plan our lessons, even those that are loosely structured due to their being deployed in an informal setting such as a home or playground or in an on-the-spot situation on the street. It is a sacrifice for us to skillfully formulate performance objectives. It is a sacrifice for us to accord detailed attention to our initial structuring of the learning situation and then to restructure it frequently as the instructional event unfolds. It is a sacrifice for us to select the right teaching method or technique from the whole repertoire of instructional methods and techniques available to us. It is a sacrifice for us to pay unremitting attention to the antecedent-consequent behavioral chaining that occurs in rapid-fire sequence throughout the instructional episode. It is a sacrifice for us to painstakingly devise and implement valid evaluation measures to validly assess the degree to which the learners have acquired the desired outcomes.

What is the result of these and the countless other sacrifices that we religious educators make in the course of a day or a week? At one level the result is that the learners will acquire the desired outcomes. At another level, the result of our unending series of sacrifices is that these learning outcomes will be placed into the realm of holiness because our own sacrifices have suffused the teaching act with the sanctity of sacrifice, with the perfume of immolation.

Looking over my own past life, I can truly affirm that whatever minute degree of personal holiness I might possibly possess is very much the result of those dedicated competent religious educators (including most especially my parents) from whom I have learned so very many things. The innumerable sacrifices that these religious educators made on behalf of the teaching act hallowed their instructional activities and hallowed me. I think that all religious educators, when reflecting on their own lives, can make a similar claim.

As to the future, we should know that the innumerable sacrifices which we religious educators will have to undergo will be as hard as they will be unending. But we should be comforted in the realization that we are made holy through the many sacrifices that we willingly endure as religious educators so that others can learn from our instructional activities.

Performance Objective: Every single time that I enter into a religious instruction event, whether with an individual or with a group, whether in a formal or an informal environment, I will ask God to bestow on me the grace to make every sacrifice, no matter how great or how difficult, in order to render each aspect of my religious instruction activity as successful as possible.

21

Renunciation

The good God is so infinitely great that no culture, no philosophical or theological system, no religious worldview, and no educational style can contain him.

Our call within a call to be a religious educator requires that each of us intentionally provide learners with opportunities to personally encounter God in the infinitely wide variety of concretizations in which the Lord reveals himself. If we religious educators are to be faithful to our special call, we first must wholly open up our own perspectives and experiences so as to be able to encounter the inexhaustibly rich and varied revelation of God that is embedded in the fabric of other cultures, philosophies, theologies, religions, and educational styles. In short, to be provincial in any way is to betray or at least corrode our call within a call to be that kind of religious educator who deliberatively leads learners to personally meet and greet the boundless expanse of the infinite Godhead.

God shines through all reality. The more authentically and existentially we touch reality, the more deeply we touch an image of the face of God. Among the myriad veils of Veronica upon which God has imprinted his face in our world is Zen Buddhism. With increasing frequency, devout and knowledgeable Christians are exploring the basic connections between Zen and the Christian faith. This is especially true for those Christians seeking a deep spiritual life, and consequently for those religious educators striving to teach others to encounter God as profoundly as possible. (Thomas Merton, the great Christian spiritual master, ingested many principles of Zen into his own life and work. In the early 1990s Robert E.

Kennedy, a Jesuit priest in good ecclesiastical standing, was officially recognized by the New York Zen community as a Zen teacher and was given the authority to teach Zen. At a special investiture ceremony, Kennedy received the black robe, staff, and other insignia of the Zen teacher's office.)

Though it has its roots in Mahayana Buddhism, which originated and developed in China, Zen is not a religion. It is not even primarily a philosophy. First and fundamentally, Zen is a highly disciplined, systematic, and focused instructional method. For its adherents, Zen is The Way, the path to enlightenment (*satori*). Zen is not equivalent to the goal of enlightenment; rather, Zen is the particular instructional method through which one arrives at enlightenment. Zen is not a revelation; it is an instructional procedure. In using Zen, therefore, religious educators are in no way adopting a new religion. Instead, religious educators are adopting another method to teach learners how to encounter God. Like all successful instructional methods, Zen is embedded in a theory of reality and a theory of teaching. Zen theory differs significantly from the Western rationalistic and dualistic matrix in which Christianity is typically situated. Zen theory does not differ from the vast preponderance of Christianity in itself as independent of any particular culture.

The object of Zen is the acquisition of a wholly new perspective on reality, a wholly new perspective on dealing with others, and a wholly new perspective on living with self. *Satori* is nothing more than this radically new perspective. Thus the use of Zen offers us religious educators an empirically proven way of providing both ourselves and our learners with a fundamentally new way of seeing and doing the spiritual life, a way that offers countless instructional riches for those who are genuinely open to growth.

Most persons and most cultures, especially in the Western world, view reality from a mixture of two fundamental perspectives, namely, dualism and rationalism. In this view, all reality is ultimately composed of radical dualities and completely separate differences, as for example existence and nonexistence, positive and negative, truth and nontruth—all instances of dualism. In this Western perspective, moreover, the way to truth is through rational, abstract, conceptual modes of thought.

In stark contrast, Zen stands against all dualism. It affirms the essential unity and oneness of all reality. For example, existence and nonexistence are two inextricably connected dimensions of the whole reality that joins these apparent contradictions in dynamic and mutually advancing oneness. Just as painters regard negative space as an essential element in a work of art, so do Zenists regard negativity as an essential dimension of the whole rather than an absence of some element in the whole.

Zen rejects rationalism and its dualistic abstract logic as a legitimate way to truth. For Zen, personal inner experience is the only way to attain truth, awareness, and *satori*. Thus Zen essentially is an instructional method that systematically enables a person to come into direct touch with the basic workings of self without resorting to any external authority or conceptual framework. The direct consequences of this view for Christian religious instruction are both powerful and far-reaching.

All effective instruction begins in, works through, and ends with the self—the self that needs to grow, the self that actively cooperates with the teacher throughout the instructional process, and the self that eventually achieves the terminal instructional objective. So it is with Zen. The journey to the true self lies at the center of Zen instructional method. Christian religious educators should note that the Zenist view of the self is that of essential oneness (nondualism), a perspective that sharply differs from the prevalent Western dualistic concept of the self.

For Zen, self is not the same as the ego, the I. Because it is basically individualistic, the ego destroys the self since it endeavors to separate the self from other areas of reality. This unnatural separation produces a chasm between the self and the nonself. All actions of the ego, of the I-process, are necessarily soaked with avidity, possession, and domination, all of which engender conflict, misery, and various forms of slavery. Because it is primary consciousness, the self is true reality whereas the ego is a twisted derivative from consciousness. In point of fact, say the Zenists, the ego, the I-process, the me, are all essentially an illusion because they fragment the essential oneness of reality into separate and often warring zones of the external and the internal. The ego is an arbitrary invention of the mind. The distinction between the ego and the nonego (the rest of the world), like all dualistic distinctions, is intelligible and meaningful only within the mind of the self. This distinction is not a function of reality itself and thus is unreal, is an illusion. A passage from the Mahayana school of Buddhism underscores this point: "The mind is the great Slayer of the Real. Let the Disciple slay the Slayer . . . Give up thy life [ego] if thou wouldst live . . . Thou canst not travel on the Path before thou has become that Path itself."

A cardinal purpose of Zen as an instructional method is to extinguish the ego so that the self can be freed to attain that genuine selfhood necessary for enlightenment. When self extinguishes the ego, it arrives at emptiness (śūnyatā). Emptiness is not nothingness. Emptiness is not absence of reality. Rather, emptiness is pure consciousness, a consciousness emptied of all dualities, a consciousness that transcends all forms of mutual relationship of subject and object, of birth and death, of God and world, of something and nothing. Emptiness does not mean vacancy; it means authentic self-actualization. Śūnyatā does not leave the self vacuous but rather enables it to be filled with direct experience. Before śūnyatā, one does not experience the world directly. What one experiences is one's ideas, one's mental conceptualizations of the world, something akin to the famous example of the cave that Plato gives in the *Republic*. In the process of attaining emptiness, one polishes the mirror of self so that one no longer views the world through the dirty layer of one's ego and its rationalities but instead learns how to merge self directly with experience so that one becomes one's experience. In Zen, voidness is not the emptiness of self but the emptiness of ego with all its false and distorting dualisms. As an ancient Zen master is reputed to have said, "No distinguishment arises—only the void-illumination reflects all manifestations within oneself."

The essence of Zen is the practice of those instructional activities intentionally designed to help the self gain a wholly new perspective on life by breaking down dualism and by obliterating rationalism in all its forms so that the person will attain enlightenment and self-sufficiency. The word "Zen" is the Japanese translation of a Sanskrit word meaning meditation. Specifically, Zen is a form of Buddhism whose axis is a well-developed set of instructional techniques for meditation. A central thread of Zen meditation is that of helping the person approach the world from the basic standpoint of intuition (immediate apprehension of reality) rather than from the standpoint of rationality (secondary, logical conceptualization about reality). Zen is nonrational, not irrational. It is nonlogical, not illogical. Zen meditation is expressly designed to liberate the person from the shackles of rationality and promote fresh flashes of intuition in all their rich experiential insights. Zen meditation exercises are structured in such a way that the person is completely involved in life rather than absorbed in rational ideas and abstractions about life. Zen in general, and Zen meditation techniques in particular, are eminently practical. Zen always deals with concrete facts and does not indulge in abstract generalizations of these facts.

Zen meditation techniques are targeted toward direct experience and away from rational explanations or categorizations of experience. Zen holds that a person cannot find meaning in experience because that person is that and only that which he or she is experiencing in the now. Zen mediation techniques are geared to help the person open up the "third eye," to experience the world directly as it really is in its essential unity. Zen theory and practice are thus forms of mysticism. Successful practice of Zen meditation techniques require a high sense of purpose and quiet discipline on the part of anyone who would learn and live this way of life.

All Zen activities, from tending a garden to techniques for meditation, are done in an atmosphere of serenity, relaxation, and simplicity. This kind of peaceful atmosphere is very important in order to melt away the tensions created by one's incessant ego-strivings to desire, possess, and dominate. This tranquil atmosphere helps an individual to let go of the ego, to let go of the sufferings attendant upon one's inner tensions.

By far the most important single Zen meditation technique is the *kōan*. This central and essential Zen meditation technique either contains a blatant contradiction or leads inevitably to a logical dead end. In a *kōan* there is not the slightest direct logical connection between the question and its direct or implied solution. The *kōan* can be solved only when one totally puts to rest one's analytical mind with its processes of discursive reasoning, relying instead on one's own experience, one's own being-in-reality, one's own nonrationality. The more one intensifies one's rational logical powers to solve the *kōan*, the more one discovers that reason is of no use. The recurring experience of the utter futility of reason to solve the *kōan* prepares the ground for letting go of reason, a complete letting go that is indispensable for solving the *kōan*. The solution can be experienced only in a sudden breakaway flash of intuition that tends to bring enlightenment (*satori*) with it.

It is a wholly new and completely different life which the *kōan* seeks to produce. Freudians and Jungians would contend that the goal of the *kōan* is to liberate one's unconscious process, an event that enables these processes to join the conscious mind in holistic unity. Zenists, for their part, regard the goal of the *kōan* as superconsciousness in which one comes to continually encounter reality directly rather than indirectly, experientially rather than rationally. The *kōan* leads the learner to a state of pure consciousness in which that person is no longer "conscious of" but instead is simply consciousness.

Over the centuries the *kōan* has been systematized, something that has preserved this central Zen meditation technique from sinking into a trance and from degenerating into a glorified tranquilizer. When an applicant has been accepted in a Zen monastery, he is given a *kōan* by his *rōshi* (recognized Zen master). The disciple lives with his *kōan* not only in the *zendō* (meditation hall where one practices Zen in a systematic and highly focused manner) but at all times of the day. Probably the most famous of all *kōans* is that proposed by Hakuin (1685–1768): "What is the sound of one hand clapping?" Another famous *kōan* is that attributed to Joshu (778–897), known as Chao-chou in Chinese: "What is the fundamental principle of Buddhism? The answer is: The cypress tree in the garden." Often the first *kōan* given to a beginning Zen student is one also proposed by Joshu: "Does a dog have a Buddha nature?

The answer is Mu." (The first of the three *kōans* given in this paragraph consists solely of a question, whereas the last two consist of both question and answer.)

Quite a few *kōans* appear in the form of a *mondō*, the pithy question-answer exchange between the Zen master and the student.

Religious educators will immediately recognize that the paradoxical nature and nonlogical essence of the *kōan*, and indeed of the entire fabric of Zen, has its Christian counterpart in the heart of the Christian mystical tradition. Meister Eckhart, for example, referred to God as "divine darkness," while another great mystic termed the upper levels of the spiritual life as "the cloud of unknowing." Down through the centuries Christian mystics have typically embarked on a progressive *via negativa* spiritual journey into the farthest reaches of the self's increasing rational and affective darkness, a journey necessary for finding the true God untainted by human cognitive speculation or rational explanations.

In the *zendō* and whenever a monk is not engaged in walking or in physical work, he meditates on his *kōan* while doing *zazen*, a particular kind of sitting position. *Zazen* is done in the famous lotus position in which an individual sits upright with legs crossed. The purpose of zazen, like all other features of Zen instructional method, is highly practical. The lotus position is used because it works. Of all bodily postures, the lotus position tends to bring with it a physical and psychological relaxation that significantly aids a learner to empty the self of conscious rational forms and break through to *satori*. As used in *zazen*, the lotus position helps still the self by felicitously aligning all bodily parts in a posture most conducive to internal harmony and the centering of self. In *zazen* one does not shut one's eyes so as to eliminate distractions because these distractions are the stuff of reality and therefore should not be shut out from the self. As a highly experiential instructional method, Zen does not seek to close the self to sensory objects but rather seeks to experience them right here and right now. Thus *zazen* is usually done with the eyes open while gazing a few feet directly ahead. Looking ahead rather than sidewards or downwards encourages a more erect posture, which in turn promotes alertness while at the same time decreasing physical stiffness and back pain. While gazing, one does not fix one's concentration on a single point, since the goal is to eliminate all ego-consciousness including the consciousness of concentration.

The ultimate goal of *zazen*, the *kōan*, the *mondō*, and all other Zen instructional techniques is to attain *satori*, enlightenment (*wu* in Chinese). *Satori* is the raison d'être of Zen. There can be no Zen without *satori* because without *satori* no one can enter the existential truth-state of Zen. *Satori* is a new birth, a birth that brings the person into enlightenment, into the realm of true seeing and true being. The luminously clear personal experience or intuitive vision of the essential oneness of reality frees persons to be who they really are. *Satori* enables the enlightened person to see into creation and the created. *Satori* can never be explained; it can only be experienced. A brilliant intellect can know all the truths and features of Zen, but only the pure and committed soul can enter *satori* and drink from its inexhaustible spring. A *satori* that can be explained or analyzed is no *satori*.

Satori brings with it detachment from things in this world, including one's very own ego with all its interests and strivings. This detachment is not the result of the enlightened person seeking detachment. Rather, detachment is one major direct outcome of *satori*. Individuals who have attained enlightenment no longer feel attachment or desire because their state of enlightenment has shown them that they are now at the heart of beings and objects and events in the whole universe, at the heart of that which is most precious and most irreplaceable in those beings and objects and events.

How should a practitioner of Zen behave in everyday life, regardless of whether that practitioner has achieved enlightenment or not? A famous Zen passage shows the way: "Monks ought to behave like a grinding stone: Chang-san comes to sharpen his knife, Li-szŭ comes to grind his axe, everybody and anybody who wants to have his metal improved in any way comes and makes use of the stone. Each time the stone is rubbed, it wears out, but it makes no complaint, nor does it boast of its usefulness. And those who come to it go home fully benefited. Some of them may not be quite appreciative of the stone. But the stone itself remains ever contented."

Our call within a call to be religious educators carries with it the imperative of being like the aforementioned grinding stone whose primary purpose is to assist others to grow and develop. In so doing, we religious educators worthily perform our sacred role in the overall sacrament of teaching.

Learners of all ages and circumstances come to us religious educators for improvement, to be helped. To what extent do we religious educators behave like the grinding stone in the Zen passage, a stone that makes no complaint but rather is content simply to have been of assistance to those who use it?

How frequently do we religious educators act like the grinding stone and renounce our egocenteredness for the sake of being of optimum use to others? Always? Sometimes? Rarely?

To what degree do we religious educators realize that the more we act like the grinding stone the more our ego-centeredness is worn away, the more our external strivings are worn away, the more our possession and domination of the learner or of anything else are worn away?

How much do we appreciate that the more wholeheartedly we merge ourselves with the experiential reality of the religious instructional dynamic, the more we gain important new perspectives on life, on learners, and on reality in general?

To what extent do we so totally enter into the dynamics of the religious instruction act that the dualism between ourselves and the learner is thereby bridged?

Do we totally become our experience in the teaching-learning act? Is our interior personal experience part of the teaching-learning dynamic or is our interior personal experience somehow apart from this dynamic? This is an important feature of our call within a call to be a religious educator, since our spiritual growth flows directly through the quality of our religious instruction activity.

Zenists believe that behaving like the grinding stone and wearing away one's ego through devoted, competent service to others is an especially salutary path to enlightenment. Christians believe much the same thing. By behaving like the grinding stone during the instructional dynamic, we religious educators die to our own egocentrism. Through this death to egocenteredness, we not only become much better teachers but in the process are born again to eternal life. How are we religious educators doing in this regard?

Performance Objective: Whenever my ego is bruised by some incident during the religious instruction event or by some critical remark made by a learner, I will instantly reflect on whether this incident or remark is actually an assault on my egoism or in fact is an incident or remark that embodies an objective reality. If I discover that the incident or remark is an assault on my egoism, I will wholeheartedly accept the gift of this hurt in the realization that such incidents or remarks constitute the grinding stones that wear away my ego, an ego that tends to stand in the way both of my achieving full selfhood and of making the religious instruction event an optimum learning experience.

22

Inconvenience

In my professional travels around the country over the years I have frequently heard religious educators who work with persons at all age levels say: "I'm not going to do such-and-such because it is inconvenient for me."

In the final analysis we do not like inconvenience because it somehow gets in the way of our personal ease and our personal agenda.

Inconvenience can be defined as anything that interferes with our comfort, wants, or plans. Consequently, we religious educators regard inconvenience as a drag on what we would like to do or on what we had intended to do.

Inconvenience is always slight. It causes us a slight annoyance. It causes us a slight unsettlement. It causes us a slight agitation. It causes us a slight vexation. It causes us a slight discomfort. It causes us a slight loss of ease. It causes us a slight unpleasantness. It causes us a slight suffering.

Inconvenience is always temporary. It causes us a temporary annoyance. It causes us a temporary unsettlement. It causes us a temporary agitation. It causes us a temporary vexation. It causes us a temporary discomfort. It causes us a temporary loss of ease. It causes us a temporary unpleasantness. It causes us a temporary suffering.

Inconvenience requires just a little more effort than we had planned for.

Inconvenience is untimely and inopportune. It crops up at the wrong time in terms of our what we had previously intended to do.

Inconvenience is a nuisance to us.

At bottom, any decision to avoid doing something because it is inconvenient means that we religious educators place our own interests ahead of the here-and-now demands of the religious instruction apostolate. A decision to avoid inconvenience is a fundamentally a decision on behalf of ego gratification.

Although none of us religious educators likes inconvenience, it is nonetheless important for us to realize that inconvenience is part and parcel of our call within a call. Our divine vocation requires us to be unreservedly willing to do everything we can in all times and in all places to be effective religious educators—and this includes embracing all manner of inconveniences for the sake of successful religious instruction. Our call within a call means that we are never free even in the slightest degree from inconveniences or from anything else that is directly related to effectively teaching religion in season and out.

Our willingness to embrace inconvenience is a clear operational test of our commitment to the religious instruction apostolate.

A religious educator's decision or series of decisions to avoid inconvenience is a sure sign of becoming stale in the religious instruction apostolate. Put another way, a religious educator's decision or series of decisions to avoid doing something because of inconvenience is the beginning of the end of that religious educator's overall effectiveness.

Every time we religious educators avoid an inconvenience we place another brick in the road leading to eventual inaction.

It is the slightness of inconvenience that sometimes causes religious educators to minimize or disvalue inconvenience. But it is attention to slight things that often makes the difference between a successful religious instruction apostolate and a mediocre one.

Inconvenience is indeed a sacrifice. But it is a little sacrifice, a minimal sacrifice in the context of the larger religious instruction task. Paradoxically, large sacrifices are often easy due to the fact that our making a major sacrifice gives us a feeling of accomplishment and oblation. But little sacrifices such as inconvenience are frequently more difficult over the long haul because they are not accompanied by any sense of performing a great task, by any feeling of satisfaction in offering up so much. As a result, we religious educators have the unfortunate tendency to falsely disvalue small sacrifices such as inconvenience, failing to realize how essential minor sacrifices are for the overall success of any endeavor.

How many fine religious instruction opportunities have been lost because the religious educator failed to do such-and-such due to its inconvenience?

Doing something that is inconvenient for the sake of optimally performing our religious instruction duties requires us to modify our plans slightly in order to attend properly to whatever is inconvenient. To what extent are we religious educators flexible and adaptable in this respect?

Our call within a call to be God's religious educator means that convenience or inconvenience are irrelevant in themselves. The only thing that is relevant is doing whatever it takes to perform our religious instruction tasks in the best manner. Thus for us religious educators, inconvenience never constitutes a valid excuse for inaction on our part.

It was surely the height of inconvenience for God to give his only begotten Son in the form of Jesus, the primal sacrament, to the world to be born, suffer and die—for us. As full-fledged participants in the sacrament of teaching, a sacrament that has its ultimate existence in Jesus the *Ursakrament*, we can never validly let even the slightest inconvenience stand in the way of doing any task that forms part of our religious instruction apostolate.

To what extent are we religious educators willing to endure the slight loss of comfort and ease brought on by an inconvenience in order to generously answer our call within a call?

To what degree are we religious educators willing to accept the slight suffering and sacrifice attendant upon inconvenience in order to be an optimally effective religious educator?

How often are we religious educators willing to make that little additional effort required to do what is inconvenient in order that we can become that kind of religious educator that God wants us to be?

Are we religious educators willing to place our own egoistic concerns in the background day in and day out so that we can pay proper pedagogical heed to the inconveniences that are so frequently strewn in the path of overall religious instruction activity?

Are we religious educators really and truly aware of the fact that inconvenience is temporary whereas the larger religious instruction apostolate is long lasting?

How many times do we religious educators rationalize our unwillingness to be inconvenienced by telling ourselves that such-and-such an inconvenient act is not really that important anyway?

Do we religious educators realize that the basic question is not convenience or inconvenience but rather what is right in terms of the religious instruction task?

To what extent to we religious educators consider the huge disproportion between the worst inconvenience that we have to suffer and the disappointment that God surely must feel because we have not done what we should in living out our call within a call?

One of the most saddest sentences which a religious educator can utter is: "I'm not going to do this because it is inconvenient."

Performance Objective: Whenever I am confronted by a worthwhile religious instruction task that requires me to inconvenience myself, I will eagerly embrace this inconvenience in the knowledge that this temporary annoyance is necessary for me in order to successfully accomplish my religious instruction objective. I will be comforted in the realization that each time I do something inconvenient in order to accomplish a worthwhile religious instruction objective, I will find it somewhat easier the next time to surmount whatever inconvenience that I encounter because I will be slowly building a habit of ignoring inconvenience during religious instruction activity—although the temptation to yield to convenience will be with me always.

23

Hard Work

Pat Riley is one of the most unusual—and winningest—professional basketball coaches in the history of this sport. On the sidelines during a game he stands out with his movie-star good looks, Giorgio Armani suits imported from Italy, gorgeous neckties, custom-made Hong Kong shirts that he designs himself complete with stylish cutaway collars, moussed hair combed straight back, and a cool composed demeanor suggesting total control of the situation both on the court and on the bench. Riley is treated with respect by his players. He is held in near awe by his adoring public who look on him as a cross between a nineteenth century European cavalry officer and a late twentieth century rock star. Women swoon and men want to follow him into battle. His intensity-with-pizazz style brings glamorous movie actors and directors, well-known television personalities, noted singers, famous athletes from other sports, and prominent politicians to attend the games he coaches. For Riley, a professional basketball contest is a combination of meticulously executed plays and Showtime.

Riley's high energy, winning intensity, flashbulb smile, and I-can-do-it style have made him one of the most sought-after motivational speakers on the corporate circuit. A 1993 survey of 311 senior corporate executives conducted by a New York public relations firm found that Pat Riley was one of five individuals most frequently cited by captains and lieutenants of industry as the person who most often influenced their business decisions in the previous year. In 1996 the readers of the prestigious men's fashion magazine *Gentlemen's Quarterly* not only voted him the most stylish man in America but also named him one of eleven individuals to receive Man of the Year (other 1996 winners included Microsoft Chairman Bill Gates, architectural pioneer I. M. Pei, and former United States president Jimmy Carter). By the late 1990s, huge corporations like International Business Machines and General Motors, as well as fast-rising smaller companies, paid $60,000 for a one-hour speech followed by a short question-and-answer session. This princely honorarium made Riley far and away the highest paid celebrity motivational speaker, earning almost twice as much as other famous celebrity motivational speakers such as former Notre Dame football coach Lou Holtz. Top corporate executives are eager to expose their senior and junior managers to dynamic inspirational speakers who are outstanding successes in their field, who are excellent motivators of their subordinates, and who believe that two major keys to success are a positive attitude and intelligent, creative hard work. Riley's electric speeches to corporate leaders are characterized by the same high level of zeal, obsession with detail, and inspiring maxims which he uses on his players both in practice and in games.

The youngest of six children, Patrick James Riley was born in Rome, New York on March 20, 1945. He had what he often refers to as a "good old-fashioned Catholic upbringing" at home. Though he was raised primarily by his mother, it was his father, Leon ("Lee") Francis Riley who exerted by far the greater influence on Pat's life. Lee Riley was a professional baseball player and manager who played very briefly for the Philadelphia Phillies but with this brief exception spent his entire career playing or managing in the minor leagues with the Phillies organization. The Phillies management promised him that he would be given a major league coaching assignment with that team. But after being repeatedly passed over to coach the Phillies, Lee Riley quit the game in disgust. In his despondency he turned to the glass crutch and became a heavy drinker. When he finally dried out, he took a job as a janitor at Bishop Gibbons High School. After a while Lee Riley was offered the additional position as school baseball coach. He accepted the offer on condition that he be allowed to coach in his janitor's uniform. Pride was one of the most important lessons that Lee Riley taught his son.

The parochial school baseball coach in his janitor's uniform and the professional basketball coach in his Armani suits are two sides of the same man. To be sure, both exist on their own terms, but both exist forever together. What looks to casual observers as the Armani suit is really the janitor's uniform in another form. Put another way, the Armani suit is the janitor's uniform turned inside out.

In many respects Pat Riley has steadfastly lived out his father's unfulfilled dreams and has more than vindicated his father's lack of success in becoming the major league field general his father so ardently desired for himself.

Besides a fierce pride, Lee Riley instilled in his son toughness in adversity together with a spirit of unceasing and uncompromising hard work. To toughen Pat and to habituate him to hard work, Lee Riley ordered his other sons to take Pat frequently to the local basketball playground and match him against older gang members who were bigger, stronger, and better players than Pat, players whose no-holds-barred style of play included smashing elbows into Pat's face during the course of a game.

Pat Riley was playing a professional basketball game in another part of the country when he learned that his father had died suddenly. He always deeply regretted that he never had a chance to say a final good-bye to his father. But Lee Riley lives on in his son, for it is the spirit of Lee Riley that has been the continual wellspring of inspiration as well as the fundamental driving force throughout Pat's entire professional career. In the deepest parts of his being, Pat still hears his father's voice urging him to work harder, to do better, to never ever give up. Pat recalls several experiences (which he terms "incredible") in which his father's presence seemed to be with him in an even deeper and more vivid way than usual. These experiences typically occurred in the turning-point moments of those crucial games that were to prove decisive in shaping his career.

The famous coach dedicated his best-selling book *The Winner Within* as follows:

To my late father, Lee Riley. I want to dedicate this book to his voice and his presence. They have been with me since his death. I never got to say goodbye or to tell you I loved you. With this book I say hello, and thank you for inspiring me to:

> Plant my feet,
> Stand firm.
> And make a point
> about who I am.
>
> Your son, "Coach"

Pat Riley has always been working hard, always pushing forward his special talents not simply to achieve the maximum but to extend this maximum to new realms of consciousness and achievement. His first big achievement on the basketball court occured as a sixth grader at St. Joseph's Academy when he led his sixth-grade team to a surprise victory over the ninth-graders. Riley was an outstanding player at Linton High School, where he began to develop his passion for the work ethic that was to become the hallmark of his career. One high school teammate said that during practice sessions Riley was always the first player in to the gym and the last one out. Practice, practice, practice became his motto, a motto that guides him down to the present day.

The legendary coach Adolph Rupp offered Pat Riley an athletic scholarship to play basketball for the University of Kentucky. Rupp's work ethic, like the work effort of Lee Riley, exerted long-lasting effect on Pat. In describing Adolph Rupp as an outstanding basketball coach, Riley once said: "He was tough and kept us thoroughly drilled. He allowed no distractions—just hard work and loads of it. That's why he produced so many winning teams."

At Kentucky Riley combined his considerable athletic talent with unrelenting hard work and self-discipline. Indeed, he played well enough to be voted the team's most valuable player in each of the years in which he played college basketball, including the season in which the Kentucky Wildcats played for the NCAA championship. A former teammate at Kentucky said that Pat Riley was driven to play as hard as he could, every minute. Little did Riley realize on the day of his graduation that his best days as a basketball player were behind him.

Because of his superb basketball career at the University of Kentucky, Riley was drafted in the very first round to play for the San Diego Rockets of the National Basketball Association (NBA). He never became more than a journeyman professional basketball player because he was a classic "tweener"—too small to play forward with the professionals but not quick or skilled enough to be a starting guard. Riley remained with the Rockets for three years and then spent the next six years successively as a player for the Portland Blazers expansion team, the Los Angeles Lakers, and finally the Phoenix Suns. After the end of the 1975-1976 season his hobbled knees and other physical problems caused him to fail the team physical examination. He was released from the Suns. At age thirty one, Riley's playing days were over and it seemed to everyone that he had nowhere to go in basketball.

Without basketball, life lost purpose and focus for Riley. Despondent and depressed, he took a year off, spending much of his time taking long walks on the beach and doing carpentry work on his house. In the fall of 1977 he took a job as the interpretive ("color") commentator on broadcasts of Los Angeles Lakers professional basketball games. Always eager to work his hardest to do the best, he hired a voice coach and an acting coach. He spent long hours at home making practice broadcast tapes and then critiquing them mercilessly.

Two years later he was offered a position as assistant coach of the Lakers. In fall 1981 head coach Paul Westhead was fired after eleven games because of an unsatisfactory record, and Riley took his place. The Lakers won the NBA championship that year.

Under Riley's leadership the Lakers became the dominant NBA team of the 1980s. In his first seven seasons with the Lakers, the team won for world championships and were in the finals six times. At the age of forty three he became the winningest coach (in percentage terms) in NBA history up to that time.

Some persons claim that the Laker players of the 1980s were so extraordinarily talented that all a coach had to do was toss the ball on to the court and the team would win. But more discerning observers recognized that the key to the Lakers' great success in the 1980s was far more complex than the single factor of enormous player talent. In this view, the success of the Lakers was ultimately to be found in how skillfully the coach blended this outstanding player talent to make a winning ball club, how well the coach motivated this talent to perform at a consistently winning level, and how hard the coach got this talent to work both in practice and in the actual game.

In large measure Riley's noteworthy accomplishments as a basketball coach stem from his deeply held view that a successful coach must necessarily accord major attention to developing a team's attitude, not just its muscles. "Effective coaching is about getting the most out of players," Riley likes to say. More than most coaches, he clearly recognizes that getting the most out of players is directly proportional to the degree to which he can get into their minds and hearts. Only in this way will players passionately desire to perform, and actually do perform on the court, at full throttle and beyond. He strongly believes that in sports, as in life, there can be no excellence without character. One way he constantly focuses on developing a player's character is to use arresting, thought-provoking maxims that he repeats often, especially at critical moments during practice.

There is nothing terribly fancy or trendy about Riley's winning formula. There are no trick plays, no complicated strategies, no razzle-dazzle maneuvers. Riley insists that his main focus as a coach is to ensure that his players coalesce into the hardest working, best conditioned, most professional, and most egoless team in the league. Players testify that Riley pushes them harder than any other head coach. As a result, no NBA team is better prepared for a game than a Riley-coached group of basketball players.

One of Riley's central beliefs is that the greatest sin in basketball, and possibly in life, is to be outworked by someone else.

Hard work, hard work, hard work—this is the mainspring and centerpiece of Riley's life as a professional. For most people, one of the most distasteful dimensions of hard work is punctilious and unrelenting attention to detail. But Riley, on the contrary, is absolutely convinced that the ultimate secret to success in any field of endeavor is meticulously detailed hard work. The practice schedules of his teams are carefully organized down to the last minute. He was not the first basketball coach to use videotapes of his players' performance. But he was the first basketball coach to raise the use of these videotapes to an almost exact science. Riley developed a three-phase utilization of videotapes to help his players constantly monitor and then improve their performance. First, he breaks down his players' individual performances into discrete and highly specific visual bytes. Second, he employs a statistical frame of reference, which he developed, to help each player measure his effort day by day—a "hard work quotient", so to speak. Finally, he splices the segmented bytes together and sets them to music as a teaching and motivational tool for his players.

Riley's scrupulous attention to detail extends to everything that happens on court. He even makes sure to wear custom-made shirts made of oxford cloth on game days because they absorb more perspiration than broadcloth shirts. He does not want to let the opposing team see him sweat because that might give them a psychological advantage over his players. Nor does he want perspiration to stain his beautiful Armani silk suits.

A primary reason why top-flight basketball players work hard for Riley is because they know that no matter how hard they themselves work, Riley works even harder. One of his star players with the Lakers and later one of his best friends, Earvin "Magic" Johnson once remarked: "There were times when I looked at him and knew he hadn't slept for days. That helped motivate me. He was always on, never off."

During a game, the players rest for stretches, catch their breath during time-outs, and take a break during the half. But Riley is working all the time during the game. "It's draining", Riley says. "It takes me a day to recover."

But even when he is recovering, Riley is hard at work. On afternoons after practice, when he was with the Lakers, Riley could usually be found poolside, spread out in a lounge chair, wearing fashionable swimming trunks and chic sunglasses, and sipping an iced drink with his left hand—the very picture of a man at leisure. But on the table next to him were very fat books detailing offensive and defensive strategies. His right hand held a felt-tipped pen with which he was scribbling notes on large (special order) powder blue sheets of paper.

Hard work, all the time and every time, is necessary to be a consistent winner. Throughout his entire professional career, Riley has never settled for just doing his best. He has always striven to do the best. Hard work is necessary if one wants to do the best.

By definition, work is something that one does not want to do. Hard work is something that one really does not want to do. But unrelenting, intelligent hard work is absolutely essential to being a true professional. "NBA basketball is a professional activity, pure and simple," Riley says. "If you want to have fun, go to the YMCA."

In 1990 Pat Riley was voted NBA Coach of the Year, an honor that many believed he should have also received several times before. That same year, in what was for him an agonizing decision, Riley resigned as head coach of the Lakers because of what he termed "a toxic environment of envy" that had built up in the Lakers organization. Very shortly afterwards the National Broadcasting Corporation gave him a $500,000 annual contract to serve as color commentator for NBA basketball games. There he worked alongside Bob Costas, one of the premier sports announcers in the country. Riley brought the same perfectionist standards and incessant hard work to his national television job as he did to coaching. Costas was particularly impressed by Riley's hunger to learn all the facets and nuances of broadcasting in order to achieve excellence as a sports analyst.

The following year the New York Knicks offered Riley a five-year $6 million contract to become its head coach. The once mighty Knicks had become chronic losers for almost a generation. In the previous seventeen seasons the Knicks had never advanced beyond the second round of the NBA playoffs. For the past six years the team had gone through five different head coaches and three general managers. Even though he enjoyed his job as NBC sports analyst, Riley accepted the Knicks offer because he "missed the fire down on the floor, the competition, the intensity," as he himself said. Riley clearly relished the enormous challenge of transforming a group of perennial losers into a group of winners. Besides, he would now be back home in New York coaching the team that he had rooted for when he was growing up in Schenectady.

Almost single-handedly Riley turned the Knicks around. In his first year, he performed one of the greatest coaching feats in the history of the NBA, piloting the previously hapless Knicks to fifty-one regular-season victories (only the team's third fifty-win campaign in eighteen seasons). That year the previously hapless Knicks played so well that they even got to the second round of the National Basketball Association championship playoffs where they were defeated in the seventh and last game by the eventual NBA champions, Michael Jordan's Chicago Bulls. Commenting on this amazing turnaround in Knick fortunes, one sportswriter said that "the Knicks under Riley evolved unlike any other professional team as their identity derived not from their star player but from their coach." The following year the Knicks won sixty regular-season games, second best in the NBA overall. In the process he again won the NBA Coach of the Year Award. Not only the team but all New York got excited about the Knicks dramatic recovery and newfound winning ways. In New York parlance, Riley brought back the buzz to the Big Apple.

Riley was able to bring about this dramatic turnaround in the Knicks fortunes by using the same successful coaching techniques he had used with the Lakers. All these techniques flowed from and centered around hard work. Riley has always recognized that people typically will not work hard or strive unrelentingly for excellence unless they have an attitude that identifies hard work and excellence with their very existence as a person. "It's all attitude" Riley says over and over again. In the end, it is attitude that determines who will be the winners and who will be the losers on the basketball court and in life as well. Winning—and losing—ultimately comes from within the person.

To develop a positive, winning attitude in the Knicks, Riley did three things. First, he inspired his players with maxims that he repeated over and over again in practice, during games, and in the locker room. These maxims were drawn from a wide variety of sources: Napoleon Bonaparte's remark that "impossible is a word to be found only in the dictionary of fools"; William Ward's observation that "adversity causes some men to break, others to break records"; and Vidal Sassoon's comment that "the only place where success comes before work is in the dictionary."

The second thing that Riley did to instill a positive winning attitude in the Knicks was to help his players rid themselves of what he calls "the disease of Me", a disease in which each player thinks primarily of himself rather than of winning. A successful team is one in which each person plays every minute with the goal of winning in mind, not with the goal of personal ego aggrandizement. Winning in a team sport like basketball means putting the team ahead of personal interests because it is the team and not the individual player that wins or loses a game. To win in a team sport is to abandon ego for the goal of attaining the goal of victory. The "disease of Me" is a sure guarantee of losing.

The third thing that Riley did to bring about a positive winning attitude in the Knicks was to have them work very hard in practice. This kind of highly disciplined hard work is reciprocally reinforcing. On the one hand unrelenting practice sharpens the team's skills. On the other hand the process of sharpening their skills makes the players feel that they are winners precisely because they are bringing their skills to perfection. Attitude conditions and sets up performance. And performance, in turn, reinforces and deepens attitude. Riley instituted grueling, carefully scripted three-hour regular practices which were so exhausting that they seemed to the players like five hours. At times the practices actually did extend to five clock hours. "Guys around the league make jokes about how hard we practice," quipped Doc Rivers, one of Riley's best players. "And sometimes in the middle of four or five hours of running up and down the court, you're thinking, This is ridiculous. But then in the same thought, you realize that Coach Riley has gotten deep into your mind and heart, and that he's won you over even as you're fighting it. The fact you're fighting it shows he's won."

The Knicks players really knew that Riley had won in his drive to get the team to work very hard when they saw the team's quiet superstar Pat Ewing on his own initiative begin to go to the weight room for an additional workout after the conclusion of fatiguing regular practice sessions.

Riley monitored each player's performance with his "effort statistics," a further refinement of the "hard work quotient" that he developed when he was with the Lakers. Every practice session and every actual game were carefully videotaped. From the videotape a computerized plus/minus report was compiled. This detailed report compared each player's level of hustle (unrelenting hard work) with that of his opponent. Using these data, Riley was able to calculate not only the published statistics of how many points a player scored or how many rebounds he got but also how many times he dove headfirst for the ball, stole the ball from an opposing player, passed off to an open man, boxed out an opponent, covered for a teammate on defense, or jumped for a rebound even if he did not get it.

As was the case when he was the Lakers, a major factor that motivated the Knicks players to work very hard is the fact that they saw their coach working even harder than they. After a game, the Knicks players usually went to bed or cruised around town looking for a night's fun. No so with Riley. After reviewing the game with assistant coaches and possibly talking with the press and visiting VIPs, the coach typically arrived at home or at his hotel around two o'clock in the morning. He then would turn on the videocassette recorder and stay up a few more hours watching and analyzing videotapes of the next opposing team.

After four years of coaching the Knicks, Pat Riley abruptly resigned. He wanted total control of player personnel decisions and a very hefty raise in salary. The Knicks refused to give him either. As an expression of contempt for the leadership of the Knicks organization, Riley did not resign in person—he sent his resignation by fax and then immediately left the city.

The Miami Heat immediately sought his services and made him an offer he could not refuse. The Heat and long been one of the NBAs worst teams, and its management was exceedingly eager to get a coach who not only was a proven winner but who also had demonstrated that he could turn losing teams into winners. The Heat gave him 10 percent of the ownership of the team, plus a salary and other kinds of financial compensation that could amount to $40 million depending on how long he remained with the team.

Pat Riley has always relished a great challenge. The previously hapless New York Knicks were a great challenge. And now the periodically wretched Miami Heat presented another supreme challenge. He did not disappoint. In Riley's very first season as head coach of the Heat, they won their division title for the first time ever, and thus made it into the NBA playoffs. They had won an amazing sixty-one games in regular season play (then a franchise record by nineteen victories) and all of this despite a wave of injuries to his players, the loss of All-Star forward Juwan Howard, and in general with a group of players possessing relatively limited talent and ability. The Heat's record the year before Riley became head coach was 32–50.

Commenting on Riley's performance, Hall of Fame coach Jack Ramsey said: "Pat Riley did a monumental coaching job. To have a contending team with this caliber of personnel—it's good but their record is much better than what the talent would seem to suggest. And Pat Riley is the reason."

New York coach Jeff Van Gundy was even more direct: "Pat Riley is the best coach in the history of team sports."

Riley followed his astounding first-year success with more seasons when the Miami Heat always did very well, despite the fact that the other teams in the NBA had players who were more talented than those on the Heat. In the 1996–1997 season, Riley was named NBA Coach of the Year.

P. J. Brown, one of Riley's players on the Heat, told why his team had done so well so quickly under their new coach: "People say 'What's the secret?' like we're down here brewing something. There's nothing to it. It's hard work. Our practices sometimes are harder than when we play other teams, and that's the truth."

Pat Riley has been such a consistently outstanding success as a basketball coach because he creates his own success through incredibly focused hard work. For Riley, the level of one's success in any field of endeavor is directly proportionate to a person's work ethic, to how much a person wants to pay for success, to how hard a person will actually work to attain success. Ultimately, the key to winning or losing lies within oneself. It is entirely fitting, therefore, that Riley gave the title *The Winner Within* to his best-selling book, that summarizes his beliefs and attitudes about how to be a winner on the basketball court and how to be a winner in life, since like any true sport, basketball is a metaphor of life.

The Winner Within is a motivational book in which Pat Riley shares with his readers how he became very successful and how everyone else can achieve success by using the same basic principles of success that he discovered and continues to live by. These principles are applicable to every person in every occupation and in every life situation.

The basic theme of Riley's book is the centrality of hard work which is dedicated totally to the task at hand. Hard work is intrinsically linked to subjugation of the ego. Hard workers (winners) do not think of their own egos but rather think exclusively of what must be done to accomplish the task perfectly. In sharp contrast, slothful persons (losers) think primarily of themselves and always calculate how much effort the task will require of them.

To help ensure uncompromising attention and total devotion to the task at hand, Riley strongly recommends that each person make a core covenant to self (or in a team sport, to the team). In the core covenant, a person pledges to self (or to the team) to work extremely hard to accomplish the task perfectly. This means conquering the ego in terms of one's own efforts and giving of oneself with total unquestioning generosity to the task. Egolessness requires the expenditure of every last drop of effort to achieve the goal.

In Riley's view, every true winner in life as well as in basketball basically is what he calls a "Showtime Warrior." This is the kind of person who, when confronted with a very difficult situation in which victory or defeat depends largely on one's own efforts, instinctively and from force of habit summons all one's inner strength in a focused manner to successfully accomplish the task at hand. "The true Warrior is someone who knows how to get the job done at a moment of truth." Riley believes that there are three traits which define a Showtime Warrior: heart, courage, and will. The successful deployment of these three defining traits requires unselfish hard work.

The margins of *The Winner Within* are adorned with maxims to play by and to live by. These maxims, drawn from a wide variety of sources, include: "We must either find a way of make one" (Hannibal); "Character is destiny" (Heraclitus); "He who stops being better stops being good" (Oliver Cromwell); "Great works are performed not by strength but by perseverance" (Samuel Johnson); "Even if you're on the right track, you'll get run over if you just sit there" (Will Rogers); "The world is full of willing people, some willing to work, the others willing to let them" (Robert Frost); "Anybody who gets away with something will come back to get away with a little bit more" (Harold Schoenberg); "When you cannot make up your mind which of two evenly balanced courses you should take, choose the bolder" (W. J. Slim); "You can only become a winner if you are willing to walk over the edge" (Damon Runyon); "Success is never final" (Winston Churchill); "Everybody wants to go to heaven, but nobody wants to die" (Joe Louis). "I have fought the good fight. I have finished the race. I have kept the faith." (2 Tim 4–7).

In the body of the text of *The Winner Within* are double-lined boxes that contain a "Riles' Rule of . . ." (Riles is Riley's nickname). All of these Riles' rules are targeted toward helping persons to work consistently hard by showing them how to gain a guiding vision, how to prevent discouragement in adversity, and how to systematically develop the winner that lies within each person. Although most of these rules are directed toward the game of basketball, they apply just as much to the game of life. For example, there is Riles' Rule of the Heart, Riles' Rule of Finishing without Being Finished, Riles' Rule of Rebirth, Riles' Rule of Raising the Stakes, and so on. Riley usually provides concrete examples from his own career to illustrate the rule. One of the rules is Riles' Rule for Triumph from the Trenches: "Never demean the time you spend in the trenches. Use any time when you aren't on center stage to strengthen your powers of perception. Keep reminding yourself that attitude is the mother of luck." Riles' Rule on Beating the Sympathy Syndrome is: "Giving yourself permission to lose guarantees a loss. Shoulda, coulda, and woulda won't get it done. In attacking adversity, only a positive attitude, alertness, and regrouping to basics can launch a comeback." Riles' Rule of the Brilliant Loss states: "When a great team loses through complacency, it will constantly search for new and more intricate explanations to explain away defeat. After a while the team becomes more innovative in thinking up how to lose than in thinking up how to win."

What is the best way to sum up Pat Riley and what he stands for? Riley himself expresses it best when he observes: "The basic philosophy of all great athletic coaches is that you have to work hard. In the beginning, players think that hard work is abnormal. But after players do it for a period of time, hard work becomes normal."

Our call within a call to be a religious educator means that we are summoned by God to be hard workers. There is no way of escaping, evading, or minimizing this incontrovertible fact. Do we realize in the core of our being that those moments during the day when we are not hard at work for the Lord are moments when we are not true to our call, when we are failing God? And to what extent do we realize that hard work is absolutely necessary for sacramenting of our religious instruction work?

Hard work and religious instruction activity go hand in hand. Do we identify hard work with our very existence as a religious educator? To what extent are we aware that we cannot be authentic religious educators unless we work hard always?

Is unrelenting hard work normal for us as religious educators? Or is it abnormal? Is hard work simply something to be endured because it goes with our call, or do we relish the opportunity God has given us to work hard for him in the religious instruction apostolate?

In my life I have consistently found that every person imagines that he or she works hard but that in actuality few persons really do work hard. Do we religious educators really work hard? Do we even think of how hard we work?

In my life I have consistently found that persons who work hard reprove themselves throughout the day for not working hard enough. I have also found that persons who work but do not work hard imagine that they are working hard. Finally, I have found that persons who are lazy and hardly working at all imagine that they are overworked. Into which of these three categories do we religious educators perceive ourselves to be?

To what extent is hard work a habit with us as religious educators? To what degree is hard work something we do automatically without even thinking about it? Or do we have to purposefully steel ourselves against the rigors of hard work at the beginning of every new day or each new religious instruction task?

How hard do we work as religious educators? Can we look God in the face and tell him without any equivocation that we are constantly working very hard, full throttle?

To what extent are we working hard as God's religious educator in all places and at all times, and not just in "official" religious instruction sites and time frames? Even at leisure, are we working hard as religious educators by ruthlessly critiquing our past performance and then devising new ways of answering our call within a call more effectively?

To what extent do we religious educators neglect unremitting attention to the nitty-gritty details of religious instruction activity? To what degree do we avoid unswervering concentration on the details of the religious instruction task because this is especially difficult? Even though we know that our success as religious educators depends on the level to which we master all the details, do we nonetheless slough these details on to someone else with the lame excuse that "I have to be involved in the major aspects of religious instruction activity and do not have time for all those little details."

We religious educators are talented in various degrees, but do we realize that talent alone will not make us effective religious educators? Talent comes to naught in the absence of hard work. Talent gets the job done in direct proportion to hard work. How hard are we religious educators working to deploy our various talents for the sake of God in the religious instruction apostolate?

Before and during the enactment of a religious instruction task, do we conquer our ego in that we do not think at all of ego but instead concentrate our whole attention on what must be done to accomplish the task as perfectly as possible? To what extent do we place the religious instruction task ahead of ourselves, ahead of our interests, ahead of our comfort? To what degree are we slothful individuals who think primarily of ourselves and always calculate how much effort one or another religious instruction task will take?

To what extent do we look on religious instruction activity as fun? Do we say that we will leave the religious instruction apostolate when it ceases to be fun? To what extent do we realize that successful religious instruction activity is hard work and is not fun? Are we aware that if religious instruction activity is a lot of fun for us, then it is bound to be unsuccessful, since in such a case the mainspring of our religious instruction activity is fun rather than doing everything it takes to be effective? To what extent do we understand that fun does not inhere in religious instruction activity in itself but lies in the enjoyment and satisfaction that flow from a job which is being well done and which has been well done?

Pride in ourselves, pride in the fact that God has called us to be his religious educators, and pride in our competence as facilitators of learning outcomes will help us work harder than we thought we could. Do we have sufficient pride in ourselves, in our call within a call, and in our instructional activities?

Ultimately, it is a guiding vision of unconditional service to God through religious instruction activity that will motivate us to work hard and will sustain us in this hard work. Without an overall guiding vision, hard work perishes, and with it our apostolate. Do we have this vision? If so, how can we nurture it? If not, how can we get it?

At the end of each day, before we go to sleep, do carefully review the day's activities in order to ascertain how hard we have worked for God in the religious instruction apostolate? Have we developed some kind of "hard work quotient" so that at the end of the day we can measure with some degree of objectivity how hard we have worked for God that day? Do we go to sleep firmly resolving to work harder tomorrow than we did today?

Performance Objective: Whenever I am tempted by the thought that I am working too hard, I will meditate for a minute on the fact that no matter how hard I work, it is still not hard enough for a person in the Lord's religious instruction service.

24

Making It Perfect

My maternal grandfather and grandmother immigrated from Germany to the United States when they were teenagers. They met each other in Brooklyn, fell in love, and after a suitable period of time got married. They saved all the money they could, and in ten years were able to have a house built for them.

Year followed upon year. Times were good. The Brenner family rented out one floor of their two-family house to supplement their income. Grandfather Brenner had a rock solid job at Worthington Pump and Machinery Company. Grandmother Brenner felt thoroughly fulfilled in her role as full-time homemaker. She also enjoyed being active in the *Frauenverein*, the German-speaking Women's Club at St. Jacobi's Lutheran Church. They had four daughters on whom they doted.

Then a series of tragedies struck. Grandfather Brenner died of heart problems. Six years later the Great Depression descended on the country. The good times soured into bad times. There was no Social Security, few company pension plans, and no government economic safety nets in those days. So Grandmother Brenner had to cut back drastically all along the line. This severe financial retrenchment even extended to the weekly donation she made to her beloved St. Jacobi Lutheran Church.

In the good times Grandmother Brenner put a crisp new one-dollar bill into the collection plate at the German-language worship service at St. Jacobi's. But now that times were hard, all she could afford was a quarter.

Every Friday afternoon just before closing time she went to the bank and withdrew a quarter. If the bank had a freshly minted quarter, she made sure she got that one. Otherwise she asked for as the newest quarter the bank had on hand.

On Sunday morning Grandmother Brenner spent the last half-hour before the worship service polishing that quarter over and over and over again. She wanted to give God as perfect and pure a gift as she possibly could.

Our call within a call as religious educators demands that we shine the quarters of our teaching as perfectly as possible so that the sacrament of teaching in which we participate will be as fulsome and as efficacious as possible.

Do we religious educators shine and reshine the quarters of our religion teaching as brightly and as perfectly as we can week in and week out?

To what extent do we religious educators earnestly strive to do everything in our teaching activity as perfectly as possible? Do we always prepare our lessons as perfectly as we can, or do we make excuses such as "I don't have enough time."

Do we constantly strive to teach as perfectly as we can, or do we make excuses such as "I'm really worn out from all this teaching, so I'll ease up now."

Do we religious educators evaluate our learners' performances as perfectly as we can, or do we make excuses such as "I really don't have to spend much time in developing excellent evaluation devices because only the Holy Spirit knows how much the learners really learned."

Do we religious educators realize that in terms of both our teaching effectiveness and our personal spiritual lives, the process of shining the quarter of our religious instruction is just as important as the shined quarter?

Performance Objective: Every time I engage in a religious instruction event, I will carefully monitor my instructional behaviors to make sure that I am doing everything perfectly. When this continuous monitoring reveals, as it inevitably will, that one or another of my teaching behaviors needs improvement, I will work relentlessly and untiringly to make it perfect.

25

Doing the Best

To be truly successful in our professional lives as religious educators and in our spiritual lives as Christians, we should not try to do *our* best. Rather, we should try unceasingly to do *the* best.

There are weak religious educators, good religious educators, and great religious educators. The essential difference among these three types is that the weak religious educators seldom try to do their best, the good religious educators consistently try to do their best, and the great religious educators try to do the best.

Our call within a call to be religious educators demands not that we try to do what we think is the best we can do, but instead what simply is the best. If we do not unceasingly press on to do the best—not the best we think we can do, but the best—we will be unfaithful to our call.

To attempt to do our best means that there exists some goal, some accomplishment which is sufficient. To attempt to do the best means that whatever we do is never sufficient. To do the best is what our call within a call is all about. It is what Jesus is all about. It is what the sacrament of teaching is all about. The call within a call, Jesus, and the sacrament of teaching are all inextricably bound up with doing the best at all times, in all places, and in all circumstances.

To endeavor to do just what we think is the best we can do is to put the locus of performance inside ourselves with all our weaknesses, complacencies, and rationalizations. To endeavor to do the best places the locus of performance outside ourselves. Such an external locus helps us attain goals that our present limited vision imagines to be out of reach.

To struggle to do the best will, by its own power and attraction, draw out of us that topmost level of performance which we otherwise would not have thought possible for us to achieve.

To strive to do the best means that we are aiming at perfection. If we do not ardently strive to do the best, we will not even do what we imagine is our potential personal best.

Failure to constantly press onward to do the best will inevitably lead to a diminished level of performance, and maybe even to mediocrity. By claiming that all we can do is our personal best, we will almost automatically become satisfied with the level of our present performance, and what is worse, satisfied with ourselves. To be satisfied with our performance as a religious educator and as a person will virtually ensure that we will be fortunate if we even attain mediocrity.

The best is both a goal and a level of performance that are unattainable for any human being. But godliness and spiritual perfection are also unattainable, as the Bible directly states (Mt 5:48). Yet godliness and spiritual perfection are incumbent on every Christian. Hence striving for the best in our professional lives is congruent with our striving for the best in our personal spiritual lives.

To try without ceasing to do the best will always keep us humble because we can never reach the best. Conversely, to be content with just trying to do our best can easily lead to a noxious pride and self-satisfaction that is debilitating to our professional life as a religious educator and to our personal spiritual life as a Christian.

It is sheer fantasy for religious educators, or anyone else for that matter, to imagine that they are doing the best they can. A good deal of solid empirical research suggests that at maximum, human beings use only about 10 percent of their abilities. Thus we can never do even a fraction of what we imagine to be our own best, to say nothing of the best. In the face of this evidence, we should set our religious instruction efforts on doing the best rather than merely doing our best.

Do we religious educators try to do the best day in and day out, year in and year out? Or do we frequently shrink from the perfectionist demands inherent in our call within a call by being content just to do our best?

To what extent are we religious educators satisfied with our level of effort? Are we ever satisfied with our performance? Are we ever satisfied with our ideals? If we answer yes to any of these three questions, then surely we are not trying to do the best.

Do we say that for the long haul we cannot do any more than we are presently doing? If we say this, if we even think this, then we are not doing the best—and maybe we are not even doing our best.

As Jesus was lifted up by doing the best, so we too can be lifted up only by doing the best. This is the true Christian vocation. This is the true religious education call within a call. This is the true sacrament of teaching.

Performance Objective: I will acquire the habit of always striving to do *the* best. I will develop this habit by never being satisfied with any aspect of my performance in the religious instruction apostolate. Instead, I will constantly exert myself to improve every dimension of my performance in the knowledge that only in this way will I be ceaselessly straining to do *the* best.

26

Extraordinarily Well

She was born into an obscure family in an obscure town in north-western France in the year of Our Lord 1873. After an uneventful childhood, she vanished behind the walls of a convent at the age of fifteen and lived there in total obscurity until her death nine years later. There was nothing remarkable about her appearance, her intelligence, or her demeanor. During her short life, only a small number of people met her or heard anything about her. At her death, just a handful of people were present at her funeral. No obituary announcing her death appeared in the newspaper. Few persons knew or even cared that she was dead. Yet this obscure young woman from an obscure family in an obscure town who lived her brief life in total obscurity became one of the most famous, most important, most beloved, and most influential Christian heroes in the twentieth century and beyond.

Why did she so deeply influence the spiritual lives of millions of people throughout the world? What did she do that gained the admiration and devotion of so many persons in so many countries for so many years? The answers to these questions hold great and immediate significance for the work and effectiveness of the religious educator.

At half past eleven on the night of January 2, 1873, Marie Françoise Thérèse Martin was born at Alençon, a small provincial town in the Normandy region of France. She was the youngest of nine children born in a thirteen year time frame to Louis and Zélie Martin. Four of the nine children died in infancy. Louis was a prosperous watchmaker and jeweler while Zélie ran a successful lace-making business. The home life of the Martin family was religiously devout and full of love. As a young man, Louis felt drawn to the monastic life. But at age thirty five he married Zélie Guérin, a skilled lace maker who earlier had been interested in entering the convent and taking the veil. Zélie was a strong-willed woman who, under the influence of the residual Jansenism still prevalent in France at the time, insisted on firm discipline in the Martin household.

Because Thérèse was the most sickly of the Martin children, she was sent a little more than two months after her birth to live with Rose Taillé, a wet nurse who resided in a farmhouse at Semallé, a nearby hamlet. This sojourn in the rural environment at Semallé proved beneficial to Thérèse's health, and after a year she returned to the Martin household in Alençon. When Thérèse was four years old, her mother died of breast cancer at the age of forty five. The death of her mother in August 1877 was a great shock to Thérèse. The happy, carefree period of her life was over.

In November of that same year Louis moved his family to Lisieux, another small provincial Norman town about fifty miles from Alençon. There his late wife's brother and sister-in-law were able to take care of the Martin family. Thérèse's older sisters Marie Louise (called Marie) and Marie-Pauline (called Pauline) also contributed significantly to raising their younger siblings and in general taking care of the entire family. Pauline became such a good substitute mother to Thérèse that she fondly called Pauline *ma petite mère* (my little mother). Thérèse's father was very tender, supportive, and nurturing toward her, so much so in fact that she later referred to him as giving her "maternal love." She was very devoted to her father throughout his life.

The second period of Thérèse's life lasted from 1877 to 1886. The death of her mother had traumatized the young Thérèse and plunged her into a state of sadness, hypersensitivity, depression, and occasional attacks of religious scruples, all of which she suffered for eight years. Later she was to call this period in her life "the winter of trial." Despite the strong undercurrent of sadness that Thérèse experienced during this period, nonetheless she did have many happy times. She kept rabbits, doves, a magpie, and a goldfish. Her favorite pet was a spaniel named Tom. She spent vacations with her family at the seaside. She had considerable talent as a mimic and entertained the family with her imitations of persons whom they all knew. There was a certain joyousness about Thérèse's natural personality that not even sadness or trauma could extinguish.

In 1881 she enrolled as a day student in the local Benedictine convent school. Though conscientious in her studies, she was by and large an average pupil. In 1883, at the age of ten, she contracted a strange illness characterized by a mixture of occasional convulsions, hysteria, and comas. For three months after the onset of her illness, physicians were unable to diagnose its cause. During this time she frequently prayed that Mary, the mother of God, would intercede with her son to deliver her from this illness. On May 13, while in prayer before a statue of Our Lady of Victories, she was instantaneously cured. From that time forward Thérèse firmly believed that her cure was miraculous and that the statue in whose presence she had been praying had actually smiled at her. She called it "Our Lady's smile."

On Christmas Eve 1886, shortly after she had returned to her house with her family after Midnight Mass, Thérèse had an intense religious experience. For the rest of her short life she referred to this deep experience as "my conversion." Her conversion marked the beginning of the third period of her life, a period that lasted for two years, This two-year period marked a major advance in Thérèse's religious development. She had always been deeply religious and had a distinct love for prayer. After her conversion, she became far more mature in her spirituality. Speaking of Thérèse's conversion and subsequent advancement to a significantly deeper religiosity, her sister Céline stated: "I was a witness to the sudden change [in Thérèse] . . . Her transformation was not limited solely to a new self-possession, but, at the same time, her soul could be seen to develop and grow in the practice of religious zeal and charity." As a result of her conversion, Thérèse developed an intense interest in the missionary apostolate and wished to suffer as a privileged way of uniting herself more closely to God. She also began to earnestly desire to enter the Discalced Carmelite Convent at

Lisieux as a contemplative nun, just her sisters Pauline and Louise had already done.

On the Feast of Pentecost in 1887, a few weeks after he had suffered his first stroke, Louis Martin gave his permission to Thérèse to enter the convent at Lisieux. Though her application was approved by the prioress of the convent, it was rejected by Jean-Baptiste Delatroëtte, the convent's ecclesiastical superior, on the grounds that at age fourteen Thérèse was too young. He counseled her to wait until she was twenty one. Thérèse, who was very persistent by nature, decided to go over the head of Delatroëtte. Accompanied by her father, she made a personal appeal to Flavien Hugonin, the scholarly bishop of Bayeaux and Lisieux. After patiently listening to Thérèse, Hugonin told her that he would take the matter under advisement.

In the autumn of that same year, Louis took his two daughters Thérèse and Céline on a pilgrimage to Rome. On Sunday, November 20, after six days of touring the sites of the Eternal City, Thérèse attended a Mass celebrated by Leo XIII for a small group of pilgrims in the private papal chapel in St. Peter's Basilica. After this Mass there was a second Mass which was followed by a papal audience. During the audience the pope, dressed in the traditional white cassock and shoulder cape, and wearing a white zucchetto on his head, sat in a big armchair as was then customary for events of this kind. One by one the pilgrims passed by the seated Leo to receive his personal papal blessing. When the spunky and precocious Thérèse was presented to the pope, she did not content herself to passively kiss his hand and receive his blessing, but in an act specifically prohibited at papal audiences of that time, boldly initiated a conversation with him. She forthrightly asked the pontiff to allow her to enter the Lisieux convent when she became fifteen. Leo was taken aback at this unexpected audaciousness on the part of the sweet teenage girl kneeling in front of him, and asked for clarification from Maurice Révérony, the vicar general of the diocese of Bayeaux/Lisieux who at that very moment happened to be standing close to the pope's right-hand side with a look of surprise and disapproval on his face. Révérony spoke to Leo: "Holy Father, this child is anxious to enter Carmel at fifteen, and her superiors are looking into the matter at this moment." The pope then looked at Thérèse with great kindness and simply said: "Very well, my child, do what your superiors tell you." Undeterred, Thérèse intrepidly pressed on, not satisfied with what the pope had told her. She put her hands on his knees, an act of boldness and familiarity unheard on the part of a laywoman in those days. "Yes," Thérèse told the pope, "but if you'd say the word, Most Holy Father, everyone would go along." Stunned but nonetheless impressed by Thérèse's obvious sincerity and tenacity, Leo fixed his eyes on her and said in a slow manner emphasizing every syllable: "All's well, all's well. If God wants you to enter, you will." Looking back on this incident a few years later, Thérèse wrote that Leo "spoke with such earnestness and conviction that I can still hear him saying it."

The pope's words gave Thérèse increased courage, and she wanted to press on some more. Two members of the papal guards then intervened in order to remove Thérèse so that other pilgrims could receive the pope's personal blessing. They attempted to lift Thérèse from her knees. Despite this effort on the part of the papal guards, Thérèse steadfastly kept her arms on the pope's knees, so that finally the exasperated papal guards had to remove her by force. As they were doing so, Leo put his right hand to her lips and then blessed her. He followed her with his eyes for quite a long time.

A little over a month later, on December 28, 1887, the bishop of Bayeaux and Lisieux gave his permission for Thérèse to enter the convent of the Discalced Carmelites at Lisieux.

The day chosen for her entrance into the Carmel was April 9, 1888, the day on which the nuns there were celebrating the feast of the Annunciation, transferred from March 25 because of Lent. On the previous evening the whole family gathered at the Martin house to bid a warm and loving farewell to Thérèse. Though she ardently desired to enter the Carmel, she was naturally sad at having to leave home. She would miss Les Buissonnets, the large and lovely house in which she and her sisters and her father had shared so many enjoyable times. She would miss her pets, especially Tom the spaniel with whom she had romped so freely. She would miss all her favorite spots, the shrubbery in which she and Céline played hide-and-seek, the place in the garden where she had built little altars, the room where her father would go to think quiet thoughts, and all these other sights and sounds and places to which she had become so attached over the years. She realized that never again would she be able to enjoy the simple pleasures that the average person takes for granted. As a young teenager she had often told others that her only wish in life was to be a saint. She left the world and entered the Carmel because she believed that in this way she could best make her fervent wish come true.

In entering the Carmel Thérèse knowingly joined one of the most austere and contemplative orders of women in the church.

The monastic Carmelite Order for men was founded by St. Berthold around 1154 on Mount Carmel in what was then called Palestine. The definitive document outlining the purpose and lifeway of the Carmelites was the Primitive Rule of Carmel, which was written by St. Albert of Jerusalem between 1206 and 1214 and was approved by Innocent 1V in 1247. The purpose of the Carmelite Order was to help its members draw closer to God through the regular practice of intense asceticism and deep contemplation in a monastic environment. In 1452 the Carmelite Order for nuns was established with the same objective as its male counterpart. A little over a century of later, the Spanish Carmelite nun and mystic Teresa of Ávila found that though the Carmelite nuns of her day still lived a relatively austere life, nonetheless with the passage of time it had become somewhat more relaxed than the life envisioned by the Primitive Rule. Under Teresa's dynamic leadership, a new branch of the Carmelite nuns was established in order to return to the spirit and practices of the Primitive Rule. The technical name for this new branch is the Reformed Carmelites. In popular parlance this branch was and still is called the Discalced Carmelites because unlike the original group, members of the new branch, out of a spirit of poverty, wear sandals rather than shoes (*calceus* is the Latin word for shoe).

The Rule of the Reformed Carmelite nuns is not permeated with an air of gloom or misery. Rather, it is suffused with a passionate, devout, and joyous enthusiasm for the cause of living one's life in as close and as intimate a relationship with God as is humanly possible. This passionate enthusiasm is nicely summed up in one of the Carmelite mottoes: *"Zelo zelatus sum pro Domino Deo exercituum."* ("With zeal have I been zealous for the Lord God of Hosts.") The goal of the Discalced Carmelites is total commitment to God as actualized in an atmosphere of holy solitude, silence, prayer, and asceticism. All these practices are intended to foster contemplation, the pure untrammeled encounter of a person with God devoid of all outside attachments or distractions. The Rule does not regard the life of a cloistered Carmelite nun to be passive or sterile, but as dynamic and fruitful. The Reformed Rule turns a person's perspective upside down. In the cloister, things that are regarded by the outside world as good or as achievements, such as riches and fame, become meaningless, whereas those things that are judged by the outside world as bad or as problems, such as discomfort and pain and hunger, are transformed by love into opportunities to grow toward deeper union with God.

In short, the life and work of a Discalced Carmelite nun is exclusively that of prayer and penance, both of which are offered up by the nun for the salvation of souls, the reparation of sins, the work of the church, and the sanctification of priests. Though theirs is not an active apostolate in the formal sense of the word, the Carmelites are deeply concerned with apostolic success in the world outside the cloister. They are convinced that their prayers and mortifications directly and powerfully influence the life of the world and success of the church in its overall mission to bring all persons to God.

For many young women entering the Carmel, life in this austere kind of convent comes as a great shock because it is so radically different from their previous existence outside the cloister. For Thérèse, however, life at the Lisieux convent was more of an extension of the deep religious life she had been living with her family than it was a wholly different lifestyle and set of perspectives.

Thérèse's life in the Lisieux convent was typical of all Discalced Carmelite nuns. It was very ordinary—nothing exceptional or unusual for a cloistered nun in an austere religious order of that time. The convent building was deliberately unheated except for a room where the nuns could go for a brief period of time to warm themselves if really necessary. The cell in which she lived was exceedingly spartan, measuring two meters in width and three meters in length (about seven feet by ten feet). It had a bare wooden floor, a small writing table for the lap, and a large hourglass. A jug of water and a basin were placed on the floor. Her bed was the same basic type found in peasant cottages in France: wooden planks lying on top of a trestle and covered with a *paillasse* (a canvas-covered bag of straw upon which to lie). Linen sheets were not used. Like all the nuns in the Carmel, she slept on a woolen sheet covered by a single woolen blanket.

Her daily life at the Lisieux Carmel occupying a red brick building on the rue de Liverot was very plain and simple—totally uneventful as measured by life in the world outside the convent walls. Like the other nuns, Thérèse arose at 5:00 A.M. in the summer, 6:00 A.M. in the winter. She washed, donned her woolen underwear and floor-length brown habit made of coarse wool, and put on her sandals. At the appointed time she, like the other nuns, filed slowly and silently into the cloistered section of the public chapel and prayed quietly behind the sturdy iron grille that concealed the nuns from other persons in the chapel and vice versa. Led by the prioress, Thérèse and the other nuns intoned or chanted, depending on the day, Prime and Terce, the third and fourth set of the daily cycle of the Liturgy of the Hours. (Formerly called the Divine Office, the Liturgy of the Hours is a monastic practice in which the monks or nuns come together in communal prayer at various times during the twenty-four-hour day to glorify God in and for each part of that day. Each of the eight monastic hours consists of the intonation or chanting of Psalms, Scripture passages, Patristic readings, hymns, and excerpts from the lives of the saints. The Liturgy of the Hours derives from the custom in the ancient church when the early Christian communities gathered for morning, daytime, and evening prayer.) After the Liturgy of the Hours, Mass began. On days permitted by the prioress, each nun received the Eucharist by successively kneeling in front of the small opening in the grille that was just large enough for the priest to place the consecrated Host on the waiting tongue. At the conclusion of Mass, the nuns spent some time in prayerful thanksgiving to God.

After the thanksgiving, Thérèse and the other nuns filed into the refectory to have breakfast. Each nun bowed before the crucifix and slipped noiselessly into her assigned place around a large wooden table. At her place were laid a crockery bowl, a dish, a pitcher, a knife, and a wooden spoon. Breakfast, like all meals at the Carmel, was simple but nonetheless sufficient to keep the nuns in adequate health. Meat was never served at any meal—perpetual abstinence was the rule. From the Feast of the Holy Cross (September 14) until Easter the Reformed Carmelites underwent their rigorous annual fast. During each meal the nuns ate silently while one of their number read aloud from some worthwhile book on spirituality. After meals there was a short time for recreation in which the nuns would chat with one another.

Five hours a day Thérèse, like the other nuns, spent at manual labor such as cooking, sewing, cleaning, nursing the sick nuns, and making the small wafers of unleavened bread for use as hosts. This work was done in a spirit of prayer. Indeed, prayer thoroughly infused whatever work the nuns were assigned. When they were not working, eating, or sleeping, the nuns were primarily at formal prayer. Formal prayer was of three types: private contemplative prayer, communal prayer during Mass, and public prayer with the other nuns in the chapel intoning or chanting the various parts of the Liturgy of the Hours. Before retiring for the night, the nuns went to the chapel where they recited or chanted Matins and Lauds (the first two sets of prayers of the Liturgy of the Hours), made an examination of conscience on what transpired during the day, and then silently filed one by one to their cells for bed.

A person who enters a particular convent of the Carmel stays there for the rest of her life, except in those cases in which she is sent to join a newly established convent. There are no vacations.

In short, Thérèse's life in the Lisieux Carmel was as outwardly ordinary, prosaic, and matter-of-fact as one could possibly imagine.

Thérèse entered the Lisieux Carmel in the traditional way, that of a postulant seeking full admission to the Order. Nine months later, on January 10, 1889, she took the habit and became a novice. On the Feast of the Nativity of Mary, September 8, 1890 she took her final (perpetual) vows. Sixteen days later she took off her novice's white veil and put on the black veil worn by nuns who have made their perpetual vows. She also took as her new name Thérèse of the Child Jesus. Some time later, on her own initiative, she added to her name the words "and of the Holy Face." In 1893 she was appointed assistant mistress of novices. These cut-and-dry events, ordinary and indeed prosaic for any sister, nun, priest, or brother in any religious order in the world, sum up all that was visibly noteworthy in the life of Thérèse.

Before she entered the convent, Thérèse had been precocious, witty, and charming. During her nine and a half years in the Carmel she retained these traits. She remained full of life, cheerful, jocular, and childlike, all quite different from the ideal of stiff and solemn spirituality so prevalent in the last quarter of the nineteenth century. But together with her sunny personality there was also a period of anguishing trial that God apparently reserves to those who love him dearly. During the Eastertide of 1896 Thérèse was beset with what the great spiritual masters call "the dark night of the soul," an invasion of the soul by a seeming absence of God and a concomitant deprivation of those personal delights that typically accompany a life lived wholly for the Lord. She was frequently buffeted with temptations against the faith. As Thérèse herself described it, "the thought of heaven, up to then so sweet to me" became "no longer anything but the cause of struggle and torment." Thérèse's dark night of the soul was to be with her until the time she died.

Thérèse was sickly as a young child, and illness continued to stalk her in the convent and finally led to her death at an early age. Throughout the sixth months prior to her death, her physical suffering became increasingly acute. Her body was racked with a fluctuating fever that sometimes "burned like fire," to use her own words. While she was enduring the fever, she perspired so intensely that her sweat soaked through her *paillasse*, dehydrating her in the process. As a consequence, she suffered continually from thirst. She could not hold food down and vomited often. Thérèse coughed frequently, often with the kind of dry cough that is so painful. She became emaciated and very weak physically. She had great difficulty in breathing. All these different forms of sickness were related to her central disease of tuberculosis, which was to kill her in the end. But despite all her sufferings, she tried as best she could to continue following the austere Carmelite way of life as perfectly as she could, until she was placed in the convent infirmary. Commenting on the physical passion she was enduring, Thérèse observed that obviously a central part of her vocation was to suffer. In this way she could draw closer to Jesus, whose sufferings were as intense as they were infinite. And in this way she could make reparation for her own sins and for the sins of others, thus enabling persons to reform their lives. There is a sense in which all suffering is ordinary in that everyone here on earth endures small or great suffering. Thérèse strove to endure her intense suffering in the best manner possible from a religious standpoint.

In early January 1895 during evening recreation, Thérèse spoke about her childhood memories to her sisters Pauline and Louise, who were living in the same convent. Pauline, now called Sister Agnes of Jesus, had become the prioress. While listening to her younger sister, Pauline thought it would be enjoyable for the other nuns during recreation periods to read about the lively Thérèse's experiences before entering the Carmel. Therefore, somewhat hesitantly, Pauline, in her role as prioress, ordered Thérèse to write down the memories of her childhood. Thérèse was then twenty-two years old.

What Thérèse did was to write an account of her spiritual journey in life. She wrote this account in the form of three distinct letters, composed between January 1895 and July 1897. She dedicated the first letter to Pauline, the second to Louise (now Sister Marie of the Sacred Heart), and the third to Marie de Gonzague, her former prioress. The letters were uneven in length and were written quickly. The handwriting in her letters progressively deteriorated, reflecting the decline in her physical condition. The final part of her last letter is almost an illegible scrawl. Her literary style was typical of the romantic, sentimental, and flushed prose of the era. Originally her three letters were intended for use exclusively by the nuns of the Lisieux Carmel. Toward the very end of her life, sensing that what she had written might be useful for others, Thérèse asked Pauline to put her three letters in book form.

It was the custom among the Carmelites to send an obituary notice to other convents when one of their number died. Rather than send an obituary notice about Thérèse after her death, the nuns at the Lisieux Carmel arranged to have her letters published privately in book form and sent to a number of other Carmelite convents. The book was so well received that it was decided to print 2,000 copies for distribution to the general public. A year later, in 1899, an additional 4,000 copies were printed. The book was given the title *L'histoire d'une âme* (*Story of a Soul*). The main theme of the book was the "Little Way", that of achieving religious perfection by doing ordinary things extraordinarily well.

The central force of both Thérèse's life and the Little Way was love. The final word she wrote in each of three letters which make up *Story of a Soul* was love. She once wrote: "You are a beggar for my love. You want my heart, Jesus, and I give it totally for you." For Thérèse and her Little Way, love is not mawkish, easy, or ethereal; rather, love is centered on the grinding, difficult, and nitty-gritty task of sacrificing oneself day in and day out for God. "To live for love is to climb Calvary with Jesus," she wrote. In another passage Thérèse stated: "In order to live in one single act of perfect Love, I offer myself as a sacrificial victim to your [God's] merciful Love." In keeping with her Little Way, Thérèse was completely convinced that it is her very ordinariness, her very incapacity with respect to achieving anything extraordinary, that gives her the boldness to offer herself totally as a victim of God's love. God's love chooses the ordinary in life because God's love is necessarily a lowering process that touches total nothingness and makes this very nothingness the fuel for its flame. In short, it was love that gave Thérèse the eyes to see how the ordinary could be transformed into something extraordinary. It was love which gave her the burning desire to do ordinary things extraordinarily well.

She liked to remind herself that what matters most is not great deeds but great love.

Thérèse was a woman of her time and country. Prior to entering the Carmel, she, like most French persons from Louis XIV onward, thirsted for *gloire* (glory). She imagined herself as a papal Zouave, dying gallantly in battle in defense of the church. She pictured herself as a missionary traveling to distant lands and majestically planting the cross on heathen soil. She earnestly desired to become a priest. But most of all she wanted to become a martyr, to give up her life in total imitation of the passion and death of the Suffering Servant. She saw herself, like so many of the saints in the ancient church, dramatically offering her neck to the executioner. All of these fantasies were extraordinary deeds sure to bring her great *gloire*. But in the end she forsook *gloire* by choosing to live an ordinary life as a cloistered Carmelite nun. By joining the Carmel, she believed that through her prayers and penances—quite ordinary for a cloistered nun in an austere religious order—she could do more good for more people than if she were a papal Zouave or a priest or a martyr or a missionary in some far-off land. For her, real martyrdom lay in offering herself as a sacrificial victim for God through the ordinary daily prayers and austerities of life in the Carmel. Such an ordinary life would not bring her *gloire*, she thought, but it would help Jesus become better known throughout the world and would bring her closer to her Lord. To do ordinary things out of total love for Jesus is a form of martyrdom, Thérèse observed, and it is the kind of unglamorous martyrdom she chose to suffer.

Today, Thérèse is best known, loved, and imitated because of her teaching of what she herself called "The Little Way" of spiritual perfection as described in her autobiography. She once defined The Little Way as "the way of spiritual childhood, the way of trust and absolute surrender." The Little Way is not a specific technique for attaining spiritual perfection. It is not a single virtue. It is not a slogan. Rather, The Little Way is a basic attitude, orientation, and pattern of life. The Little Way is a lifestyle that is focused on on objectively trivial events and minor details all of which are entered into and performed extraordinarily well. The Little Way centers on sanctity as achieved through the exemplary performance of minutiae.

It was in the period from the end of 1894 to the beginning of 1895 that Thérèse made her discovery of The Little Way. She was acutely aware of her own ordinariness as a person and the ordinariness of her way of life as a Carmelite nun. She desired to be a saint. But how could she achieve holiness in light of the fact that she was so very ordinary and lived such an ordinary life? She knew that she was, objectively speaking, a "helpless nonentity", a "poor little soul", to use her own words. She believed that she did not have the capability of practicing great virtues. She was profoundly cognizant of the vast abyss that separated her, an obscure grain of sand as she called herself, from persons like Paul, Augustine, and Teresa of Ávila, whose enormous personal gifts and divine graces had enabled them to be spiritual giants. And she was well aware that her life spent in a walled-in Carmelite convent situated in a backwater town did not afford her the opportunity of performing great deeds of sanctity that would electrify the world. She felt that she was much too little in a spiritual sense to successfully climb the steep path to perfection. How could she, despite her littleness, achieve sanctity? Then one day the light hit her. Sanctity does not lie in the achievement of great deeds but in the way in which one performs any deed, large or small. Any deed, no matter how great or how small, is rendered great in the spiritual realm to the extent that it is performed extraordinarily well. She resolved to achieve sanctity not despite her spiritual littleness but through it.

She came to see that The Little Way constituted the preeminent path to sanctity, not just for her with her limited gifts and opportunities but for all those millions of other persons who had ordinary talents, ordinary jobs, and ordinary lifestyles. "I implore you, O Jesus, to look down in mercy on a whole multitude of souls that share my littleness," she wrote. In another place, she observed: "In my Little Way there are only very ordinary things: it is essential that little souls should be able to do everything I do." She saw that her vocation, and the vocation of countless other average persons throughout the world, was to do ordinary things extraordinarily well. "I am very little," she wrote, "and want to remain little."

Thérèse's Little Way was perceived as really little and anything but extraordinary in the eyes of the nuns who lived with her in the Lisieux Carmel. As far as the other nuns could ascertain, her life was no different from any other member of the community. During the process that, after her death eventually led to Thérèse's canonization, Sister Saint Vincent de Paul, a nun in the Lisieux Carmel, remarked to her interrogators: "I do not know why people are talking so much about Sister Thérèse of the Child Jesus. She didn't do anything extraordinary. One does not even see her practicing virtue. You wouldn't even say that she is a good nun."

But it was love, great love, that elevated Thérèse's Little Way to the level of true greatness. It was out of complete love that she did ordinary things extraordinarily well. She frequently reminded herself that "love is not a matter of lofty sentiments: love means doing things." She liked to say that "love needs to be proved by action." Because she was an ordinary person living an ordinary life, all she could offer Jesus was, as she herself put it, "mere nothings, but done with great love."

By ability, vocation, and location, Thérèse could not attain notable or dazzling achievements. Central to her view of The Little Way is that she lays emphasis not on the successful attainment of any task large or small but entirely on the love that motivates and accompanies this attainment. Although the successful achievement of a small task is not in itself great, the love that motivates and accompanies this achievement is truly great. And it is love that enables a person day in and day out to perform ordinary tasks extraordinarily well. Thus it was out of love, and with the awareness that love is tested in action, that Thérèse habitually rendered the nuns in the convent all sorts of services which were in themselves so insignificant that the other nuns did not even notice these helpful acts as, for example, regularly folding with great care the mantles forgotten by one or another nun.

For Thérèse, nothing is really true or holy unless and until it is perfected in the moment-to-moment fulfillment of God's will. This fulfillment comes about for most people, including Thérèse, by doing ordinary things extraordinarily well. It is genuinely difficult to strive on a habitual basis to do ordinary things extraordinarily well. This kind of habitual action involves dying to one's ego because the very ordinariness of a task does not elicit intrinsic motivation to perform the task in anything but an ordinary way, if even that. Going against the personal and objective grain by habitually doing ordinary things extraordinarily well involves a strong measure of heroism. Yet it is precisely heroism in the service of God that is the hallmark of holiness and the badge of sanctity.

Sanctity is doing something heroic for God. Great sanctity is doing something heroic for God on a habitual basis. Thérèse's Little Way of habitually doing ordinary things extraordinarily well represents an especially high form of sanctity because it is high form of heroism. It gets no rewards. It gets no plaudits. It gets no place in the limelight. It does not give the person any of the psychological rewards that typically follow the performance of a heroic act. But habitually doing ordinary things extraordinarily well is a true and authentic form of martyrdom, all the more so because such activity is totally devoid of the glamorous trappings or front-page recognition that often come with martyrdom. It is the seemingly unheroic and totally unromantic character of habitually striving to do ordinary things extraordinarily well that elevates such acts to a top tier of the heroic.

In one of the most famous passages of her spiritual autobiography, Thérèse wrote: "This shall be my life, to scatter flowers—to miss no single opportunity of making some small sacrifice, here by a smiling look, there by a kindly word, always doing the tiniest things right, and doing them for love." Down to our own day, Thérèse is often called "The Little Flower."

In April 1897 Thérèse entered the terminal and most excruciating phase of her tubercular condition. In addition to her seemingly unendurable physical sufferings there came the darkest of dark nights of the soul, enormous and searing temptations against faith that were to be with her until the end. Shortly before her death she said; "I didn't think it was possible to suffer so much." She offered her sufferings to God as a victim soul, a victim who was privileged to place her physical agonies at the foot of the throne of God in reparation for her own sins and the sins of others.

During her physical and spiritual agony those final months, the other nuns enjoyed visiting Thérèse in the infirmary because she was so cheerful. This delightful cheerfulness in the teeth of excruciating physical and spiritual pain was not only a manifestation of her great love for God but also a sign of her authentic love for the other nuns. She did not wish them to feel at all sad that one of their number was dying.

A few minutes after seven o'clock in the evening of September 30, 1897, gazing steadfastly at a crucifix and surrounded by the nuns of her community, Thérèse of the Child Jesus breathed her last. Her final words were: "My God, I love you."

She was twenty-four years old when she died.

A photograph of her taken shortly after her death shows a face that was fresh, young, and at peace.

A few days later, on October 4, 1897, Thérèse was buried in the cemetery at Lisieux. On the cross over her grave are inscribed the words she once had spoken: "I will spend my heaven in doing good upon earth." Thérèse believed that the purpose of her whole existence was to help others become holy. It was in this spirit that she once wrote: "I shall be more useful in heaven than on earth." And it was in the spirit of usefulness to others that she lived and died.

Not long before Thérèse's death, one of the nuns in her convent remarked: "Our Sister Thérèse will soon be dead. I really can't imagine what Reverend Mother will find to say about her once she is gone. It won't be easy for Reverend Mother, I can tell you, because this little sister, charming as she is, has certainly never done anything worth the telling."

The world outside the Lisieux Carmel saw things differently.

Thérèse's spiritual autobiography, *L'histoire d'une âme*, became an international best-seller not long after her death. It is quite possibly the most widely read book on spirituality in the entire world in the entire twentieth century. It has been translated into nearly forty languages ranging from English to Arabic, Chinese to Swahili. As Thérèse's autobiography spread like wildfire throughout the world, letters inundated the Lisieux Carmel. There were countless reports from persons in every continent attesting to spiritual and even material favors coming to persons who sought the intercession of the Little Flower before the throne of God. In Thérèse's case, the Holy See took the extraordinary step of waiving its virtually ironclad fifty-year waiting period prior to the beginning of an official Vatican investigation on whether or not a person of outstanding holiness should be beatified. On May 17, 1925, a scant twenty-eight years after her death, Thérèse was canonized a saint, a time frame unprecedented for its brevity in the modern world, and all the more amazing when one considers the intense rigor of the investigatory process. The canonization ceremony took place in the magnificent basilica of St. Peter's in Rome in the presence of thirty-four cardinals, over two hundred archbishops and bishops, innumerable priests and nuns, and legions of laypersons. It was reliably estimated that over 60,000 persons jammed St. Peter's Basilica for the event. Half a million more packed the square outside the basilica. St. Peter's itself was lavishly decorated with garlands of roses. The following year she was officially declared, along with the great Apostle to the Indies Francis Xavier, principal co-patron of the missions. Later the French government declared her the secondary patron of France, along with Joan of Arc. In 1997 John Paul II proclaimed her Doctor of the Church, only the third woman ever to receive that title. (Catherine of Siena and Teresa of Ávila were the other two women who had earlier been declared as official universal teachers of the Church. Thirty males have been declared Doctor of the Church.) One or another statue of Thérèse stands in thousands and thousands of churches in every corner of the globe. Her patronage is invoked by millions of persons devout and not so devout throughout the world. Countless persons of every age, clime, and social station wear around their necks a medal bearing the likeness of St. Thérèse—including Tara Lipinski on the day that she won the 1998 Winter Olympic gold medal for women's figure skating to become, at fifteen, the youngest person ever to win that event. Every October 3 her feast day is publicly celebrated at Mass in all Catholic churches worldwide: in cities and in rural hamlets, in poor parishes and in wealthy ones, in industrialized countries and in woefully underdeveloped nations, in church buildings or at worship service on the battlefield,

In the end, Thérèse got her *gloire*. It was a *gloire* far more extravagant than anything the child Thérèse could have ever imagined or hoped for.

What was it that gave Thérèse her outstanding sanctity and the worldwide *gloire* that flowed from this sanctity? In his formal announcement of her canonization, Pius XI gave the answer: Thérèse had fulfilled her vocation and had achieved sanctity "without going beyond the common order of things." In short, the key to Thérèse's incredible success in answering her own call within a call was doing ordinary things extraordinarily well.

For the most part, the religious instruction apostolate is by and large a vocation to, in, and for the ordinary. Our daily activities as religious educators almost always lie within the realm of the ordinary. The only thing that we religious educators can do to make our apostolate exceptional is to perform ordinary tasks extraordinarily well. Our success as religious educators does not primarily lie in the achievement of great deeds because our apostolate typically does not present us with the opportunity of performing monumental or even noteworthy deeds. Just as Thérèse's call within a call meant that she spent her life in the prosaic tasks of cooking, sewing, cleaning, nursing the sick, praying, and penance, so too our call within a call as religious educators means that we spend our lives in the prosaic tasks of motivating learners, preparing the nitty-gritty details of the pedagogical event, evaluating the degree to which learning takes place, engaging in professional reading, and all the other small but essential details involved in religious instruction activity. If we religious educators are to be successful and holy in what we do, then should we not immediately adopt as our touchstone The Little Way—in our case, The Little Way of Religious Instruction? Does anything else make sense? Is not any other course of action on our part an exercise of fantasized grandiosity?

The sacrament of teaching is, in large measure, a sacrament of the ordinary. It is a sacrament that, if performed extraordinarily well, can accomplish truly great and wonderful things.

To what extent do we realize that our success as religious educators (as well as success in our spiritual lives) comes through the moment-to-moment fulfillment of God's will, which in the case of the religious instruction apostolate means performing our ordinary teaching tasks extraordinarily well? To what degree do we religious educators hunger down deep for *gloire* and concomitantly chafe because we have to regularly engage in the prosaic demands of religious instruction activity? How much do we secretly thirst to attain *gloire* by winning thousands of souls to God by the force of our eloquence or by dazzling programs we establish or by going out into the streets and converting all whom we meet? But all these noteworthy deeds will almost never cover us with *gloire* because they rarely happen. What will surely win *gloire* for us religious educators is the habitual performance of all the ordinary tasks of our apostolate extraordinarily well. It was The Little Way that brought *gloire* to Thérèse and of a certainty it will be The Little Way of Religious Instruction that will bring *gloire* to almost every religious educator.

Our success as religious educators will not be visibly noteworthy or famous because our religious instruction activities by and large are not visibly noteworthy or famous. But there is a vast difference between visibly noteworthy on the one hand and noteworthy in the eyes of God on the other hand. In the divine perspective, what is truly noteworthy is not so much what we do but how we do it. From God's perspective, what is important is not so much the objective nature of the deed we perform but rather the quality (the degree of extraordinariness), which we invest in the performance of that deed. Thus we religious educators must ask ourselves the question: To what extent do we want to be famous in front of others or to what extent to we want to be famous in the eyes of God? To what extent to we seek human adulation by performing flashy and monumental tasks, and to what extent do we seek God's affirmation through doing ordinary things extraordinarily well?

Generally speaking, most of us religious educators are ordinary people. Thus in many respects we are not equipped by talent or disposition to perform extraordinary deeds. But each of us can acquire the skill and the will to perform in an extraordinary manner the ordinary tasks that consume almost all of our apostolate. How deeply do we appreciate the fact that the only thing that will make us extraordinary is transforming our ordinariness into extraordinariness by doing ordinary things extraordinarily well?

The mainspring of habitually striving to do ordinary things extraordinarily well is love. As Thérèse of Lisieux liked to say, what matters is not great deeds but great love. Love is the only force powerful enough to motivate us religious educators to accept the drudgery and grinding difficulty of doing ordinary things extraordinarily well. Love is not primarily a feeling. Love consists primarily of doing things with all our heart. What elevated Thérèse to greatness, what gained her immeasurable *gloire,* was not great deeds but great love. What can each of us religious educators do both now and on a regular basis to make love the foundation and mainspring of all the ordinary things we are called upon to do in our apostolate?

Habitually performing our ordinary religious instruction tasks in an extraordinary fashion is true heroism. Performing ordinary religious instruction deeds extraordinarily well is very difficult because this kind of activity does not give us the rush of excitement which comes from extending ourselves beyond the limit for a prominent cause which all can see. Being engaged in the ordinary does not give us a sense of being involved in something very important. Yet this very lack of rush of excitement, this very lack of visibility, this very lack of feeling part of a great cause is precisely what contributes so significantly to the heroic character of doing ordinary things extraordinary well. The heroism involved in The Little Way of Religious Instruction is more heroic than the highly visible deeds of heroism because it involves the absence of the kind of praise and adulation that accrues to those who perform visible deeds of heroism. To what extent do we religious educators joyfully accept the unnoticed heroic tasks we are called upon to endure in the extraordinary discharge of our ordinary religious instruction activities?

The Little Way of Religious Instruction involves martyrdom, a martyrdom of ego by striving in each and every instance to do ordinary things extraordinarily well—when we are tired, when we are aggravated, when we face an unappreciative learner, when our work does not seem to be having much impact on others. To what extent do we warmly embrace the martyrdom that God has sent each of us through the exercise of our religious instruction apostolate?

Every one of us religious educators has to suffer, though most of us are not asked by God to suffer as intensely as Thérèse. How often do we religious educators consciously offer up our sufferings in union with God for the success of our religious instruction apostolate?

The Little Way of Religious Instruction is possibly the best single way to sanctify our religious instruction work and to sanctify ourselves in the process. Our success as religious educators, and our success as Christians seeking to draw close to God, depends in no small measure on how wholeheartedly and how habitually we clothe ourselves from head to toe with The Little Way of Religious Instruction.

Performance Objective: Each morning I will select from my repertoire of religious instruction activities one very small task. During the day I will work hard to accomplish this small task extraordinarily well, knowing that by acting in such a way I will be truly living The Little Way of Religious Instruction.

27

A Matter of Love

There hangs in my home a lovely framed reproduction of the famous painting of Thomas More made by his onetime houseguest Hans Holbein. From the very first time I came to know about More many years earlier, I have always entertained a special admiration for this deeply principled and incorruptible Englishman.

At all times and in all circumstances, More was his own man. His was a life completely committed to uncompromising personal integrity to himself and to his fundamental principles. As far as it is possible for a human being, More never sold out, whether in matters large or small, personal or political, familial or ecclesiastical.

In the last years of his life, when the chips were really down for him, More held fast to his honor and integrity when almost all of the English nobility, bishops, university professors, and even close family members forsook their own honor and integrity for the sake of expediency. More's supreme and unswerving allegiance was always to God who, while immanently present in secular and ecclesiastical affairs, nevertheless simultaneously surpasses terrestrial phenomena.

Another major aspect of More's personality that I very much savor is the way in which apparent anomalies coexisted in a ready and easy manner in his everyday behavior, often at the same time and under the same set of circumstances: jest together with profundity, wisecracking together with expressions of deep religious conviction, exquisitely constructed shafty remarks that cut an adversary to the quick together with words and prayers and acts of charity toward those selfsame adversaries.

221

More was a major bridge figure between the medieval and modern eras. He was simultaneously a medieval and a modern, both in his personal life and his professional life. He merged the medieval trust in stability with the modern desire for change. He combined the medieval thirst for integrity with the modern striving for productive opportuneness. He blended the medieval pursuit of honor with the modern quest for honors. He melded the medieval conviction of the absoluteness of conscience with the modern tendency toward circumstantial flexibility in matters affecting conscience. He intermingled the medieval fondness for humility with the modern appetite for ambition. He admixed the medieval thrust toward the otherworldly with the modern inclination toward the this-worldly. He interlaced the medieval orientation toward the interior life with the modern pursuit of the exterior life. And finally, he coalesced the medieval vision of the seamless international unity of Christendom with the modern emphasis on the substantial separateness of national differences and spiritualities.

It was toward the beginning of February 1478 that Thomas More was born in London. His mother Agnes died when he was still a small child. His father John was an up-and-coming lawyer. Thomas completed his first years of schooling at a classically grounded grammar school in which all subjects were taught and learned in Latin. More was fortunate to spend the next few years as a boarding student and page in the household of John Morton at Lambeth Palace. The learned and politically astute Morton was a cardinal, Archbishop of Canterbury, Henry VII's Lord Chancellor of England, and a fine canon lawyer. At Morton's prompting, More entered the University of Oxford at about the age of fourteen to continue his classical education. John More was so upset by this turn of events that he pressured his son emotionally and financially to abandon classical studies and become a lawyer. After two years at Oxford, and somewhat against his will, Thomas More transferred to the University of Cambridge to pursue education in the law.

For about four years during his legal studies, More lived at the Charterhouse. This was a monastery of the Carthusians, the most austere order then and now in the church. More did not totally live the life of a Carthusian monk during his stay at the Charterhouse, but rather came and went as he pleased. Nonetheless he did attempt to participate in monastic life as much as his legal studies permitted. During much of his time at the Charterhouse, More seriously contemplated becoming a Carthusian monk. But in the end, he decided that his own passionate attraction to women was a sign from God that his vocation was not to be a celibate monk but instead to consciously serve God as a married man in the legal profession.

Though More decided against becoming a monk, he nonetheless warmly embraced some the ascetic practices and deeply pervasive spirituality that he learned while living among the Carthusians. It was during his years in the monastery that More began his lifelong practices of always wearing a hairshirt, daily devout recitation of the Little Office, and the use of the discipline. Throughout his life, he often spent long nightly vigils in prayer.

Holbein's famous portrait of Thomas More shows the Englishman resplendent in the finest clothes of the day and wearing an impressive chain of office. To understand the real More, one must look not only at the gorgeous garments but also realize that under the fine linen and cushy velvet and costly fur he was wearing an exceptionally irritating hairshirt next to his skin. The only two people who knew that More always wore a hairshirt were his confessor and his eldest daughter who regularly washed it.

Not long after he left the Charterhouse More married seventeen-year-old Jane Colt, the eldest daughter of a country squire of modest means. Jane, whom More later called his *"cara uxorcula"* ("dear little wife") was an uneducated rustic girl to whom More taught the humanities during their marriage. She gave birth to four children in rapid succession and then died in the summer of 1511 at the age of 23. Within a month More married again, this time to Alice Middleton, the widow of a prosperous merchant. Alice, who was six years older than More, was a blunt, rude, shrewish, and in many ways an ignorant woman. More married her because he felt he needed an experienced housewife, an efficient manager of his household, and a structured caring stepmother to his four children. Alice admirably fulfilled these tasks. But she really never understood Thomas or his fundamental principles of life.

Family life in the More household was religious, cultured, and delightful. His house at Chelsea included a chapel and a library, joining under one roof the two chief engines of More's life, namely, piety and learning. Prayers were said at meals, and passages from Scripture and from the Fathers of the Church were read aloud. More could not bear to waste a minute; thus he did not allow idleness and frivolous games in his house. Instead, everyone was encouraged to pursue learning and to engage in useful tasks. More hired a series of outstanding tutors to teach religion and the humanities to his children. For More, true education involves teaching persons to lead an upright, God-filled life and to engage in lifelong liberal studies.

Three of More's four natural children were girls, and, far ahead of his time, he provided an education to his daughters that was equal to if not superior to that available to bright young men of the era. He was a strong advocate of equal educational opportunities for both males and females. More believed that a woman attains her perfection when she is submissive to a good husband. But he also believed that a woman should receive that quality of liberal and religious education that was equal to a man's, so that she can be a fine companion to her husband and a liberating mother to her children. More's eldest daughter Margaret (Meg) became especially well educated, entering into lengthy sophisticated discussions with many persons, including Henry VIII. She even composed Latin poems that she read aloud to the delighted monarch.

From the time he first began to practice law, More's career progressed in a straight uninterrupted upward trajectory. From his earliest days as a practicing lawyer, More gained a fine reputation as a hardworking, oratorically gifted, incorruptible, and skilled lawyer who emphasized fairness. These admirable qualities made him much sought after by clients far and wide. Henry VIII, who became king in 1509, and for whose coronation More composed a series of Latin poems, appointed him to a royal mission to the Low Countries in 1515. Six years later More was knighted, and in 1523 he was selected as Speaker of the House of Commons, where he was instrumental in establishing the parliamentary right of free speech. In 1529 Henry appointed More to the highest political office available to a commoner, that of Lord Chancellor of England. In 1532 More resigned this post and went back to private life, citing ill health, which was factual. It is more probable, however, that More resigned because he could not in conscience work for a government that he strongly believed was attempting to violate the inviolable law of God.

For virtually all his adult life, More was at the center of the "new learning" that was sweeping all over Europe. Michelangelo was three years older than More; Raphael was three years younger. Together with his friends Desiderius Erasmus, John Colet, Peter Giles, William Grocyn, Thomas Linacre, and Jerome Busleyden, More emphasized the humanistic culture and values of ancient Athens and Rome as the foundation of true liberal learning. This stress on humane studies was not intended to replace or deemphasize religious studies or piety but rather to place religious life and learning on a firmer, more expansive, and more incarnational foundation. Erasmus referred to More as "England's only genius."

Despite his very busy life as a lawyer and public servant, More found time to do a great deal of writing. In his best-known book, *Utopia,* More sharply criticized the inequitable socioeconomic conditions in Europe and proposed an ideal state based on reason. He also wrote two important historical books, *History of Richard III* and *Life of John Picus.* His Latin writings include his lovely *Epistles* and also his *Epigrams.* He also wrote some tracts in defense of his faith. His spiritual writings are admirable, touching, and inspirational. Two of the finest of these devotional works are the *Dialogue of Comfort against Tribulation* and the moving *Treatise on the Passion of Christ*, both of which were written toward the end of his life while he was imprisoned in the Tower of London.

Like More, Henry VIII was a jovial, well-read, classically educated humanist. Thus it was natural that the two became warm friends. So when Henry tired of his wife Catherine of Aragon because she did not produce a male heir to the throne, he consulted More. After lengthy reflection and study, More told Henry that he could not support the king's desire to divorce Catherine and marry his ambitious passionate mistress Anne Boleyn because such an action was directly contrary to Scripture and therefore contravened the immutable law of the church.

Unable to obtain from the pope an annulment from his marriage, Henry resolved to marry Anne. He put great pressure on the university professors and the nobility to support him, which virtually all of them did. On May 15, 1532, almost all the English hierarchy made their complete submission to the king. The very next day More, pleading ill health, resigned as Lord Chancellor. The king, of course, suspected that an even stronger, more underlying reason prompted More's resignation.

After his retirement from public office with its concomitant loss of income, More had to fire his extensive household staff. Always a man of great fairness, he found places for most of them with his friends among the nobility and hierarchy. His family, especially his wife, Alice, found it difficult to adjust to diminished circumstances. She frequently complained about this to More and to anyone else who would listen. Ever the optimist, More wrote to his friend Erasmus that at long last he had a great deal of time to devote to God and to his own spiritual welfare, adding, in the manner of a loyal subject to the crown, that this felicitous turn of events came about because of the "favor of an indulgent prince."

More declined to attend Anne Boleyn's coronation as queen on July 1, 1533, telling close friends that though he might be devoured, he would never be deflowered.

Early in 1534 Parliament passed the Act of Succession. There were two major parts to the Act. One of these parts stated that Anne was now queen and her children by Henry were to be recognized as legitimate heirs to the throne. The other major part stated that the marriage of Henry and Catherine was null and that matters of this sort would henceforth be settled not by the pope but by the hierarchy of the Church of England. The Act further stated that every person, under pain of high treason, had to consent to all the contents and effects of the Act. Everyone had to take an oath to agree with and uphold the entire Act of Succession. More agreed with the first part of the Act, but not with the second, since this would take away what he regarded as the supreme authority of the pope, which Jesus personally gave to Peter the Apostle while still on earth.

More refused to take the oath. Until the time he was formally condemned to death, More never told anyone why he refused to sign the oath, not even his closest friends or members of his own family. As a skilled lawyer, More knew full well that he could not be convicted on the basis of silence; lawful conviction required a treasonous statement or action. More faced relentless and intense pressure to sign the Act by Henry's minions, notably Thomas Cromwell and the Duke of Norfolk (Ann Bolyn's uncle). More steadfastly refused to take the oath, and so was imprisoned in the Tower of London. His family visited him as frequently as the authorities allowed. It was a source of great anguish to More that his family, whom he loved so much, never really understood why he clung so dearly to his conscience.

On July 1, 1535, in Westminster Hall, More was tried for high treason. He was convicted because of the perjury of Richard Rich, who was paid off by being appointed Attorney General for Wales.

Immediately after the death sentence was pronounced, More gave a brief speech that was typical of this high-minded man, a speech that tied together More's strong belief that he was simultaneously a citizen of England and a citizen of heaven. ". . . Like the Blessed Apostle Paul (as we read in the Acts of the Apostles) was present and consented to the death of St. Stephen, and kept their clothes that stoned him to death, and yet be they now both twain Holy Saints in heaven, and shall continue there friends together for ever, so I verily trust, and shall therefore right heartily pray, that though your lordships now here in earth been judges to my condemnation, we may hereafter in heaven merrily all meet together, to our everlasting salvation. And thus I desire Almighty God to preserve and defend the King's Majesty, and send him good counsel."

Shortly afterward, More composed a beautiful prayer asking God to have mercy on all those who bear evil will against him and would do him harm, so that the glorious Trinity, through the bitter passion of Christ, would bring them and him to heaven together.

At about nine o'clock in the morning of July 6, 1535, Thomas More was executed on Tower Hill. None of his immediate natural family was present; only his adopted daughter Margaret Clement was there. His beloved daughter Meg was so overcome with grief that she could not bring herself to attend. On the way to his execution a kindly stranger offered him a glass of wine. More refused, saying that Jesus had been offered only gall while on the cross. In accordance with the custom of the time, More gave a short speech on the scaffold just prior to his execution. He asked the throng in attendance to pray for the king and ask God to continually give the king good counsel.

He ended his speech with a glorious summary of his life and what he stood for: "I die the king's good servant, but God's first."

More's last moments on earth combined the wittiness and religious depth that characterized his life. More told the executioner not to put his beard on the block, since his beard had committed no treason. He then knelt down and recited the *Miserere*: "Have mercy on me, O God, in your faithful love, and in the fullness of your mercy wipe away all my offenses . . ." The axe fell, and one of England's greatest personages of all time was dead.

More's body was buried in the small church of St. Peter ad Vincula inside the Tower of London. His severed head was exhibited for all to see on Tower Bridge and was then buried in the Roper vault at St. Dunstan, Canterbury.

In the centuries following his death, Thomas More has been the subject of innumerable biographies and other kinds of historically based accounts. One of the most celebrated of these is the magnificent play *A Man for All Seasons*, written in the early 1960's by Robert Bolt. In a scene having great import for religious educators, some of More's family come to his prison cell in the Tower of London to persuade him to take the oath and return home to Chelsea. His beloved daughter Meg tries in vain to persuade him to take the oath and return home to Chelsea. Frustrated by her failure, Meg emotionally cries out to her father: "Haven't you done as much as God can reasonably want?" To which More replies, "Well . . . finally . . . it isn't a matter of reason; finally it's a matter of love."

In giving us our call within a call to be his religious educators here on earth, God does not ask us so much to be reasonable as to love. God asks us to give everything we have and everything we are to religious instruction activity not because this is the reasonable thing to do but because this is the loving thing to do.

To do things for the sake of reasonableness is to do things that make sense in terms of logic, prudence, and self-preservation. To do things for love is to do things that make sense in terms of all-giving sacrifice, complete commitment, and unswervering dedication to a goal that lies beyond what reason can legitimately be expected to embrace on its own grounds. In the end, religious instruction of the authentic sort is not so much a matter of reason as it is a matter of love.

Is any sacrament primarily an act of reasonableness or is it an act of love? Can it be any different for the sacrament of teaching?

From the standpoint of reasonableness, the grinding sacrifices and self-consuming efforts that we make as religious educators are utterly foolish. But from the standpoint of love, these sacrifices and efforts are the only course of action we can legitimately take if we are to be true to our call within a call.

As religious educators we must adhere to and live the highest principles. Our principles should shine forth in our work as religious educators. Ultimately, these principles are more existential than logical because they are rooted in love much more than they are in reason.

To assert that ultimately our call to and our work as religious educators is less a matter of reason and more a matter of love suggests very hard work and continuous sacrifice on the part of the religious educator. It suggests no stinting and no holding back, even in the slightest, to the exigencies of the religious instruction task. When we are tired, exhausted, discouraged, overwhelmed with work, do we settle for reasonableness or do we press forward unrelentingly because of love?

Sometimes, even oftentimes, it happens that friends, relatives, clergy, and even mediocre religious educators do not understand why we are making so many large and small sacrifices in our efforts to be optimally effective religious educators. Surely in the light of all this lack of understanding and support it is reasonable for us not to press on wholeheartedly, or at least to scale back our efforts somewhat. But ultimately, religious instruction, like our call within a call, is not so much a matter of reason as it is a matter of love. So we press forward unabated and undaunted, frequently alone in the world save for the love of God for whom we basically toil and who gives us the strength and courage to persevere.

Reasonableness is often just an excuse for inaction, a rationalization for a lack of complete self-sacrifice, an escape from the constant enervating hard work that is essential for that level of religious instruction to which God has called us. "Ah," we say, "I am tired. I am no longer a teenager and so don't have a young person's level of energy. I am working hard enough as a religious educator. It just isn't reasonable to ask me to do any more." But love responds in a very different—and unreasonable—fashion when there is a learner to teach, when there are persons whom we could help draw closer to Jesus if we would just work harder and sacrifice more.

Although we religious educators should never agree with or respect another religious educator's desire to be ultimately motivated by reasonableness rather than by love, we should never look down on such persons as persons. Rather, like Thomas More, we should pray that God grant them the grace to go beyond reasonableness and to root their religious instruction motivations and efforts in love. Moreover, by the all-giving sacrifices we make in carrying out our own religious instruction tasks, we concretely model for "reasonable" religious educators the love that is the ultimate motivation and mainspring of authentic religious instruction activity.

If our all-embracing love for our religious instruction work is to remain alive and not tumble into the shallows of reasonableness, it must be nourished by a vigorous, ongoing prayer life. This prayer life must of necessity be holistic, encompassing the cognitive, affective, and lifestyle domains of our existence. Our love, like that of Thomas More, should not be unduly serious lest it fall flat and lose its vigor and humanity. Rather, our love for religious instruction activity should be seasoned with the salt of wit. And finally, our love for religious instruction ministry should not be an ignorant love but a love that is in vital touch with the deepest drafts of learning in the humanities, the sciences, and the field of religious instruction. A love that is unaccompanied by learning is foolishness, and love is never foolish.

To what extent do we religious educators allow "reasonableness" to sometimes blind us to the all-important basic motivation of love?

To what degree do we religious educators do things out of reasonableness rather than out of love? What can we concretely do now to ensure that everything we do in our religious instruction apostolate is done not so much out of reasonableness as out of love?

Ultimately, we can never justify our call within our call or anything we do concretely as religious educators on the basis of "reasonableness." Ultimately, we can only justify our call and our activities on the basis of love.

Let us go one step further. As seen exclusively from the light of our call within a call to be religious educators, is not all-giving love on our part the only true reasonableness?

Performance Objective: Whenever I am confronted with a worthwhile religious instruction task that seems unreasonable in terms of the great amount of time and effort it will involve or that my colleagues and friends say is unreasonable, I will spur myself onward to accomplish this task out of great love in the full realization that love, especially great love, is always unreasonable.

28

Cost

One of the most influential financiers and international bankers of his era, or of any other era in the history of the world, was John Pierpont Morgan.

He was born on April 17, 1837, in Hartford, Connecticut. His father, Junius, a successful local merchant, sent him to Boston's academically distinguished English High School. Pierpont—or Pip as he was called in his school days—completed his secondary education at a private school in Vevey, Switzerland, because his father accepted an invitation to join a private banking house in London in 1853. He then matriculated in the University of Göttingen to study mathematics. Pip was such an outstanding student at this distinguished German university that one of his teachers, Professor Ulrich, urged him to pursue a career as a university professor of mathematics.

During his student days in Europe, Morgan expanded his lightening mathematical mind which was to be of great use to him in his later financial career. In Europe he also acquired a deep love for art, which remained with him for the rest of his life.

In 1857 Morgan began his financial career as an accountant in a New York banking house. Four years later he set himself up as an independent banker, acting as New York agent for the London banking firm of George Peabody. In the years that followed he expanded his financial operations enormously because the rapidly-growing large corporations in America required great infusions of capital to further accelerate their rapid expansion. Morgan engineered a series of major financial coups, such as financing the merger out of which the first billion-dollar American company, United States Steel, was formed. He also financed the formation of many other giant corporations such as General Electric and International Harvester.

J. P. Morgan became heavily involved in railroads and was responsible for financing the reorganization of many of the largest lines including New York Central Railroad, Pennsylvania Railroad, and Northern Pacific Railroad. Indeed, he became one of the world's most powerful railroad magnates, financially controlling as many as 5,000 miles of track.

During the severe depression that followed the Panic of 1893, Morgan formed a syndicate that two years later supplied the U.S. government with the then huge sum of $62 million in order to relieve the acute Treasury crisis. Morgan was beginning to rule the U.S. government, at least financially.

In 1907 he almost single-handedly mobilized the New York banking community to successfully avoid a nationwide financial collapse following the Wall Street panic of that year. This successful action showed the entire nation the tremendous power that J. P. Morgan actually wielded. As a result, the Federal Reserve system was established in 1913 out of the belief that no single individual or small group of individuals should be able to wield such enormous financial power over the whole nation.

Because Morgan controlled a significant portion of the expanding American institutional sources of capital such as major commercial banks and large insurance companies, and even in a certain sense the federal government, his influence spread not just to the world of business but to each man and woman and child throughout the United States.

In short, Morgan ruled money at the exact time in American history when money was the most important thing to rule.

Yet it is generally agreed, in the words of one of his contemporaries, that "Morgan never knowingly abused his almost incredible power."

Why were large and shrewd investors not only willing but indeed eager to place their financial resources into the hands of J. P. Morgan and trust him completely to invest these monies well?

Morgan himself provided the answer (which each of his investors already knew intuitively) by repeatedly insisting that commercial credit is not based primarily on the amount of money or property a person possesses. Rather, affirmed Morgan, commercial credit is based on character, the character of the person into whose hands the investors place their money. Morgan was perceived, and rightly so, as being honest in his business dealings.

As a worldly and sophisticated man who appreciated culture and the finer things of life, J. P. Morgan greatly enjoyed international travel since his high school days. In the last fifteen years of his life he spent a great deal of time abroad, sometimes up to a half a year. Whether cruising the Adriatic, lolling about in fashionable Continental spas and resorts like Aix-les-Bains, sipping tea with England's king or quaffing beer with Germany's kaiser, sailing around the Greek Isles, or leisurely enjoying the sights of ancient Egypt, Morgan always combined business with pleasure. He thought about, planned, and sometimes even consummated business deals wherever he was in the world. He never let pleasure interfere with business.

Toward the end of an extended trip to Egypt in the winter of 1913, Morgan's health took a decided turn for the worse. Before sailing home to New York, he decided to recuperate in Rome, a city that he had come to love dearly. At first he grew stronger in the Eternal City. But after some days his health began to severely deteriorate. Just a few minutes after midnight on the morning of March 31, J. P. Morgan expired. His last words, uttered as he pointed upward, were: "I've got to go up that hill."

Upon learning of J. P. Morgan's death, the New York Stock Exchange closed for a day, a rare tribute for a private person then or now.

J. P. Morgan had four great loves in his life. One of these great loves was his first wife, Mimi, who died tragically of an acute pulmonary disease after only four months of marriage. She was only twenty-seven years of age; Pierpont was twenty-five. For the rest of his life, Morgan visited her grave whenever he could, but always on either February 17, the date of Mimi's death, or October 7, the date of their wedding.

The second great love of Morgan's life was art. He was the most important collector and donor of his era. He commissioned Charles McKim, the leading American architect of his time, to design and build the beautiful Pierpont Morgan Library in New York in the general style of an Italian Renaissance *palazzo*. The exclusive purpose of this library was to house Morgan's own rich collection of precious manuscripts, rare books, priceless paintings, magnificent tapestries, superlative bronzes, exquisite ivories, gorgeous enamels, delicate porcelains, marvelous miniatures, ravishing jewelry, and beautiful furniture. He donated many art treasures to the Wadsworth Atheneum in Hartford, the city of his birth. On a visit to London, he noticed that the spacious and beautiful proportions of the interior of the great dome of St. Paul's Cathedral were not able to be readily appreciated by worshipers or sightseers because of the dim light there. He suggested to cathedral officials that electric lighting be installed and offered to pay for it, which he did quietly. His financial generosity was responsible for establishing and later expanding the American Academy in Rome for the study of architecture and art. An especial object of his lavish munificence was the Metropolitan Museum of Art in New York, which he helped organize and to which he donated innumerable art treasures. He also continued to cover the Metropolitan's large annual deficit, enlisting the assistance of other generous magnates such as Henry Frick and Edward Harkness. During very difficult financial times at the turn of the century, Morgan put up to money to save the venerable publishing house of Harper & Brothers because he firmly believed that its demise would be harmful to American letters. He was, in many ways, akin to an Italian Renaissance prince, a contemporary Lorenzo il Magnifico, and on that account was sometimes called *Pierpontifex Maximus.*

Religion was the third great love of Morgan's life. When he was in residence in New York City, he attended worship services every Sunday at his beloved St. George's Protestant Episcopal Church, where he was warden. In the warmer months, when he frequented his country estate Cragston located in Highland Falls, he regularly attended church services at Holy Innocents Church, where he was a vestryman. Sunday evenings were devoted to hymn singing with his family at home where Morgan sang lustily though not always on pitch. He frequently attended regional and national conventions of the Episcopal Church as a lay delegate. On a trip to Palestine one year, he fell to his knees in the Church of the Holy Sepulchre. Morgan apparently did not perceive any serious contradiction between his strong abiding attachment to his religion and major strands of his own personal behavior. His life evinced an almost total lack of humility and self-denial, two central Christian virtues. Like some rich men with unexciting wives and burdensome business cares, he frequently sought the company of sexually exciting and intellectually titillating women. In fact, Morgan was an insatiable womanizer. He had innumerable liaisons with all sorts of women at home and abroad. He installed short-term and long-term mistresses on his private yacht as well as at various localities in New York City and in foreign lands. When he traveled to Europe and the Near East, he was always seen in the company of beautiful women on whom he lavished expensive and exquisite gifts. After finishing a session in the private gaming rooms in Monte Carlo or in Camille Blanc's even more restricted salon, he typically retired to a special room or to an elegant nearby hotel with of one or another of Europe's most gorgeous cocottes who were always available to help a wealthy man top off a successful run at the tables. He even showed up at an important church convention with a woman other than his wife on his arm.

Morgan's fourth great love was his yacht. He had four yachts in his lifetime. He named the second one Corsair; subsequent yachts were christened Corsair II and Corsair III respectively. The last of these Corsairs was 302 feet long. The fittings and furnishings on Corsair II and Corsair III were luxurious but not ostentatious, as was the case, for example, with James Gordon Bennett's magnificent yacht, which had on board a Turkish bath and an Alderney cow to provide fresh milk and cream daily. Morgan spent a great deal of time on the Corsair, sometimes on trips to his country estate Cragston situated up the Hudson River at Highland Falls, at other times on leisurely cruises up the New England coast, but most often either at its regular pier or lying at anchor in the waters off New York. He even made extensive cruises throughout the

Mediterranean on the Corsair, after his crew had first had sailed it to Europe while he traveled there via a much larger commercial luxury ocean liner. The Corsair was not just a leisure yacht; Morgan regularly conducted business there, and some of his most important financial deals were thrashed out on the Corsair. One of his greatest thrills came when he was elected Commodore of the New York Yacht Club. He loved it when friends and acquaintances addressed him as Commodore.

J. P. Morgan had a distinct knack of immediately piercing to the essence of a problem or situation in a blunt and direct manner. As a result, a great many anecdotes were told about him. One of the most famous of these is of special pertinence to religious educators. One day a Wall Street acquaintance came up to him and, after exchanging pleasantries, said: "Mr. Morgan, you know a great deal about yachts. You are a leading member of the New York Yacht Club and are personally acquainted with the owners of many of America's most luxurious yachts. And you yourself have a splendid yacht, the Corsair. Tell me, Mr. Morgan, how much does a fine private yacht cost, and how much are the annual operating costs?"

Looking at his Wall Street acquaintance squarely in the eyes, Morgan replied: "If you have to *even think* about the cost, you can't afford it."

Cost is the price we pay for something. Most persons think of cost in terms of money. But there are other kinds of cost that are more important than money and indeed explain why money is itself a cost. Among the major components of cost are time, effort, and sacrifice.

Nothing in life is free. Everything costs something. Mediocre things cost little, but they still cost something. Good things cost a good deal. Excellent things have a very high cost. Even bad things have their cost, a cost in direct proportion to how bad the thing is.

There are three very different psychological stages at which every person approaches the cost of something. The first and lowest stage is that of asking the cost. The second stage is that of counting the cost. The highest stage is that of just thinking about the cost.

In his reply to his Wall Street acquaintance, J. P. Morgan said that his questioner should not *even think* about the cost if he genuinely wanted to purchase and operate a large yacht. Morgan obviously thought that either asking the cost or counting the cost was so insignificant in terms of attaining what a person really and truly desires that he did not even have to mention these two lesser stages.

Our call within a call as religious educators necessarily demands that we pay an exceptionally high price to walk our call. Because the religious instruction is such an extraordinarily exalted apostolate, it has an extraordinarily high cost. Our call exacts from us the cost of placing everything that we are as a person at the disposal of the religious instruction apostolate. Our call demands from us the cost of placing everything we do throughout the day at the direct disposal of the religious instruction apostolate. Do we ask the cost of what it is to be Christ's religious educator? Do we count the cost? Do we *even think* of the cost?

To paraphrase J. P. Morgan, if we even as much as think about what our religious instruction apostolate costs us, then we cannot afford it. If we cannot afford the cost, we should not be a religious educator.

Every sacrament, including the sacrament of teaching, bestows. Each bestows because each first costs. The Eucharist bestows so very much because its cost to Jesus was enormous. The sacrament of teaching will bestow in proportion to its cost to us religious educators.

Our call to be religious educators necessarily demands that we put the apostolate ahead of our family, our friends, and our personal interests. Do we ask how much this costs? Do we count this cost? Do we even think about this cost? If we ask how much this costs, if we count the cost, if we even think of how much this costs, then we have to ask ourselves whether we can really afford the cost of being God's religious educator?

Our call to be a religious educator necessarily demands that we completely and unreservedly sacrifice all that we are and all that we do for the sake of the apostolate. Do we ask how much this total sacrifice costs? Do we count the cost? Do we even think about the cost? Can we afford the cost of being God's religious educator?

To answer the call to be God's religious educator is to totally live the cost of the call in everything we do day in and day out. If we are to answer God's call truly, then we have to undergo a three-tiered process of conversion in which we first learn not to ask the cost of any activity that our religious instruction call requires of us, then learn not to count the cost, and finally learn not to even think of the cost. When we arrive at this final stage of conversion and when we concretely live this conversion in our daily lives, then we can truly say that we are answering God's call to us to be his religious educator.

Performance Objective: Whenever I approach a worthwhile religious instruction task large or small, I will not even as much as think of what it will cost me in terms of time, effort, or energy. Rather I will concentrate completely on the task and on whatever it will take to successfully accomplish it.

29

Generosity

Once upon a time in a small town in Europe there lived a very poor man. He was so destitute that he had nothing he could really call his own. Having no house, he slept in a deserted cave. The only clothes he owned were the tattered rags in which he was habitually clothed. Around his neck he wore a small shabby leather purse to hold whatever grains of wheat he was able to find in the fields in order to feed himself.

One early December morning the man looked into his small weathered purse and discovered to his great dismay that he only had enough grains of wheat to make just a single meal for himself. He grew very disconsolate because the harvest had long since past, the wheat fields lay bare, and the birds had eaten all the grains of wheat that somehow remained on the ground.

"After my next meal, what?" he asked himself. "Starvation?"

Having nothing to do and feeling extremely dejected, the man walked to the main square of the town hoping that the sights and sounds and bustle of the people there would take his mind off his impending tragedy. After a little while, four of the king's men, resplendent in their official uniforms, rode their horses into the town square. Three of them blew their trumpets very loudly in order to gain everyone's attention. When the people in the square had turned quiet, the fourth man read an announcement which declared that in mid-afternoon of that very day the king himself would be coming to town to pay a royal visit.

The poor man thought that the king's visit represented a providential opportunity to rescue him from his dire circumstances. "If only I can get close enough to the king to tell him of my tragic plight, I'm sure he will help me. After all, the king is famous in all corners of the realm for his great generosity to all his subjects," he thought.

Sometime after two o'clock on that sunny brisk afternoon the king's entourage slowly but majestically processed into the town square. It was a gorgeous sight. Twelve men, three abreast, and attired in resplendent blue, gold, and white uniforms, led the procession. These were followed by six of the king's finest Horse Guards riding superb, immaculately groomed stallions. Like the soldiers on foot, they were also decked out in the royal colors of blue, gold, and white. At the end of the procession, riding a magnificent white steed, came the king himself wearing a crown on his head and holding the royal scepter.

The crowd cheered and cheered for their beloved monarch as he rode slowly and majestically around the square so that everyone, even those far in the back, could see him.

Finally the king alighted from his mount and handed his scepter to one of his retinue. As good fortune would have it, the king dismounted from his horse directly in front of the poor man. Now was the opportunity for which the poor man was so eagerly waiting, the opportunity to beg the king of assistance.

Before the poor man was able to open his mouth to speak, the king asked him if he had any present to offer the monarch as a welcoming gift for his visit to the town. The poor man was at first taken aback at the king's question. Then he became shocked. He had fully expected to receive something from the king rather than to give something. "Aren't kings supposed to give?" he asked himself quietly under his breath.

After a minute or two of silence, the poor man responded: "Your Majesty, I am a very poor man. Therefore I have no gift for you to welcome you into our town."

At hearing the man's words, a sad expression passed over the king's face. The monarch started to turn away.

"Oh wait, Your Majesty," exclaimed the poor man nervously. "I just remembered that there is one thing I do have. It's my small beat-up purse holding some grains of wheat, just enough for tonight's meal."

Slowly and with great sadness in his heart the poor man opened his small leather purse. He really did not want to give its contents away to anyone. He desperately needed each and every grain in order to feed himself one more time. After that, who knows how he would feed himself. "Besides," he thought, "the king has plenty. He is rich. What does he need from me, a poor man? But the king is the king, and it would not do for any man, even a very poor man as myself, not to offer the king some sort of welcoming present."

Reluctantly, very reluctantly in fact, the man removed a single grain of wheat from the purse. He then presented the solitary grain to the king. The monarch graciously thanked the poor man for his gift and then proceeded to move away in order to speak with another person in the crowd.

The poor man could not believe the incredibly bad luck that had befallen him. He had so ardently hoped to come out richer from his encounter with the king. Astoundingly, he emerged poorer from the whole affair.

Shaking his head in disbelief, the poor man went back to the deserted cave where he lived and slept. When it came time for the evening meal, he sat down and emptied the contents of his small worn leather purse into his hand and began to count the grains. As he moved his fingers slowly through the grains of what, he noticed one grain that was different from the rest. He looked carefully at that single grain, and found to his great astonishment that it was made of gold.

The man slumped forward and let out a wail. "What a fool I have been!" he cried remorsefully. "If I had only been generous to the king! I didn't have much, but if I had given the king the contents of my whole purse, I would be a rich man now. All my problems would be over. I would be well on my way to fulfilling all my desires and dreams. I just wasn't generous enough. As a matter of fact, I really wasn't generous at all."

At the core of our call within a call to be religious educators is generosity, giving our whole heart and soul and efforts without any reserve whatsoever to the religious instruction apostolate. A religious educator who is not generous to every aspect of religious instruction work is automatically not generous to the Lord. Generosity, all-giving generosity to others and to every single exigency of the religious instruction apostolate, is one of the hallmarks of our call within a call to be God's religious educator.

By its very nature, a sacrament is intrinsically and unabashedly generous. A sacrament gives to others and keeps on giving, looking for no reward for itself. So it is also with the sacrament of teaching.

God has a special place in his heart for persons who are generous. Consequently, few things will bless our religious instruction work and make it fruitful more than our generosity. The reason for this is simple: When we are totally generous to the Lord in doing religious instruction work, we are not only giving ourselves completely to God but we are also establishing those instructional conditions that bring about a high degree of outcomes in the learners whom God has given us. Grace does not only build upon nature; it works through the nature that it thoroughly suffuses.

It has been my consistent experience that persons who are not too generous with the Lord perceive themselves to be extremely generous. It has also been my experience that persons who are extremely generous to the Lord frequently chastise themselves for failing to be more generous. Where do we religious educators fit in with this kind of self-evaluation?

To what extent do we religious educators give our whole selves to the religious instruction apostolate?

How often do we religious educators hold something back and not give totally of ourselves in doing our religious instruction work?

Generosity means giving ourselves egolessly in trying to make each and every religious instruction event the very best it can be. Do we do as much as we can do to make each teaching event the very finest experience it can be for learners?

When we are tired or out of sorts, do we still press forward and give as generously to the religious instruction apostolate as we do when things are going well?

Authentic Christian generosity is done cheerfully and with a good heart, realizing that we are indeed incredibly fortunate to have received the divine call to give ourselves with total generosity to the Lord's service. To what degree are we cheerful and of good heart when one or another act of generosity proves very difficult for us?

Generosity does not mean going the extra mile; it means going all the way. How frequently do we go all the way for the Lord in the discharge of our religious instruction mission?

If we religious educators are not as generous to our call within a call as the Lord wants, when will we convert to a total axis of generosity? Now? Tomorrow? Ever?

Performance Objective: In everything I do with my religious instruction colleagues and learners, I will focus on how much I can give to them rather than how much I can get from them in one way or another. One of the entries I will regularly make in my professional journal will be to describe how much I am giving to colleagues and learners, and how much I am striving consciously or unawaredly to receive from them.

30

Conversion

He was the preeminent bridge figure between two of the three great eras in Western civilization, the ancient world and the medieval world. It is for this reason that he has been called the last of the ancients and the first of the medievals.

His name was Augustine and he was one of the most enduringly influential Christians who ever lived. Augustine's wide-ranging religious thought, his ardent religious love, and his deep religious life have profoundly affected Christianity from his own time down to the present. There is a sense in which every Christian one way or another must come to grips with Aurelius Augustinus and what he stood for.

Augustine was primarily a bishop, religious educator, philosopher, and theologian. Combining deep piety, great energy, a heart on fire, and an enormous intellect, Augustine created a vision of personal spirituality and a system of philosophy/theology that became lasting landmarks for Christianity. His placement of philosophy and theology squarely within the context of his interpretation of Plato thoroughly dominated Western Christian thought until the rediscovery of Aristotle in the thirteenth century.

If Augustine's philosophical/theological system is no longer dominant in Christianity, his profound personal piety and intense love for God are as bright, inspirational, and educational as they have always been.

Aurelius Augustinus was born in 354 in the small town of Thagaste (now Souk-Arras in Algeria), a hill town in the North African province of Numidia, about fifty miles inland and south of Hippo

Regius (today Annaba also in Algeria). As was the frequent practice in that era, Augustine was not baptized shortly after birth. He
was instead given the sign of the cross on his forehead and cleans-
ing salt on his lips. He was reared as a Christian and even was inscribed as a catechumen in his early youth.

After attending the local school in Thagaste, Augustine was sent
at the age of fifteen to the nearby city of Madaura to further his
classical education. It was in Madaura that Augustine began a life
of unbridled sensual pleasure that was enormously profligate, even
by modern standards. Somehow Augustine managed to be a superb
student while he was concomitantly satisfying his voracious sexual
appetites. From Madaura he went to Carthage where he pursued
advanced studies in rhetoric and Latin literature. There Augustine
studied diligently, engaged in the bohemian student life, frequented
the licentious theaters, and continued to live a life of debauchery.
After a while, he settled down a little in the sense that he took a
more or less permanent mistress by whom he had a son. Though
Augustine later referred to his son as "the child of my sin," he gave
him at birth the name Adeodatus, which means "gift of God." Augustine loved his son dearly.

After completing his studies, Augustine became a teacher of
rhetoric successively at Thagaste, Carthage, Rome, and finally at
Milan, where he was appointed municipal professor late in 384. To
further his knowledge and skill in rhetoric, he attended sermons delivered by the famous bishop Ambrose, who was a magnificent or-
ator and a cultural leader in Milan. Augustine received from Ambrose three great treasures which were to lead to his conversion and
which would remain cornerstones of his own spirituality, religious
instruction work, and theology: Neoplatonism, the Bible, and strict
moral standards.

Slowly but surely Augustine became intellectually convinced
that he should become a Christian and devote his life entirely to
God in one way or another. It was probably sometime in 385 when
Augustine gave his complete intellectual assent to the truths of the
Christian religion. The great conflict between the Christian moral
standards that Augustine accepted intellectually and his lascivious
behavior now became even more acute. He felt fenced in on all

sides by God, whose wisdom as given in the Bible had struck the deepest intellectual chords in his mind. But his lust-filled habits proved to be too heavy a weight to bear. The agonized Augustine desperately wanted to surrender his heart and life to God, just as he had given his intellect to the Lord, but he could not. Time and time again Augustine cried out in anguish to God for the grace of chastity in these words: "Grant me continence and chastity, but not yet." Augustine was deeply afraid that God would hear his pleas too soon.

One day in the summer of 386 a fellow North African named Ponticianus came to visit Augustine. Ponticianus, a devout Christian who held an important position in the imperial court, told Augustine about the life of St. Anthony of Egypt. Ponticianus recounted the story of how Anthony renounced all his material possessions and went into the desert to devote himself entirely to God by practicing prayer, severe mortification, silence, and manual labor, all the while resisting alluring sensual temptations sent to him by the devil.

On hearing the story of St. Anthony, Augustine's disgust at his own moral state reached the boiling point. Overcome with emotion and convulsed psychologically, he sought peace and surcease in the garden that was next to his house. Once in the garden, the tormented Augustine kept repeating to himself, "Let it be now, let it be now." In anguish, he flung himself down under a fig tree and broke down completely. In the midst of his soul-searing agony, Augustine heard a child's sing-song voice coming from another house and saying over and over again, *"Tolle lege, tolle lege!"* ("Take it and read it! Take it and read it!") Augustine returned to the bench where he had been sitting. Heeding the child's voice, he opened the Bible at random. His eyes fell on the text: "Not in revelry and drunkenness, not in debauchery and wantonness, not in strife and jealousy; but put on the Lord Jesus Christ. As for the flesh, take no thought for its lusts" (Rom 13:13–14). At that instant Augustine was converted morally, and a great sense of calm and tranquility washed over him. He resigned his prestigious professorship and went to a country villa in Cassiciacum to study Christianity more intensely and to go on a personal spiritual retreat.

On Holy Saturday evening in the year 387, Augustine, together with his son Adeodatus, received baptism from the hands of Ambrose.

In the autumn of 388 he returned to Thagaste, sold all his possessions, and together with some likeminded idivudals, founded and lived in an austere monastery for laypersons. Against his initial wishes, he was later ordained a priest in Hippo. In 395 he became its bishop. Soon afterward he turned his episcopal residence into a monastery. During his thirty-five years as bishop he proved to be a tireless shepherd of souls, religious educator, theologian, and philosopher.

In the year 430 the Vandals laid siege to Hippo. In the third month of this siege Augustine came down with a fever and took to his bed. He realized that the end was not far off. Since his conversion he had very frequently prayed the seven penitential Psalms. Now that the end was near, he arranged for the seven penitential Psalms to be written on leaves of vellum and hung on the wall by his bed so that he could have these Psalms right before his eyes to repeatedly pray and weep at these Psalms as death drew closer. On August 28, while reciting the seven penitential Psalms, he breathed his last. Augustine died as he had lived.

A thoroughgoing religious educator to the end, Augustine wrote in his will that he wished for his own extensive library not to be destroyed. He obviously wanted his own writings and the writings of others to remain at the disposal of all those who wished to be educated in the Christian life. Augustine's wish came to pass, and his library was spared destruction by the Vandals. (Only with the Arab conquest centuries later was the library laid to ruin.)

The life and work of Augustine have much to say to us religious educators, especially the agony and resolution of his conversion.

Have we been converted to be that kind of religious educator whose first and all-consuming priority is religious instruction activity? Have we been converted to such a degree that we completely accept and honor the call God has given to us to be his religious educator? Have we been completely faithful to our divine call? Are we totally committed to the religious instruction apostolate? Do we hold any part of ourselves back from the total giving of ourselves to religious instruction work? Are we always and everywhere at work on behalf of religious instruction? Do we gladly accept all the large and small sacrifices that the religious instruction profession demands of us? Do we ask the price of these sacrifices? Are we wholly converted or just partially converted to the religious instruction apostolate?

The fact that we are now religious educators indicates that at one time or another we were intellectually converted to accept God's call within a call to be a religious educator. But have we been converted in our wills and in our actions? Or do we cry out to God: "Let me live the sacrificial and committed life of a religious educator, but not yet!"

If we have not yet been converted to complete and holistic acceptance of the divine call to be a religious educator, have we even advanced to the level at which we are deeply anguished and pained by the fact that we have intellectually accepted God's call while at the same time continuing to resist the volitional and lifestyle aspects of God's call?

Intellectual conversion to the grinding rigors of the religious instruction apostolate is far easier than volitional and lifestyle conversion. For most persons, including Augustine, a deeply-felt interior experience is required for authentic volitional and lifestyle conversion to a great cause. We can have this kind of experience only if we are open to its possibility and acceptant of its actuality.

We need a strong desire to be converted in will and in lifestyle if we are ever to totally follow God's call within a call to be his religious educator. If God's converting grace is to touch our hearts and move our lives, we must surrender ourselves to his grace totally and without reserve. Do we pray often and earnestly to God: "Let my total conversion to be a religious educator be now! Let it be now!"

Intellectual conversion to the total renunciation of self in the complete service of our divine call gives us the light to know what we should do in order to be that kind of religious educator who is worthy of the call. Volitional and lifestyle conversion gives us the heat to follow the call with our whole hearts and strength.

In the moments immediately preceding his final and complete conversion, Augustine made himself ready to accept the grace of God. Have we prepared ourselves adequately for total conversion to a full acceptance of everything the religious instruction apostolate continually demands of us? Are we currently preparing ourselves?

At the time of his final and complete conversion, Augustine hung in the balance between a life of self-serving pleasure and a life of unconditional abandonment to God. What tipped the balance for him was his answer to the call *"Tolle lege, tolle lege!"* ("Take it and read it, take it and read it!") In like manner, religious educators who truly seek to become totally converted to the religious instruction apostolate or who seek to remain converted should read on a daily basis both the Bible and top-flight professional religious instruction books. To what extent are we religious educators doing this? If not now, when? If not now, ever?

Our total conversion of intellect, will, and lifestyle to the difficult demands of the religious instruction apostolate involves great personal sacrifice on our part. In a word, it involves the cross. Those religious educators who try to live their religious instruction lives by some easy or streamlined version of the cross will discover with Augustine that evasion of the cross is the hardest cross to bear.

The cross of sacrifice, of blood, of total giving hangs over and suffuses every Christian sacrament, including the sacrament of teaching.

Perhaps our most inward and paralyzing fear of being totally converted to the religious instruction apostolate is that somehow we have to diminish or even relinquish our humanity. The whole life of Augustine shows us that our fears are not well founded. What made Augustine such a respected a religious educator, such a revered bishop, and such an influential philosopher/theologian down through the ages was his own deeply human set of qualities which pervades all his written and oral teachings. Augustine's human qualities were not only positive but also negative. Through his once and continuing total conversion, his negative human qualities were transmuted by God's grace and Augustine's great love into shining positive qualities. Augustine's personal consciousness is clearly the most telling trait of his genius and still remains the most decisive source of his enormous influence on the history of the world. It is precisely because of his humanity in all its aspects that of all the great leaders whom Christianity has had for two millennia, it was to Augustine that the church awarded the official title of Doctor of Grace.

The key to Augustine's teachings lies with his own personal life as he lived it with great intensity from beginning to the very end. In the process of his conversion, Augustine discovered a central teaching of Jesus: The person who totally surrenders self to God finds more humanity than that individual ever dreamed possible. So it is also with religious educators. It is first by surrendering our life through total and complete conversion to the divine call to be God's religious educator that we find our truest and most human self.

The weight of the religious instruction cross lifts us up.

For Augustine, total conversion was extremely hard. Like Augustine, we religious educators sometimes resist the difficult demands of our call within a call. And like Augustine, we religious educators can exclaim: "I did even bay against you, O Christ!" What enables our true and complete conversion to fully living out our divine call, what seals our conversion, what continues our conversion is precisely what enabled, sealed, and continued Augustine's conversion to his divine call, namely, the sovereignty of love. In the beginning, middle, and end, love is always the basic motivator and the ultimate context. Religious educators do their work according to the measure of their love. Those religious educators who deeply love their call will do the best work, and vice versa. Virtue is its own reward, since persons inevitably become what they love. Religious educators who are truly converted to the call will end up living the call, since the call gives what it promises.

It is not too late for us religious educators to become converted to full and unconditional acceptance of our divine call, to make our call the preeminent priority in our life, to sacrifice everything we have and everything we are for the sake of the religious instruction call. In one of the most memorable passages in all his writings, Augustine cries out in remorse: "Late have I loved you, O Beauty so ancient and yet so new. Late have I loved you." In one sense it is always too late for religious educators to love and live our call from God. But in a more important and ultimate sense, it is never too late. The life and religious instruction work of Augustine proved that. Our lives will also prove it as well—if we become totally and fully converted to our religious instruction call.

Only when we become completely converted in every way to our religious instruction call within a call can be truly be ready to successfully enact the sacrament of teaching.

Performance Objective: Every day I will throw myself upon the Lord and pray earnestly for the grace of total and immediate conversion in mind, heart, and action so that I will successfully accomplish all the performance objectives set forth in this meditation book and in the two volumes of meditations that follow this one. I will resolve never to yield to the temptation that says: "Lord, let me be converted to the accomplishment of these performance objectives, but not yet." Instead, I will ardently ask for the grace to cry out: "Lord, let it be now that I am fully converted to the accomplishment of these performance objectives! Let it be now!"

Notes

MEDITATION 1: THE FIRST CALL

1. Paul Marshall, *The Kind of Life Imposed on Man: Vocation and Social Order from Tyndale to Locke* (Toronto: University of Toronto Press, 1996), pp. 3–9; David T. Hansen, *The Call to Teach* (New York: Teachers College Press, 1995), pp. 1–18; Kenan B. Osborne, *Ministry* (New York: Paulist, 1993), 596–609; Francis Dewar, *Called or Collared: An Alternative Approach to Vocation* (London: S.P.C.K., 1991), pp. 1–12; Romney M. Moseley, *Becoming a Self before God: Critical Transformations* (Nashville, Tenn.: Abingdon, 1991), p. 101; Donald R. Heiges, *The Christian's Calling*, rev. ed. (Philadelphia: Fortress, 1984), pp. 27–51; James W. Fowler, *Becoming Adult, Becoming Christian: Adult Development and Christian Faith* (San Francisco, Cal.: Harper & Row, 1984), pp. 1–3, 71–75, 93–105, 125–126, 128–138; Jean-Pierre de Caussade, *The Sacrament of the Present Moment*, trans. Kitty Muggeridge (San Francisco, Cal.: Harper & Row, 1982), pp. 5–27; John Spencer Hill, *John Milton Poet, Priest and Prophet: A Study of Divine Vocation in Milton's Poetry and Prose* (Totowa, N.J.: Rowman and Littlefield, 1979), pp. 1–26; Malcolm Muggeridge, *Something Beautiful for God* (New York: Harper & Row, 1971), p. 19; James Michael Lee, "Layhood as Vocation and Career," in *Evolving Religious Careers*, ed. Willis E. Bartlett (Washington, D.C.: Center for Applied Research in the Apostolate, 1970), pp. 144–166; Joseph A. Novak, *Christian Witness: Response to Christ* (New York: Holt, Rinehart and Winston, 1967), pp. 10–60; James Michael Lee and Nathaniel J. Pallone, *Guidance and Counseling in Schools: Foundations and Processes* (New York: McGraw-Hill, 1966), pp. 488; Einar Billing, *Our Calling*, trans. Conrad Bergendoff (Philadelphia: Fortress, 1964), pp. 1–12; Maurice Bellet, *Vocation et Liberté* (Bruges, Belgique: Desclée de Brouwer, 1963), pp. 19–41; Wade H. Boggs Jr., *All Ye Who Labor* (Richmond, Va.: Knox, 1961), pp. 36–64; Pierre Teilhard de Chardin, *The Divine Milieu*, trans. Bernard Wall (New York: Harper, 1960), pp. 17–43; Dietrich Bonhoeffer, *The Cost of Discipleship*, 2d ed., trans. R. H. Fuller, rev. Irmgard Booth (New York: Macmillan, 1959), pp. 61–86; W. R. Forrester, *Christian Vocation* (London: Lutterworth, 1951), pp. 15–66; Douglas Horton, "To Whom Must We Look?", in *Christian Vocation*, ed. Douglas Horton, William Blakeman Lampe, and Ernest Fremont Tittle (Boston: Pilgrim, 1945), pp. 9–14.

For specifically religious education treatments of the vocation to the religious instruction apostolate, see W. Larry Richards, *The Abundant Bible Amplifier; 1 Corinthians; The Essentials and Nonessentials of Christian Living* (Nampa, Id.:

253

Pacific, 1997), pp. 141–147; Gloria Durka, *The Joy of Being a Catechist* (Mineola, N.Y.: Resurrection, 1995), pp. 57–58; Anne Streaty Wimberly, *Soul Stories: African American Religious Education* (Nashville, Tenn.: Abingdon, 1994), pp. 26–32; Perry G. Downs, *Teaching for Spiritual Growth* (Grand Rapids, Mich.: Zondervan, 1994), pp. 23–30; Robert W. Pazmiño, *By What Authority Do We Teach?* (Grand Rapids, Mich.: Baker, 1994), pp. 71–76; Jack L. Seymour, Margaret Ann Crain, and Joseph V. Crockett, *Educating Christians* (Nashville, Tenn.: Abingdon, 1993), pp. 21–34; Jerry M. Stubblefield, *The Effective Minister of Education: A Comprehensive Handbook* (Nashville, Tenn.: Convention, 1993), pp. 45–46; Ronald Habermas and Klaus Issler, *Teaching for Reconciliation* (Grand Rapids, Mich.: Baker, 1992), pp. 52–54; C. Doug Bryan, *Relationship Learning* (Nashville, Tenn.: Broadman, 1990), pp. 234–235; Marianne Sawicki, *The Gospel in History: Portrait of a Teaching Church: The Origins of Christian Education* (New York: Paulist, 1988), pp. 60–63; Grant W. Hanson, *Foundations for the Teaching Church* (Valley Forge, Pa.: Judson, 1986), pp. 61–62; Thomas H. Groome, "Walking Humbly with Our God," in *To Act Justly, Love Tenderly, Walk Humbly: An Agenda for Ministers*, by Walter Brueggemann, Sharon Parks, and Thomas H. Groome (New York: Paulist, 1986), pp. 57–58; Robert J. Hater, *Parish Catechetical Ministry* (Encino, Calif.: Benziger, 1986), pp. 24–28; Kent L. Johnson, *Called to Teach* (Minneapolis, Minn.: Augsburg, 1984), pp. 39–41; Ugo Vanni, "Commitment and Discipleship in the New Testament," in *Biblical Themes in Religious Education*, ed. Joseph S. Marino (Birmingham, Ala.: Religious Education Press, 1983), pp. 156–168; John H. Westerhoff III, "A Catechetical Way of Doing Theology," in *Religious Education and Theology*, ed. Norma H. Thompson (Birmingham, Ala.: Religious Education Press, 1982), pp. 239–241, 240–242; Mary C. Boys, introduction to *Ministry and Education in Conversation*, ed. Mary C. Boys (Winona, Minn.: St. Mary's Press, 1981), p. 7; Carl F. H. Henry, "Restoring the Whole Word for the Whole Community," in *The Religious Education We Need*, ed. James Michael Lee (Birmingham, Ala.: Religious Education Press, 1977), pp. 68–69; H. W. Byrne, *Christian Education in the Local Church*, 2d ed. (Grand Rapids, Mich.: Zondervan Academie, 1973), pp. 25–26; Johannes Hofinger, *The Art of Teaching Christian Doctrine*, 2d ed. (Notre Dame, Ind.; University of Notre Dame Press, 1962), p. 8; Warren Sten Benson, "The Pedagogy of Paul according to the Acts of the Apostles" (master's thesis, Dallas Theological Seminary, 1956), pp. 18–19; Herman Harrell Horne, *The Philosophy of Christian Education* (New York: Revell, 1937), pp. 48–50.

2. James Michael Lee, *The Shape of Religious Instruction* (Birmingham, Ala.: Religious Education Press, 1971), pp. 281–287; James Michael Lee, *The Content of Religious Instruction* (Birmingham, Ala.: Religious Education Press, 1985), pp. 608–618, 629–633, 653–657.

MEDITATION 2: VISION

1. The story about the three stonecutters came from a sermon delivered in the early 1970s by William Burgess, an ordained minister in the Church of the Brethren. While I was doing research at the University of Cambridge in the summer of 1996, a colleague on the faculty at that university told me that he believes that this story originally was told in one of the plays of Dorothy Sayers, an Englishwoman.

For Michelangelo's theory of sculpture, see Joachim Poeschke, *Michelangelo and His World*, trans. Russell Stockman (New York: Abrams, 1987), pp. 23–26, 31; Nathan Leites, *Art and Life: Aspects of Michelangelo* (New York: New York University Press, 1986), pp. 10–14; Linda Murray, *Michelangelo: His Life, Work, and Times* (New York: Thames and Hudson, 1984), pp. 174–176; David Summers, *Michelangelo and the Language of Art* (Princeton, N.J.: Princeton University Press, 1981), pp. 203–233; Nicholas Waddley, *Michelangelo* (Feltham, England: Hamlyn, 1975), p. 90; Martin Weinberger, *Michelangelo the Sculptor*, vol. 1, *Text* (London: Routledge and Kegan Paul, 1967), pp. 380–384; Michelangelo Buonarroti, *Michelangelo: A Self-Portrait*, ed. and trans. Robert J. Clements (Englewood Cliffs, N.J.: Prentice-Hall, 1963), p. 11 (here can be found two key poems written by Michelangelo beautifully encapsulating his theory of sculpture, namely "Se Ben Concetto...", and "Non Ha L'Ottimo Artista..."); Robert J. Clements, *Michelangelo's Theory of Art* (New York: New York University Press, 1961), pp. 19–31; Adrian Stokes, *Michelangelo: A Study in the Nature of Art* (New York: Philosophical Library, 1956), pp. 95, 99; Charles de Tolnay, *The Youth of Michelangelo*, 2d ed. (Princeton, N.J.: Princeton University Press, 1947), p. 33; Gerald S. Davis, *Michelangelo*, 2d ed. (London: Methuen, 1924), pp. 60, 103, 109, 185.

2. James Michael Lee, *The Shape of Religious Instruction* (Birmingham, Ala.: Religious Education Press, 1971), pp. 298–314; James Michael Lee, *The Flow of Religious Instruction* (Birmingham, Ala.: Religious Education Press, 1973), pp. 41–43, 212–215; James Michael Lee, *The Content of Religious Instruction* (Birmingham, Ala.: Religious Education Press, 1985), pp. 746–766.

MEDITATION 3—PRIORITIES

1. Plato, *Apology*. This dialogue deals with the trial of Socrates. Persons who wish to read further on those aspects and teachings of Socrates treated in this meditation might wish to also read the following three dialogues of Plato: (1) *Euthyphro* (the events leading up to the trial of Socrates and then Socrates awaiting his trial); (2) *Crito* (Socrates in prison); (3) *Phaedo* (Socrates' last moral and religious education discourse and finally his death).

Other source materials that I used in writing this meditation include Paul W. Gooch, *Jesus and Socrates* (New Haven, Conn.: Yale University Press, 1996), pp. 244–254, 291–297; James W. Hulse, *The Reputations of Socrates: The After-life of a Gadfly* (New York: Lang, 1995), pp. 11–33; Thomas C. Brickhouse and

Nicholas D. Smith, *Plato's Socrates* (New York: Oxford University Press, 1994), pp. 10–14, 23–29; Gregory Vlastos, *Socratic Studies*, ed. Myles Burnyeat (Cambridge: Cambridge University Press, 1994), pp. 8–11; Gregory Vlastos, *Socrates: Ironist and Moral Philosopher* (Ithaca, N.Y.: Cornell University Press, 1991), pp.. 209–232; Thomas C. Brickhouse and Nicholas D. Smith, *Socrates on Trial* (Princeton, N.J.: Princeton University Press, 1989), pp. 87–100; Mario Montuori, *Socrates: An Approach*, trans. Marcus de la Pae (Amsterdam: Gieben, 1988), pp. 9–18, 79–83; I. F. Stone, *The Trial of Socrates* (Boston: Little, Brown, 1988), pp. 52–67; Mary P. Nichols, *Socrates and the Political Community* (Albany, N.Y.: State University of New York Press, 1987), pp. 48–56, 133–138, 153–156; Kenneth Seeskin, *Discovery: A Study in Socratic Method* (Albany, N.Y.: State University of New York Press, 1987), pp. 73–95, 117–134; Luis E. Navia, *Socratic Testimonies* (Lantham, Md.: University Press of America, 1987), pp. 3–33, 185–193; Michael C. Stokes, *Plato's Socratic Conversations* (Baltimore, Md.: Johns Hopkins University Press, 1986), pp. 41–44, 420–437; Luis E. Navia, *Socrates* (Lanham, Md.: University Press of America, 1985), pp. 299–330; James Beckman, *The Religious Dimension of Socrates' Thought* (Waterloo, Canada: Wilfred Laurier University Press, 1979), pp. 5–111; Meg Parker, introduction to *Socrates: The Wisest and Most Just?* (Cambridge: Cambridge University Press, 1979), pp. 1–4; W. K. C. Guthrie, *Socrates* (Cambridge: Cambridge University Press, 1971), pp. 58–89; J. L. Fischer, *The Case of Socrates*, trans. Iris Lewitová (Praha: Academia Nakladatelství Československé Akademie Věd, 1969), pp. 57–66; A. E. Taylor, *Socrates* (Boston: Beacon, 1951), pp. 94–137; Werner Jaeger, *Paideia: The Ideals of Greek Culture*, vol. 2; *In Search of the Divine Centre*, trans. Gilbert Highet (New York: Oxford University Press, 1943), pp. 13–76; Diogenes Laertius, *Lives of Eminent Philosophers*, trans. Robert Drew Hicks. (Cambridge, Mass.: Harvard University Press, 1925), 1: 149–177; J. T. Forbes, *Socrates* (Edinburgh: Clark, 1913), pp. 53–72, 241–264.

2. James Michael Lee, *The Shape of Religious Instruction* (Birmingham, Ala.: Religious Education Press, 1971), pp. 24–27, 48–55, 302–304; James Michael Lee, *The Flow of Religious Instruction* (Birmingham, Ala.: Religious Education Press, 1973), pp. 28–38.

MEDITATION 4:
GIVING EVERYTHING WE HAVE

1. This story is adapted from Penninnah Schram, *Jewish Stories: One Generation Tells Another* (Northvale, N.J.: Aronson, 1987), pp. 128–132. Actually, my adaptation is more closely aligned to the way I heard Schram tell this story in February 1988 at Temple Beth-El in Birmingham, Alabama, than the way she narrated it in her book.

2. James Michael Lee, *The Flow of Religious Instruction* (Birmingham, Ala.: Religious Education Press, 1973), pp. 157–160; James Michael Lee, *The Content*

Notes 257

of Religious Instruction (Birmingham, Ala.: Religious Education Press, 1985), pp. 240–241.

MEDITATION 5: COMMITMENT

1. The story narrated in this meditation comes from Robert Considine, *The Maryknoll Story* (New York: Doubleday, 1950, p. 22.

Other source materials on the Japanese invasion of China that I used for this meditation include John King Fairbank, *China: A New History* (Cambridge, Mass.: Belknap, 1992), pp. 312–321; Jonathan D. Spence, *The Search for Modern China* (New York: Norton, 1990), pp. 443–466; Ikuhiko Hata, "Continental Expansion," trans. Alvin D. Cox, in *The Cambridge History of Japan*, ed. Peter Duus, (Cambridge: Cambridge University Press, 1988), 6: 290–309; Lloyd Eastman, "Nationalist China during the Sino-Japanese War 1937–1945," in *The Cambridge History of China*, ed. John K. Fairbank and Albert Feuerwerker (Cambridge: Cambridge University Press, 1986), 13: 547–575; Immanuel C. Y. Hsü, *The Rise of Modern China*, 3d ed. (New York: Oxford University Press, 1983), pp. 582–599; Hsi-Sheng-Ch'I, *Nationalist China at War: Military Defeats and Political Collapse, 1937–1945* (Ann Arbor, Mich.: University of Michigan Press, 1982), pp. 41–63; Marius B. Jansen, *Japan and China: From War to Peace, 1894–1972* (Chicago: Rand McNally, 1975), pp. 425–431; F. F. Liu, *A Military History of Modern China* (Princeton, N.J.: Princeton University Press, 1956), pp. 197–208.

On commitment in psychology, see Richard L. Gorsuch, "Toward Motivational Theories of Intrinsic Religious Commitment," in *The Psychology of Religion: Theoretical Approaches*, ed. Bernard Spilka and Daniel N. McIntosh (Boulder, Colo.: Westview, 1997), pp. 11–22; Rodney Stark and William Sims Bainbridge, "Toward a Theory of Religion: Religious Commitment, in *The Psychology of Religion: Theoretical Approaches*, pp. 27–42; Rachel Karniol and Michael Ross, "The Motivational Impact of Temporal Focus: Thinking about the Future and the Past," in *Annual Review of Psychology*, vol. 47, ed. Janet T. Spence, John M. Darley, and Donald J. Foss (Palo Alto, Calif.: Annual Reviews, 1996), 47: 593–620; Paul Karoly, "Mechanisms of Self-Regulation: A Systems View," in *Annual Review of Psychology*, ed. Lyman Porter and Mark R. Rosenzweig (Palo Alto, Calif.: Annual Reviews, 1993), 44: 28–29; Thomas W. Lee et al., "Commitment Propensity, Organizational Commitment, and Voluntary Turnover: A Longitudinal Study of Organizational Entry Processes", *Journal of Management* 18 (March 1992): 15–32; Charles A. O'Reilly III, "Organizational Behavior: Where We've Been, Where We're Going," in *Annual Review of Psychology*, ed. Mark R. Rosenzweig and Lyman Porter (Palo Alto, Calif.: Annual Reviews, 1991), 42: 437–438; Beverly Fehr, "Prototype Analysis of the Concepts of Love and Commitment," in *Journal of Personality and Social Psychology* 55 (October 1988): 557–579; Michael E. Bratman, *Intention, Plans, and Practical Reason* (Cambridge, Mass.: Harvard University Press, 1987), pp. 14–27, 107–110; Margaret A. Farley, *Personal Commitments* (New York: Harper & Row, 1986), pp. 12–37, 110–135; Peter G. Stromberg, *Symbols of Community* (Tuscon,

Ariz.: University of Arizona Press, 1986), pp. 9–14; Robert Lawrence Kuhn and George Thomas Geis, *The Firm Bond* (New York: Praeger, 1984), pp. 101–172; Wade Clark Roof, *Community and Commitment* (New York: Elsevier, 1978), pp. 19–24, 79–106; James M. Smith, *Understanding Religious Convictions* (Notre Dame, Ind.: University of Notre Dame Press, 1975), pp. 7–8; T. R. Miles, *Religious Experience* (London: Macmillan, 1972), pp. 53–59; Charles A. Kiesler, *The Psychology of Commitment* (New York: Academic Press, 1971), pp. 30–33, 63–64, 167–172; John Finley Scott, *Internalization of Norms: A Sociological Theory of Moral Commitment* (Englewood Cliffs, N.J.: Prentice-Hall, 1971), pp. 35–37, 110–126; Gabriel Marcel, *Creative Fidelity*, trans. Robert Rosthal (New York: Farrar, Straus, 1964), pp. 107–110; Ian Ramsey, *Religious Language* (London: SCM Press, 1957), pp. 28–37.

For material dealing more or less with commitment in religious instruction, see Luther E. Lindberg, "Teaching Matters: The Role of the Teacher," in *Lifelong Learning*, ed. Rebecca Grothe (Minneapolis, Minn.: Augsburg, 1997), p. 95; Robert L. Browning and Roy A. Reed, *Models of Confirmation and Baptismal Affirmation* (Birmingham, Ala.: Religious Education Press, 1995), pp. 24–25, 34–38, 48, 149, 162–163; Blake J. Neff, "Family Communication." in *Handbook of Family Religious Education*, ed. Blake J. Neff and Donald Ratcliff (Birmingham, Ala.; Religious Education Press, 1995), p. 145; Jeff Astley, *The Philosophy of Christian Religious Education* (Birmingham, Ala.: Religious Education Press, 1994), pp. 208–212; Richard Robert Osmer, *Teaching for Faith* (Louisville, Ky.: Westminster/Knox, 1992), pp. 106–148; Michael Warren, *Faith, Culture and the Worshipping Community* (New York: Paulist, 1989), pp. 36–37; Muriel Fontenot Blackwell, *Called to Teach Children* (Nashville, Tenn.: Broadman, 1983), pp. 84–91; Lawrence O. Richards, "Experiencing Reality Together: Toward the Impossible Dream", in *Religious Education and Theology*, ed. Norma H. Thompson (Birmingham, Ala.: Religious Education Press, 1982), p. 205; Mary K. Cove and Mary Louise Mueller, *Regarding Religious Education* (Mishawaka, Ind.: Religious Education Press, 1977), pp. 41–41; Johannes Hofinger, *Evangelization and Catechesis: Are We Really Proclaiming the Gospel?* (New York: Paulist, 1976), pp. 61–76; Gabriel Moran, *Design for Religion* (New York: Herder and Herder, 1970), p. 143; Gabriel Moran, *Catechesis of Revelation* (New York: Herder and Herder, 1966), pp. 37–38, 70–73, 127–130; L. Harold DeWolf, *Teaching Our Faith in God* (New York: Abingdon, 1963), pp. 26–27; Georgia Harkness, "An Underlying Philosophy for Christian Education," in *Studies in Religious Education*, ed. Philip Henry Lotz and L. W. Crawford (Nashville, Tenn.: Cokesbury Press, 1931), pp. 58–59.

2. James Michael Lee, *The Flow of Religious Instruction* (Birmingham, Ala.: Religious Education Press, 1973), pp. 195–196; James Michael Lee, *The Content of Religious Instruction* (Birmingham, Ala.: Religious Education Press, 1985), pp. 133, 242.

MEDITATION 6: A HOLY ACT

1. It is important to underscore that my treatment of sacrament in this meditation is primarily phenomenological rather than theological in the propositional
and formal senses of classical Christian theology. In this meditation I am not suggesting that religious instruction is technically a sacrament in the formally defined doctrinal meaning of that term in conventional Christian sacramental theology and especially in classical Catholic sacramental theology. I am using the term
"sacrament" as it appears both in Christian and non-Christian faith traditions, not
just as a metaphor of "true sacrament" but as an active participation both in Jesus
the *Ursakrament* and in Jesus' ongoing grace-flowing activity in the holy work of
his Church. In this dual phenomenological and extended theological sense, religious instruction is not simply a "little sacrament" or even a sacramental, but
more importantly is a kind of ontic and functional sharing in the whole of authentic sacramental reality.

On the etymology of the word "sacrament," see D. A. Simpson, ed., *Cassell's
New Latin Dictionary* (New York: Funk and Wagnalls, 1959), p. 529; Charlton T.
Lewis and Charles Short, *Latin Dictionary* (Oxford: Clarendon, 1879), pp.
1611–1612; Robertus Stephanus, *Thesaurus linguae latinae*, tomus IV, p. 142.

Some complementary theological treatments of sacrament that I consulted as a
background to composing this meditation include John Macquarrie, *A Guide to the
Sacraments* (New York: Continuum, 1997), pp. 1–11; Louis-Marie Chauvet, *Sym-
bol and Sacrament: A Sacramental Reinterpretation of Christian Existence*, trans.
Patrick Madigan and Madeleine Beaumont (Collegeville, Minn: Liturgical Press,
1995), pp. 180–189; Bernard Cooke, *Sacraments and Sacramentality*, 2d ed.
(Mystic, Conn.: Twenty-Third, 1994), pp. v-vi, 6–28, 171–173, 224–231; Michael
G. Lawler, *Symbol and Sacrament* (New York: Paulist, 1987), pp. 29–63; Mary
Peter McGinty, *The Sacraments of Christian Life* (Chicago: Thomas More, 1992),
pp. 26–46; Wayne Ward, "Sacrament," in *Holman Bible Dictionary*, ed. Trent C.
Butler (Nashville, Tenn: Holman, 1991), pp. 1217–1218; Theodore W. Jennings Jr.
and Monika K. Hellwig, "Sacrament," in *The Encyclopedia of Religion*, ed.
Mircea Eliade (New York: Macmillan, 1987), 12: 500–554; Joseph Martos, *Doors
to the Sacred* (Garden City, N.Y.: Doubleday, 1981), pp. 9–151; John P. Dourley,
C. G. Jung and Paul Tillich: The Psyche as Sacrament (Toronto: Inner City Press,
1981), pp. 31–47; Tad Guzie, *The Book of Sacramental Basics* (New York: Paulist,
1981), pp. 71–91; Gerhard Ludwig Müller, *Bonhoeffers Theologie der Sakramente*
(Frankfurt am Main: Knecht, 1979), ss. 230–243; Raphael Schulte, "Sacraments,"
in *Sacramentum Mundi*, ed. Karl Rahner et al. (New York: Herder and Herder,
1970), 5: 378–384; Victor W. Turner, *The Ritual Process* (Chicago: University of
Chicago Press, 1969), pp. 1–43; G. C. Berkouwer, *The Sacraments*, trans. Hugo
Bekker (Grand Rapids, Mich: Eerdmans, 1969), pp. 13–26; Raj Bali Pandey,
Hindu Samskāras: Socio-Religious Study of the Hindu Sacraments, 2d ed. (Delhi:
Motilal Banarsidass, 1969), pp. 15–47, 106–152; Hans Küng, preface to *The
Sacraments: An Ecumenical Dilemma*, ed. Hans Küng, trans. Theodore L. Westow
(New York: Paulist, 1966), pp. 1–3; E. Schillebeeckx, *Christ the Sacrament of the
Encounter with God*, trans. Paul Barrett, Mark Schoof, and Laurence Bright (New

York: Sheed and Ward, 1963), pp. 7–20, 179–222; Bernard Piault, *What Is a Sacrament?* trans. A. Manson (New York: Hawthorn, 1963), pp. 17–28, 40–100; E. O. James, *Sacrifice and Sacrament* (New York: Barnes and Noble, 1962), pp. 13–35, 232–251; Kendig Brubaker Cully, *Sacraments: The Language of Faith* (Philadelphia: Christian Education Press, 1961), pp. 11–21; Arnold van Gennep, *The Rites of Passage,* trans. Monika B. Vizedom and Gabrielle L. Caffee (Chicago: University of Chicago Press, 1960), pp. 1–14, 41–165, 189–194; F. Gavin, *The Jewish Antecedents of Christian Sacraments* (London: Society for Promoting Christian Knowledge, 1928), pp. 1–25.

For a treatment of sacrament in the religious instruction literature, see Iris V. Cully, *The Bible in Christian Education* (Minneapolis, Minn.: Fortress, 1995), pp. 123–125; Padraic O'Hare, *Busy Life, Peaceful Center: A Book of Meditating* (Allen, Tex.: Thomas More, 1995), pp. 32–38; Timothy Arthur Lines, *Functional Images of the Religious Educator* (Birmingham, Ala.: Religious Education Press, 1992), pp. 484–492; Thomas H. Groome, *Sharing Faith* (San Francisco, Calif.: HarperSanFrancisco, 1991), pp. 341–347; Marianne Sawicki, "Tradition and Sacramental Education," in *Theological Approaches to Christian Education,* ed. Jack L. Seymour and Donald L. Miller (Nashville, Tenn.: Abingdon, 1990), pp. 43–49, 53–60; Matías Preiswerk, *Educating in the Living Word,* trans. Robert R. Barr (Maryknoll, N.Y.: Orbis, 1987), pp. 8–11; Berard L. Marthaler, *The Creed* (Mystic, Conn.: Twenty-Third, 1987), pp. 347–368; Robert L. Browning and Roy A. Reed, *The Sacraments in Religious Education and Liturgy* (Birmingham, Ala.: Religious Education Press, 1985), pp. 3–116; Jack L. Seymour, Robert T. O'Gorman, and Charles R. Foster, *The Church in the Education of the Public: Refocusing the Task of Religious Education* (Nashville, Tenn.: Abingdon, 1984), pp. 139–142; Johannes Hofinger, *Pastoral Life in the Power of the Spirit* (Staten Island, N.Y.: Alba, 1982), pp. 179–205; Joannes Paulus II, "Catechesi Tradendae," [n.t.], in *John Paul II, Catechist* ed. Robert J. Levis and Michael J. Wrenn, presented and endorsed by a number [8] of [Pontifical] Catechetical Institutes in the United States (Chicago; Franciscan Herald Press, 1980), p. 88 (No. 23); Alfred McBride, *Catechetics: A Theology of Proclamation* (Milwaukee, Wis.: Bruce, 1966), pp. 64–74; Marshall C. Dendy, *Changing Patterns in Christian Education* (Richmond, Va.: Knox, 1964), pp. 51–52.

2. James Michael Lee, *The Shape of Religious Instruction* (Birmingham, Ala.; Religious Education Press, 1971), pp. 55–74, 81–88, 258–297; James Michael Lee, *The Flow of Religious Instruction* (Birmingham, Ala.: Religious Education Press, 1973), pp. 10–13; James Michael Lee, *The Content of Religious Instruction* (Birmingham, Ala.: Religious Education Press, 1985), pp. 318–326, 521–522, 608–638.

MEDITATION 7: A HOLY PLACE

1. Karate instructors hold one of four ranks. The highest rank is that of *Saiko Shihan* (grand master), followed in descending order by *Shihan* (master), *Sensei*

(teacher and mentor), and finally *Sempai* (senior student who has attained the black belt).

Karate learners hold various degree depending on their demonstrated proficiency. Each degree is signified by a different color belt that the learner wears at the midsection to hold in place the two-piece *dōgi* (karate uniform). From the beginner to the most advanced, the rank progression of learners in the World Oyama Karate Organization (which is quite similar to the ranking system in other karate groups) is: white belt (10th *Kyu*), white belt with blue stripe (9th *Kyu*), blue belt (8th *Kyu*), blue belt with yellow stripe (7th *Kyu*), yellow belt (6th *Kyu*), orange belt (5th *Kyu*), green belt (4th *Kyu*), green belt with brown stripe (3d *Kyu*), brown belt (2d *Kyu*), brown belt with black stripe (1st *Kyu*), and finally black belt (1st *Dan Sempai*). There are nine grades within the rank of black belt. The brown belt marks the beginning of very serious acquisition of karate practice. A brown belt at World Oyama Karate is the equivalent of a black belt in many other reputable karate institutions in the United States. At World Oyama Karate, the brown belt examination takes two and a half hours, not counting the written examination. Parents are not allowed to attend brown belt examinations and higher because they often wince and become frightened if their children get hurt during the examination. (Most of the learners in the karate training sessions which my three young sons attended were adults.)

In order to attain each degree, the learner must demonstrate during a special promotion examination a designated level of performance in both form (*kata*) and fighting skill (*kumite*). Typically a learner is admitted to the formal promotion exercise for the next degree only when the karate teacher believes that the learner has reached that level of *kata* and *kumite* performance necessary to pass the promotion test.

In addition to the knowledge of karate that I gained from watching my three sons practicing three times a week on the *dōjo* I consulted some written sources when preparing this meditation, including U.S. Oyama Black Belt Association, *Student Handbook* (New York: The Association, n.d.); John C.H. Wu, *The Golden Age of Zen,* 2d ed. (New York: Doubleday Image, 1996), pp. 34–42; Gui-Young Hong, "Buddhism and Religious Experience," in *Handbook of Religious Experience*, ed. Ralph W. Hood Jr. (Birmingham, Ala: Religious Education Press, 1995), pp. 87–121; Nathan Johnson, *Zen Shaolin Karate: The Complete Practice, Philosophy, and History* (Rutland, Vt.: Tuttle, 1994), pp. 19–31, 64–68, 232–236; S. Oyama, Y. Oyama, M. Miura, *Full Contact Karate: Perfect Karate I* (New York: Oyama Publishing, 1992); Christopher J. Goedecke and Rosmarie Hausherr, *The Wind Warrior: The Training of a Karate Champion* (New York: Four Winds Press, 1992), pp. 4–15, 20–24; *The Transmission of the Lamp: Early Masters*, ed. Tao Yuan, trans. Sohaku Ogata (Wolfeboro, N.H.: Longwood, 1990), pp. xxi–xxiv, 57–77; Heinrich Dumoulin, *Zen Buddhism: A History,* vol. 1; *India and China*, trans. James W. Heisig and Paul Knitter (New York: Macmillan, 1988), pp. 85–94; Doris Buchanan Smith, *Karate Dancer* (New York: Putnam's, 1987), pp. 163–175; Tadasshi Nakamura, *Karate Technique and Spirit: Respect, Love, Obedience* (Tokyo: Shufunotomo, 1986), pp. 13–19, 22–33, 40–41, 53–55; Hideyuki Ashihara, *Fighting Karate*, trans. [Kodansha translation team] (Tokyo: Kodansha, 1985), pp. 4–5, 62–63, 82–85, 126–131; George R. Parulski, Frankie

"Dr. Speed" Mitchell, and the East Coast Demo Team, *Karate Power: Learning the Art of the Empty Hand* (Chicago: Contemporary Books, 1985), pp. 3–9; Morio Higaonna, *Traditional Karate-Do—Okinawa Goju Ryu:* vol. 1: *The Fundamental Techniques* (n. p.: Minato Research/Japan, n.d. [1985], p. 13; Thomas Hoover, *The Zen Experience* (New York: New American Library, 1980), pp. 21–27; P.M.V. Morris, *The Karate-dō Manual* (London: Stanley Paul, 1978), pp. 12–22, 28–49; Tak Kubota, *The Art of Karate* (New York: Peebles Harrington House, 1977), pp. 11–13, 26–27, 58–61, 100–101; Shigeru Egami, *The Heart of Karate Dō* (Tokyo: Kodansha, 1976), pp. 9–23, 36–37, 122–123; Shoshin Nagamine, *The Essence of Okinawan Karate-Do (Shorin-ryu)* (Rutland, Vt.: Tuttle, 1976), pp. 13–30; Masutatsu Oyama, *Advanced Karate* (Tokyo: Japan Publications, 1970), pp. 13–26, 137–143, 237–241; Bruce Tegner, *Bruce Tegner's Complete Book of Karate*, 2d ed. (Ventura, Calif.: Thor, 1970), pp. 7–42; Daisetz Teitaro Suzuki, *The Training of the Zen Buddhist Monk* (New York: University Books, 1965), pp. 3–13, 148–155, 159–161; Masutatsu Oyama, *This Is Karate* (Tokyo: Japan Publications, 1965), pp. 37–44, 60–67, 137–191; 223–254, 308–323, 352–360; Daisetz Teitaro Suzuki, *An Introduction to Zen Buddhism* (New York: Grove Weidenfeld, 1964), pp. 118–132; Bobby Lowe, *Mas Oyama's Karate as Practiced in Japan* (New York: Wehman, 1964), pp. v-vi, 1–9, 30–33, 69–75; Hidetaka Nishiyama and Richard C. Brown, *Karate* (Rutland, Vt.: Tuttle, 1959), pp. 13–37.

Some related religious instruction treatments include Helen Goggin, "Process Theology and Religious Education," in *Theologies of Religious Education*, ed. Randolph Crump Miller (Birmingham, Ala.: Religious Education Press, 1995), pp. 137–138; Jerome W. Berryman, *Godly Play: A Way of Religious Education* (San Francisco, Calif.: HarperSanFrancisco, 1991), pp. 80–87; Thomas P. Walters and Rita Tyson Walters, *Making a Difference: A Catechist's Guide to Successful Classroom Management* (Kansas City, Mo.: Sheed and Ward, 1986), pp. 24–32; Norma J. Everist, *Education Ministry in the Congregation* (Minneapolis, Minn.: Augsburg, 1983), pp. 15–17; Parker J. Palmer, *To Know As We Are Known: A Spirituality of Education* (San Francisco, Calif.: Harper & Row, 1983), pp. 69–105; Paul H. Vieth, *Worship in Christian Education* (Philadelphia: United Church Press, 1965), pp. 104–107.

2. James Michael Lee, *The Shape of Religious Instruction* (Birmingham, Ala.: Religious Education Press, 1971), pp. 74–88; James Michael Lee, *The Flow of Religious Instruction* (Birmingham, Ala.: Religious Education Press, 1973), pp. 65–73, 240–248; James Michael Lee, *The Content of Religious Instruction* (Birmingham, Ala: Religious Education Press, 1985), pp. 442–445, 506–512.

MEDITATION 8: RELIGIOUS EXPERIENCE

1. John Wesley, "Journal" (October 14, 1735—November 3, 1738), in *The Complete Works of John Wesley*, 3d ed. (Grand Rapids, Mich.: Baker, 1872), 1: 17–164; John Wesley, "Last Will and Testament," in *Complete Works*, 4:500–502; John Wesley, "On the Education of Children" (sermon 95), in *Complete Works*,

7:86–98; John Wesley, "On the Duty of Constant Communion" (sermon 101), in *Complete Works*, 7:86–98; John Wesley, "An Act of Devotion," in *Complete Works*, 8: 185; John Wesley, "An Address to the Clergy," in *Complete Works*, 10: 480–500; John Wesley, "How Far Is It the Duty of a Christian Minister to Preach Politics?" in *Complete Works*, 11:154–155; John Wesley, "Plain Account of Christian Perfection," in *Complete Works*, 11:366–446; John Wesley, "Thoughts on the Single Life," in *Complete Works*, 11:456–463; John Wesley, "Reasons against Separation from the Church of England," in *Complete Works*, 13:225–231.

Sources that I consulted on the life, conversion, and spirit of John Wesley include Bufford W. Coe, *John Wesley and Marriage* (Bethlehem, Pa.: Lehigh University Press, 1996), pp. 39–44, 55–57, 72–79; Richard B. Steele, *"Gracious Affection" and "True Virtue" according to Jonathan Edwards and John Wesley* (Metuchen, N.J.: Scarecrow Press, 1994), pp. 103–110; Ted A. Campbell, *John Wesley and Christian Antiquity: Religious Vision and Cultural Change* (Nashville, Tenn.: Abingdon Kingswood, 1991), pp. 58–67; Mary Elizabeth Mullins [sic] Moore, "Our Teaching Task," in *By What Authority: A Conversation on Teaching among United Methodists*, ed. Elizabeth Box Price and Charles R. Foster (Nashville, Tenn.: Abingdon, 1991), pp. 107–108; Henry Abelove, *The Evangelist of Desire: John Wesley and the Methodists* (Stanford, Calif.: Stanford University Press, 1990), pp. 24–39; Henry D. Rack, *Reasonable Enthusiast: John Wesley and the Rise of Methodism* (Philadelphia: Trinity, 1989), pp. 45–161, 353–360, 535–554; Gregory S. Clapper, *John Wesley on Religious Affections: His Views on Experience and Emotion and Their Role in the Christian Life and Theology* (Metuchen, N.J.: Scarecrow Press, 1989), pp. 1–15, 154–177. (On p. 13, Clapper, a Methodist, states in a telling footnote: "Many who have *not* ignored these issues [of the interrelation between affectivity and theology and between religious experience and theology], like Bernard of Clairvaux, Bonaventure or even Søren Kierkegaard, are often exiled from the (often more prestigious) realm of 'theology' proper and related to the supposed nether-region of 'spirituality.' Others, like Augustine and Aquinas, discuss the nature of the heart and the affections, but these analyses are often ignored (especially by Protestants)"; Frances Young, "The Significance of John Wesley's Conversion Experience." in *John Wesley: Contemporary Perspectives,* ed. John Stacey (London: Epworth Press, 1988), pp. 37–46; Aelred Burrows, "Wesley the Catholic," in *The Significance of John Wesley's Conversion Experience*, pp. 54–66; Richard P. Heitzenrater, *The Elusive Mr. Wesley* (Nashville, Tenn: Abingdon, 1984), 1:37–115, 174–198, 216–220; 2:15–70, 83–89, 143–158; Howard A. Snyder, *The Radical Wesley and Patterns for Church Renewal* (Downers Grove, Ill.: Inter-Varsity Press, 1980), pp. 13–52; Stanley Ayling, *John Wesley* (Cleveland. Ohio: Collins, 1979), pp. 44–103, 291–315; Robert G. Tuttle Jr., *John Wesley: His Life and Theology* (Grand Rapids, Mich.: Zondervan, 1978), pp. 15, 31–68, 99–102, 113–142, 181–229, 259–310, 351–354; Willie Snow Edwards, *Strange Fires: The True Story of John Wesley's Love Affair in Georgia* (New York: Vanguard, 1971), pp. 76–81, 148–240, 246–247; Albert C. Outler, preface to *John Wesley,* ed. Albert Outler (New York: Oxford University Press, 1964), pp. vii–xii (quotation about Wesley's chief endeavor on p. vii; also see p. 20); Albert Outler, introduction to *John*

Wesley, pp. 3–33, 51–53, 306–307; A. B. Lawson, *John Wesley and the Christian Ministry* (London: SPCK, 1963), pp. 71–98; Umphrey Lee, *The Lord's Horseman* (Nashville, Tenn.: Abingdon, 1954), pp. 16–91, 122–134, 143–167, 198–214; Maximin Piette, *John Wesley in the Evolution of Protestantism*, trans. J. B. Howard (New York: Sheed & Ward, 1937), pp. 212–392, 436–442; John W. Prince, *Wesley on Religious Education* (New York: Methodist Book Concern, 1926), pp. 64–76, 97–136.

On religious experience, which constituted the central feature of John Wesley's conversion and subsequent religious instruction activities, see Kilian McDonnell, "Spirit and Experience in Bernard of Clairvaux," *Theological Studies* 58 (March 1997): 203–233; Rodney Stark, "A Taxonomy of Religious Experience," in *The Psychology of Religion: Theoretical Approaches*, ed. Bernard Spilka and Daniel N. McIntosh (Boulder, Colo.: Westview, 1997), pp. 209–221; Ralph W. Hood Jr., "The Empirical Study of Mysticism," in *The Psychology of Religion*, pp. 222–232; Raymond F. Paloutzian, *Invitation to the Psychology of Religion*, 2d ed. (Boston: Allyn and Bacon, 1996), pp. 176–198; Frederica R. Halligan, "Jungian Theory and Religious Experience," in *Handbook of Religious Experience*, ed. Ralph W. Hood Jr. (Birmingham, Ala.: Religious Education Press, 1995), pp. 568–597; Ralph W. Hood Jr., "The Facilitation of Religious Experience," in *Handbook of Religious Experience*, pp. 568–597; Kevin Fauteux, *The Recovery of Self: Regression and Redemption in Religious Experience* (New York: Paulist, 1994), pp. 7–13, 90–91, 158–191; David M. Wulff, *Psychology of Religion: Classic and Contemporary Views* (New York: Wiley, 1991), pp. 184–192, 501–507, 529–532, 555–565, 601–605; William P. Alston, *Perceiving God: The Epistemology of Religious Experience* (Ithaca, N.Y.: Cornell University Press, 1991), pp. 14–67; Kenneth E. Hyde, *Religion in Childhood and Adolescence* (Birmingham,, Ala.; Religious Education Press, 1990), pp. 164–193; Caroline Franks Davis, *The Evidential Force of Religious Experience* (Oxford: Clarendon, 1989), pp. 5–65; J. Harley Chapman, *Jung's Three Theories of Religious Experience* (Lewiston, N.Y.: Mellen, 1988), pp. 152–159; William James, *The Varieties of Religious Experience* (Cambridge, Mass.: Harvard University Press, 1985), pp. 262–339; Wayne Proudfoot, *Religious Experience* (Berkeley, Calif.: University of California Press, 1985), pp. 179–189, 226–227; André Godin, *The Psychological Dynamics of Religious Experience: It Doesn't Fall Down from Heaven*, trans. Mary Turton (Birmingham, Ala.: Religious Education Press, 1985), pp. 85–99; Joseph F. Byrnes, *The Psychology of Religion* (New York: Free Press, 1984), pp. 179–214; C. Daniel Batson and W. Larry Ventis, *Religious Experience: A Social-Psychological Perspective* (New York: Oxford University Press, 1982), pp. 56–96; Marilyn May Mallory, *Christian Mysticism: Transcending Techniques: A Theological Reflection on the Empirical Testing of the Teaching of St. John of the Cross* (Amsterdam: Van Gorcum, 1977), pp. 23–69, 166–178, 299–300; Carlos Castaneda, *A Separate Reality: Further Conversations with Don Juan* (Simon and Schuster Touchstone, 1972), pp. 218–237, 266–275, 284–298; Morton Kelsey, *Encounter with God* (Minneapolis, Minn.: Bethany Fellowship, 1972), pp. 143–153; T. R. Miles, *Religious Experience* (London: Macmillan, 1972), pp. 9–14, 33–44; Seely Beggiani, "Revelation and Religious Experience", in *New Dimensions in Religious Experience*, ed. George

Devine (Staten Island, N.Y.: Alba, 1971), pp. 39–51; Carlos Castaneda, *The Teachings of Don Juan: A Yaqui Way of Knowledge* (Berkeley, Calif.: University of California Press, 1968), pp. 13–19, 131–140, 175–179; Thomas Merton, *The Ascent to Truth* (New York: Harcourt, Brace, 1951), pp. 274–306; Gordon W. Allport, *The Individual and His Religion: A Psychological Interpretation* (New York: Macmillan, 1950), pp. 135–141; George Albert Coe, *The Psychology of Religion* (Chicago: University of Chicago Press, 1916), pp. ix, xv, 152–174, 263–285.

For some treatments of religious experience as discussed by religious educators or persons interested in religious education, see James Michael Lee, "Religious Instruction and Religious Experience," in *Handbook of Religious Experience*, ed. Ralph W. Hood Jr. (Birmingham, Ala.: Religious Education Press, 1995), pp. 535–567; John L. Elias, *Psychology and Religious Education*, 3d ed. Malabar, Fla.: Krieger, 1990), pp. 9–11; C. Ellis Nelson, *How Faith Matures* (Louisville, Ky.: Westminster/Knox, 1989), pp. 75–77; Michael Grimmitt, *Religious Education and Religious Development* (Great Wakering, England: Mc-Crimmon, 1987), pp. 179–179–182, 187–191; William E. Reiser, "Jesuit Spirituality and the Religious Educator", in *The Spirituality of the Religious Educator*, ed. James Michael Lee (Birmingham, Ala.: Religious Education Press, 1985), pp. 128–129; David Arthur Bickimer, *Christ the Placenta* (Birmingham, Ala.: Religious Education Press, 1983), pp. 9–14; James Michael Lee, "Religious Education and the Bible: A Religious Educationist's View," in *Biblical Themes in Religious Education*, ed. Joseph S. Marino (Birmingham, Ala.: Religious Education Press, 1983), pp. 8–11; Joseph S. Marino, "The Bible in Religious Education: A Biblicist's View", in *Biblical Themes in Religious Education*, pp. 80–81; William Bedford Williamson, *Language and Concepts in Christian Education* (Philadelphia: Westminster, 1979), pp. 68–76; André Brien, "Catechetics as a Task for Our Age," in *Teaching All Nations*, ed. Johannes Hofinger, trans. and ed. Clifford Howell (Freiburg im Breisgau, Deutschland: Herder, 1959), pp. 4–7; Josef Andreas Jungmann, *Handing on the Faith*, trans. and rev. A. N. Fuerst (New York: Herder and Herder, 1959), pp. 204–217.

2. James Michael Lee, *The Shape of Religious Instruction* (Birmingham, Ala.: Religious Education Press, 1971), pp. 13–19, 271–272; James Michael Lee, *The Flow of Religious Instruction* (Birmingham, Ala.: Religious Education Press, 1973), pp. 73–75; James Michael Lee, *The Content of Religious Instruction* (Birmingham, Ala: Religious Education Press, 1985), pp. 42–49, 63–67, 649–653, 661–672.

MEDITATION 9: THE JOURNEY

1. During my last two years on the faculty of the University of Notre Dame, my instructional duties centered around teaching the Great Books to undergraduate students. Wishing to make the Great Books vivid and operational in the consciousness and lives of these sophomores, I used highly personal instructional procedures. During my two years of teaching the course, it became increasingly

apparent to me that a central and recurrent theme of the world's greatest fictional and nonfictional literature is the journey into oneself. A great deal of previous social-scientific study, especially in the area of depth psychology, had taught me that the journey into oneself constitutes a major axis of the human psyche. Through teaching the Great Books I came to realize that the authors of the enduring great works of fiction and nonfiction, being students of human nature in their own right, were themselves deeply aware of the pivotal quest for a personal coming home. (I greatly enjoyed those two years of teaching the Great Books to very bright undergraduates.)

2. James Michael Lee, *The Shape of Religious Instruction* (Birmingham, Ala.: Religious Education Press, 1971), pp. 24–27; James Michael Lee, *The Flow of Religious Instruction* (Birmingham, Ala.; Religious Education Press, 1973), pp. 119–141; James Michael Lee, *The Content of Religious Instruction* (Birmingham, Ala.: Religious Education Press, 1973), pp. 78–128, 557–559, 633–643, 676–678.

MEDITATION 10: SMOKEHOUSE

1. Lue Park and Ed Park, *The Smoked-Foods Cookbook* (Harrisburg, Pa.: Stackpole, 1992), pp. 1–35; Sylvia G. Bashline, *Sylvia Bashline's Savory Game Cookbook* (Harrisburg, Pa.: Stackpole, 1983); Brian Paust and John Peters, "Smoked Fish Manual," Alaska Sea Grant Report 82–89, December 1982; Eliot Wigginton, *Foxfire 3* (Garden City, N.Y.: Doubleday Anchor, 1975), pp. 354–360. (I am indebted to James S. Davidson III, a Domer who loves not only people but also the land, for pointing me to the Foxfire series.)
See also James Michael Lee, "Lifework Spirituality and the Religious Educator," in *The Spirituality of the Religious Educator*, ed. James Michael Lee (Birmingham, Ala.: Religious Education Press, 1985), pp. 7–42; Parker J. Palmer, *To Know As We Are Known: A Spirituality of Education* (San Francisco, Calif.: Harper & Row, 1983), pp. 106–125.

2. James Michael Lee, *The Shape of Religious Instruction* (Birmingham, Ala.: Religious Education Press, 1971), pp. 302–304; James Michael Lee, *The Flow of Religious Instruction* (Birmingham, Ala.: Religious Education Press, 1973), pp. 73–75, 79–89, 284, 290–291.

MEDITATION 11: STATE OF CONSCIOUSNESS

1. For some treatments giving different perspectives on consciousness and the construction of self and its orientation, see Güven Güzeldere, The Many Faces of Consciousness: A Field Guide," in *The Nature of Consciousness*, ed. Ned Block, Owen Flanagan, and Güven Güzeldere (Cambridge, Mass.: MIT Prress, 1997), pp. 1–67; David J. Chalmers, "Facing Up to the Problem of Consciousness," in *Toward a Science of Consciousness*, ed. Stuart H. Hamerhoff, Alfred W. Kaszniak, and Alwyn C. Scott (Cambridge, Mass.: MIT Press, 1996), pp. 5–28; John

R. Searle, "The Problem of Consciousness", in *Scale in Conscious Experience*, ed. Joseph King and Karl H. Pribram (Mahwah, N.J.: Erlbaum, 1995), pp. 13–22; Antti Revonsuo, Matti Kamppinen, and Seppo Sajama, "The Riddle of Consciousness," in *Consciousness in Philosophy and Cognitive Neuroscience*, ed. Antti Revonsuo and Matti Kamppinen (Hillsdale, N.J.: Erlbaum, 1994), pp. 1–23; Antti Revonsuo, "In Search of the Science of Consciousness", in *Consciousness in Philosophy and Cognitive Neuroscience*, pp. 249–285; Norton Nelkin, "The Connection between Intentionality and Consciousness", in *Consciousness: Psychological and Philosophical Essays*, ed. Martin Davies and Glyn W. Humphries (Oxford: Blackwell, 1993), pp. 224–239; David M. Rosenthal, "Thinking That One Thinks", in *Consciousness: Psychological and Philosophical Essays*, pp. 197–223; Nicholas Humphrey, *A History of Mind* (New York: Harper Perennial, 1992), pp. 115–128; Ernest Keen, "Being Conscious Is Being-in-the-World," in *Self and Consciousness: Multiple Perspectives*, ed. Frank S. Kessell, Pamela M. Cole, and Dale L. Johnson (Hillsdale, N.J.: Erlbaum, 1992), pp. 45–63; Owen Flanagan, *Consciousness Reconsidered* (Cambridge, Mass: MIT Press Bradford, 1992), pp. 193–211; Daniel C. Dennett, *Consciousness Explained* (Boston: Little, Brown, 1991), pp. 21–42; Anthony J. Marcel, "Phenomenal Experience and Functionalism," in *Consciousness in Contemporary Science*, ed. A. J. Marcel and E. Bisiach (Oxford: Clarendon, 1988), pp. 121–158; Alan Allport, "What Concept of Consciousness?" in *Consciousness in Contemorary Society*, pp. 159–182; Natalino Caputi, *Guide to the Unconscious* (Birmingham, Ala.: Religious Education Press, 1984), pp. 1–14; Henri Ey, *Consciousness*, trans. John H. Flodstrom (Bloomington, Ind.: Indiana University Press, 1978), pp. 267–291; Julian Jaynes, *The Origin of Consciousness in the Breakdown of the Bicameral Mind* (Boston: Houghton Mifflin, 1976), pp. 84–125, 255–292; Arthur Deikman, "Bimodal Consciousness and the Mystic Experience," in *Symposium on Consciousness*, ed. Philip R. Lee et al. (New York: Viking, 1976), pp. 67–88; Arnold M. Ludwig, "Altered States of Consciousness," in *Altered States of Consciousness*, ed. Charles T. Tart (New York: Wiley, 1969), pp. 225–234; G. Dawes Hicks, J. Laird, and Alan Dorward, "Symposium: The Nature of the Self and Self-Consciousness," in *Mind, Matter, and Purpose*, supp. vol. 8, ed. Aristotlean Society (New York: Johnson Reprint, 1964), pp. 189–221.

For some treatments on consciousness as related to religious instruction in one way or another, see Michael Warren, *Communications and Cultural Analysis: A Religious View* (Westport, Conn.: Bergin & Garvey, 1992), pp. 11–19; Michael Grimmitt, *Religious Education and Human Development* (Great Wakering, England: McCrimmon, 1987), pp. 109–111; 114–121, 135–138, 155–159, 167–173; David Arthur Bickimer, *Christ the Placenta* (Birmingham, Ala.: Religious Education Press, 1983), pp. 11, 40–64; Mary Elizabeth Moore, *Education for Continuity and Change* (Nashville, Tenn.: Abingdon, 1983), pp. 50, 138–139; Russell Crescimanno, *Culture, Consciousness, and Beyond* (Lantham, Md.: University Press of America, 1982), pp. 41–53; John H. Westerhoff III, "Spiritual Life: Ritual and Consciousness," in *Learning through Liturgy*, by Gwen Kennedy Neville and John H. Westerhoff III, (New York: Seabury Crossroad, 1978), pp. 121–122; Malcolm L. Warford, *The Necessary Illusion: Church Culture and Educational Change* (Philadelphia: United Church Press, 1976), pp. 63–74; Gabriel Moran,

Religious Body (New York: Seabury Crossroad, 1974), pp. 92–95; Gabriel Moran, *The Present Revelation* (New York: Herder and Herder, 1972), pp. 97–101.

See also Pierre Teilhard de Chardin, *The Future of Man*, trans. Norman Denny (New York: Harper & Row, 1964), pp. 64–66, 113–120, 295–323; Pierre Teilhard de Chardin, *Hymn to the Universe*, trans. Simon Bartholomew (New York: Harper & Row, 1961), pp. 94–95; Pierre Teilhard de Chardin, *The Phenomenon of Man*, trans. Bernard Wall (New York: Harper, 1959), pp. 46–47, 54–61, 87–90, 147–152, 164–178, 254–263, 301–308.

2. James Michael Lee, *The Shape of Religious Instruction* (Birmingham, Ala.: Religious Education Press, 1971), pp. 184–189, 302–304; James Michael Lee, *The Flow of Religious Instruction* (Birmingham, Ala.: Religious Education Press, 1973), pp. 279–286; James Michael Lee, *The Content of Religious Instruction* (Birmingham, Ala.: Religious Education Press, 1985), pp. xiii-xiv, 484–512.

MEDITATION 12: INFLUENCE

1. Henry Adams, *The Education of Henry Adams* (Boston: Houghton Mifflin, 1918), p. 300.

2. James Michael Lee, *The Shape of Religious Instruction* (Birmingham, Ala.: Religious Education Press, 1971), pp. 87–88, 251–253, 259–261, 309–313; James Michael Lee, *The Flow of Religious Instruction* (Birmingham, Ala.: Religious Education Press, 1973), pp. 39–43, 51–55, 146–147, 212–215, 279–289; James Michael Lee, *The Content of Religious Instruction* (Birmingham, Ala.: Religious Education Press, 1985), pp. 17–23, 255–256, 753–758.

MEDITATION 13: LEADERSHIP

1. Chaim Herzog, *The Arab-Israeli Wars* (New York: Random House, 1982), pp. 247–362; Trevor N. Dupuy, *Elusive Victory: The Arab-Israeli Wars, 1947–1974* (New York: Harper & Row, 1978), pp. 387–633. Both of these books, the first written by a high-ranking American military officer and the second by a senior Israeli military officer, are very professional and are good examples of military science. Each of these books is quite objective and nonpartisan, no small achievement on a topic so frequently characterized by self-serving subjectivity and rabid partisanship.

On leadership in general and educational leadership in specific, see Robert K. Greeenleaf, *On Becoming a Servant-Leader*, ed. Don M. Frick and Larry C. Spears (San Francisco, Calif.: Jossey-Bass, 1996), pp. 127–148; Robert K. Greenleaf, *Seeker and Servant: Reflections on Religious Leadership*, ed. Anne T. Fraker and Larry C. Spears (San Francisco, Calif.: Jossey-Bass, 1996), pp. 9–48 (on p. 12 Greenleaf defines leadership as "going ahead and showing the way"); Diane Dreher, *The Tao of Personal Leadership* (New York: HarperCollins, 1996), pp. 206–233; Edgar H. Schein, "Leadership and Organizational Culture," in *The*

Leader of the Future, ed. Frances Hesselbein, Marshall Goldsmith, and Richard Beckhard (San Francisco, Cal.: Jossey-Bass, 1996), pp. 59–69; James M. Kouzes and Barry Z. Posner, *Credibility: How Leaders Gain It and Lose It, Why People Demand It* (San Francisco: Jossey- Bass, 1993), pp. 2–11; Don Hellriegel, John W. Slocum Jr., and Ronald W. Woodman, *Organizational Behavior*, 7th ed. (Minneapolis, Minn: West, 1992), pp. 342–384; James W. Guthrie, "The Evolution of Educational Management: Eroding Myths and Emerging Models," in *Educational Leadership and Changing Contexts of Families, Communities, and Schools,"* ed. Luvern L. Cunningham, Eighty-ninth Yearbook of the National Society for the Study of Education, pt. 2 (Chicago: The Association, 1990), pp. 210–231; William A. Cohen, *The Art of the Leader* (Englewood Cliffs, N.J.: Prentice-Hall, 1990), pp. 25–26; Bernard M. Bass, *Bass and Stogdill's Handbook of Leadership*, 3d ed. (New York: Free Press, 1990), pp. 37–55; John Heider, "The Leader Who Knows How Things Happen," in *Contemporary Issues in Leadership*, ed. William E. Rosenbach and Robert L. Taylor (Boulder, Colo.: Westview, 1989), pp. 161–167; Glenn L. Immegart, "Leadership and Leader Behavior", in *Handbook of Research on Educational Administration* ed. Norman J. Boyar (New York: Longman, 1988), pp. 259–275; James M. Kouzes and Barry Z. Posner, *The Leadership Challenge* (San Francisco, Calif: Jossey-Bass, 1987), pp. 11–12, 187–216; Robert K. Greenleaf, *Teacher as Servant* (New York: Paulist, 1979), pp. 144–152; Robert K. Greenleaf, *Servant Leadership* (New York: Paulist, 1977), pp. 14–15; Robert Tannenbaum, Irving R. Weschler, and Fred Massarik, *Leadership and Organization: A Behavioral Science Approach* (New York: McGraw-Hill, 1971), pp. 22–42; Douglas MacArthur, *Reminiscences* (New York: McGraw-Hill, 1964), p. 70.

For a treatment of leadership in overall ministry and especially in religious instruction ministry, see Robert Pazmiño, *By What Authority Do We Teach?* (Grand Rapids, Mich.: Baker, 1994), pp. 29–32, 37–58; Ndubuisi B. Akuchie,"The Servants and the Superstars: An Examination of Servant Leadership in Light of Matthew 20:20–28", *Christian Education Journal* 14 (Autumn 1993): 39–46; Bernard J. Lee, "God as Spirit," in *Empirical Theology: A Handbook*, ed. Randolph Crump Miller (Birmingham, Ala.: Religious Education Press, 1992), pp. 132–133; Helen Goggin, "Process Theology and Religious Education," in *Empirical Theology*, p. 146; Rex E. Johnson, "Philosophical Foundations of Ministry," in *Foundations of Ministry: An Introduction to Christian Education for a New Generation*, ed. Michael J. Anthony (Grand Rapids, Mich.: Baker, 1992), pp. 61–66; Michael J. Wrenn, *Catechisms and Controversies* (San Francisco, Calif.: Ignatius, 1991), pp. 199–206; Gail Thomas McKenna, *300 Questions DREs Are Asking about People and Programs* (New York: Paulist, 1990), pp. 7–15; David Arthur Bickimer, *Leadership in Religious Education* (Birmingham, Ala.: Religious Education Press, 1990), pp. 15–54, 151–232; Donald G. Emler, *Revisioning the DRE* (Birmingham, Ala.: Religious Education Press, 1989), pp. 95–114; G. Temp Sparkman, "The Pastor as Leader of an Educational Team," in *The Pastor as Religious Educator*, ed. Robert L. Browning (Birmingham, Ala.: Religious Education Press, 1989), pp. 126–145; James W. White, *Intergenerational Religious Education* (Birmingham, Ala.: Religious Education Press, 1988), pp. 162–163; Howard G. Hendricks, "The Teacher as Leader," in *The Christian*

Educator's Handbook on Teaching, ed. Kenneth O. Gangel and Howard G. Hendricks (Grand Rapids, Mich.: Baker, 1988), pp. 241–256; Larry Richards, *Living in Touch with God* (Grand Rapids, Mich.: Zondervan Pyranee, 1988), pp. 109–119; Léon Lauraire, *Jacques Piveteau: frère des écoles chrétiennes* (Paris: Secretariat Fréres des Ecoles Chrétiennes, 1988), pp. 82–85 (in Piveteau's words, ". . . *dans l'école ou dans la catéchèse, la piorité doit être donnée aux personnes: à leurs capacités, à leurs besoins, à leur promotion*" [p. 82]); Brennan R. Hill, *Key Dimensions of Religious Education* (Winona, Minn.: St. Mary's Press, 1988). pp. 155–156; Lawrence O. Richards, *A Practical Theology of Spirituality* (Grand Rapids, Mich.: Zondervan Academie, 1987), pp. 233–240; Robert J. Hater, *Parish Catechetical Ministry* (Encino, Calif.: Benziger, 1986), pp. 26–31; Kenneth O. Gangel, *Building Leaders for Church Education* (Chicago: Moody Press, 1981), p. 76; Edward Schillebeeckx, *Ministry: Leadership in the Community of Jesus Christ*, trans. John Bowden (New York: Crossroad, 1981), pp. 21–22; Lawrence O. Richards and Gilbert R. Martin, *Lay Ministry: Empowering the People of God* (Grand Rapids, Mich: Zondervan, 1981), pp. 73–85; J. Gordon Myers, "Decision Making—Goal of Reflection in Ministry," in *Method in Ministry*, ed. James D. Whitehead and Evelyn Eaton Whitehead (San Francisco, Calif.: Harper & Row, 1980), pp. 99–112; Lawrence O. Richards and Clyde Hoeldtke, *A Theology of Church Leadership* (Grand Rapids, Mich.: Zondervan, 1980), pp. 88–124; H. W. Byrne, *Improving Church Education* (Birmingham, Ala.; Religious Education Press, 1979), pp. 13–20; Lawrence O. Richards, *Christian Education: Seeking to Become Like Jesus Christ* (Grand Rapids, Mich.: Zondervan, 1975), pp. 131–134; Norman Wegmeyer, "The Pastor's Leadership Role", in *The Pastor's Role in Educational Ministry*, ed. Richard Allan Olson (Philadelphia: Fortress, 1974), pp. 225–226; Iris V. Cully, *Change, Conflict, and Self-Determination: Next Steps in Religious Education* (Philadelphia; Westminster, 1972), pp. 99–103; Lois E. LeBar, *Focus on People in Church Education* (Old Tappan, N.J.: Revell, 1968), pp. 239–241; C. Ellis Nelson, *Where Faith Begins* (Richmond, Va.: Knox, 1967), pp. 198–202; David W. Jewell, "Leadership Theory and Practice," in *An Introduction to Christian Education*, ed. Marvin J. Taylor (Nashville, Tenn.: Abingdon, 1966), pp.134–135; Kenneth L. Cober, *The Church's Teaching Ministry* (Valley Forge, Pa.: Judson, 1964), pp. 99–100.

2. James Michael Lee, *The Flow of Religious Instruction* (Birmingham, Ala: Religious Education Press, 1973), pp. 153–158, 166–169, 218–221.

MEDITATION 14: AT WORK ALWAYS

1. Niels Bohr, *Atomic Theory and the Description of Nature* (Cambridge: Cambridge University Press 1934), pp. 25–51; Niels Bohr, *Atomic Physics and Human Knowledge* (New York: Wiley, 1958), pp. 67–82; Niels Blaedel, *Harmony and Unity: The Life of Niels Bohr*, trans. Geoffrey French (Madison, Wis.: Science Tech, 1988), pp. 114–118, 156–202, 169–197, 212–221, 274–275; Peter Robertson, *The Early Years: The Niels Bohr Institute 1921–1930* (Copenhagen: Akademisk Forlag, 1979), pp. 28, 53, 57, 62, 88, 105, 111–112. 118–119,

128–155; David Jens Adler, "Childhood and Early Years," in *Niels Bohr: His Life and Work as Seen by His Friends and Colleagues*, ed. S. Rozenthal (Amsterdam: North-Holland, 1967) pp. 11–37; Léon Rosenfeld and Erik Rüdinger, "The Decisive Years 1911–1918," in ibid., pp. 38–73; Werner Heisenberg, "Quantum Theory and Its Interpretation", in *Niels Bohr: His Life and Work as Seen by His Friends and Colleagues*, pp. 94–108; Hendrick B. G. Casimir, "Recollections from the Years 1929–1931," in *Niels Bohr: His Life and Work as Seen by His Friends and Colleagues*, pp. 109–113; Léon Rosenfeld, "Niels Bohr in the Thirties: Consolidation and Extension of the Conception of Complementarity," in *Niels Bohr: His Life and Work as Seen by His Friends and Colleagues*, pp. 114–136; Aage Bohr, "The War Years and the Prospects Raised by the Atomic Weapons," in *Niels Bohr: His Life and Work as Seen by His Friends and Colleagues*, pp. 191–214; Ruth Moore, *Niels Bohr* (New York: Knopf, 1966), pp. 3–30, 152–161, 414–436; Werner Heisenberg, "The Development of the Interpretation of the Quantum Theory," in *Niels Bohr and the Development of Physics*, ed. Wolfgang Pauli (London: Pergamon, 1955), p. 15.

2. James Michael Lee, *The Shape of Religious Instruction* (Birmingham, Ala: Religious Education Press, 1971), pp. 300–304; James Michael Lee, *The Flow of Religious Instruction* (Religious Education Press, 1973), pp. 198–202, 206–212; James Michael Lee, *The Content of Religious Instruction* (Birmingham, Ala.: Religious Education Press, 1985), pp. 608–615.

MEDITATION 15: DESIRE

1. By 1998 Béla Karolyi had sold his gym in Houston and had concentrated his regular professional activities on conducting gymnastics training camps, gymnastics clincs, and gymnastics summer camps. He is also an official consultant of the U.S National Team in gymnastics.

Bela Karolyi, personal correspondence, April 9, 1998; Bela Karolyi, professional and personal resumé, 1998; Mary Lou Retton and Bela Karolyi, with John Powers, *Mary Lou: The Making of an Olympic Champion* (New York: McGraw-Hill, 1986), pp. 25–75, 127–137; Bela Karolyi and Nancy Ann Richardson, *Feel No Fear: The Power, Passion, and Politics of a Life in Gymnastics* (New York: Hyperion, 1994), pp. 168–177, 42–64, 76–90, 189–222.

See also Jane Leavy, "Happy Landing", *Sports Illustrated*, 87 (11 August, 1997), pp. 55–59; Karolyi, Béla, in *Current Biography Yearbook: 1996*, ed. Judith Graham (New York: Wilson, 1996), pp. 247–249; Richard Zoglin, "Kerri's Leap of Faith," *Time* 148 (5 August 1996), pp. 42–44; Mark Starr, "Leap of Faith," *Newsweek* 128 (5 August 1996), pp. 40–42, 46, 48; E. M. Swift, "Profile in Courage," *Sports Illustrated* 85 (5 August 1996), pp. 58–65; Tom Weir, "Commentary: Pain Hardly a Stranger to Gymnasts," *USA Today* (25 July 1996), p. E2; E. M. Swift, "Sports People: Dominique Moceanu," *Sports Illustrated* (8 May, 1995), pp. 54–55; Barbara Kantrowitz, "Living with Training,." *Newsweek* 120 (10 August 1992), pp. 24–25; Richard O'Brien, "Lord Gym," *Sports Illustrated* 77 (27 July 1992), pp. 46–52; Mark Starr, "The Little Pumpkin," *Newsweek* 120

(27 July 1992), pp. 54–57; Kathryn Casey, "Friends and Rivals," *Seventeen* 51 (June 1992), pp. 86–89; E. M. Swift, "A Wow at the Worlds," *Sports Illustrated* 75 (23 September 1991), pp. 40–41; Christine Brennan, "Bent Over Backwards," *Sport* 79 (October 1988), pp. 38–43; David Hutchings, "10 is His Number," *People Weekly* 30 (12 September 1988), pp. 44–47; Craig Neff, "Hardly Tiny in Talent," *Sports Illustrated* 68 (14 March 1988), p. 73; Anita Verschoth, "Ride 'Em Bela!," *Sports Illustrated* 64 (30 June 1986), pp. 56–57; Herma Silverstein, *Mary Lou Retton and the New Gymnasts* (New York: Watts, 1985), pp. 3–15; Rosemary G. Washington, *Mary Lou Retton: Power Gymnast* (Minneapolis, Minn.: Lerner, 1985), pp. 5–46; Francis Moriarty, "The Making of a Gymnast", *Women's Sports* 7 (January/February 1985), pp. 51–54, 66–67; Karen Freifeld and Sheldon Engelmayer, "The Next Nadia?" *Health* 16 (March 1984), pp. 48–49, 52; Bob Ottum, "The Double Romanian Twist," *Sports Illustrated*, 68 (13 June 1983), pp. 68, 70.

2. James Michael Lee, *The Shape of Religious Instruction* (Birmingham, Ala.: Religious Education Press, 1971), p. 52; James Michael Lee, *The Flow of Religious Instruction* (Birmingham, Ala.; Religious Education Press, 1973), pp. 89–98; James Michael Lee, *The Content of Religious Instruction* (Birmingham, Ala. Religious Education Press, 1985), pp. 21–22, 512–513, 743–744.

MEDITATION 16: CARE

1. On the etymology of the word "care," see Louis Guilbert et al. redacteurs, *Grand Larousse de la langue française* (Paris: Larousse, 1972), 1: 1095; Ernest Klein, *A Comprehensive Etymological Dictionary of the English Language* (Amsterdam: Elsevier, 1967), 1: 385; Eric Partridge, *Origins* (New York: Macmillan, 1966), pp. 135–136; *The Oxford Dictionary of English Etymology*, ed. C.T. Onions (Oxford: Clarendon, 1966), p. 236; *The Oxford Latin Dictionary*, fasc. 2 (Oxford: Clarendon, 1965), pp. 473–474; *Cassell's New Latin Dictionary*, ed. D. A. Simpson (New York: Funk & Wagnalls, 1959), pp. 162–163); *Cassell's Latin Dictionary* rev. ed., ed. R. V. Marchant and Joseph F. Charles (New York: Funk & Wagnalls, n.d.), p. 146; *Oxford English Dictionary* corrected reissue (Oxford: Clarendon, 1933), 2: 1262–1263; *Latin Dictionary*, rev. ed., ed. Charlton T. Lewis and Charles Short (Oxford: Clarendon, 1879), pp. 500–501; Robertus Stephanus, *Thesaurus linguae latinae* (Basileae, Helvetia: Thurnisiorum, 1743), 1: 738–740.

On the empirical research study discussed in this meditation, see René A. Spitz, "Hospitalism: An Inquiry into the Genesis of Psychiatric Conditions in Early Childhood," in *The Psychoanalytic Study of the Child* (New York: International Universities Press, 1945), 1: 53–74.

For an examination of care, see Grace Clement, *Care, Autonomy and Justice: Feminism and the Ethic of Care* (Boulder, Colo.: Westview, 1996), pp. 1–9, 109–122; Roy B. Zuck, *Teaching As Jesus Taught* (Grand Rapids, Mich.: Baker, 1995), pp. 82–89; Joel B. Green, "Caring as Gift and Goal: Biblical and Theological Reflections," in *The Crisis of Care: Affirming and Restoring Caring Practices in the Helping Professions*, ed. Susan S. Phillips and Patricia Benner

(Washington, D.C.: Georgetown University Press, 1994), pp. 149–167; Dianne Bergant, "Compassion in the Bible," in *Compassionate Ministry*, ed. Gary L. Sapp (Birmingham, Ala.: Religious Education Press, 1993), pp. 9–34; Wayne Whitson Floyd Jr., "Compassion in Theology," in *Compassionate Ministry*, pp. 35–63; James Michael Lee, "Compassion in Religious Instruction", in *Compassionate Ministry*, pp. 171–216; Nel Noddings, *The Challenge of Care in Schools* (New York: Teachers College Press, 1992), pp. 15–27, 44–62; Jeffrey Blustein, *Care and Commitment* (New York: Oxford University Press, 1991), pp. 27–65, 145–153; Uwe Gielen, "Research on Moral Reasoning," in *The Kohlberg Legacy for the Helping Professions*, ed. Lisa Kuhmerker (Birmingham, Ala: R.E.P. Books, 1991), pp. 48–51; Julie A. Gorman, *Let's Get Together* (Wheaton, Ill.: Victor, 1991), pp. 126–129; Jim Wilhoit and Leland Ryken, *Effective Bible Teaching* (Grand Rapids, Mich.: 1988), p. 68; Charlene J. Langdale, "A Re-vision of Structural-Developmental Theory," in *Handbook of Moral Development*, ed. Gary L. Sapp (Birmingham, Ala.: Religious Education Press, 1986), pp. 15–54; Carol Gilligan, *In a Different Voice* (Cambridge, Mass.: Harvard University Press, 1982), pp. 24–63; Nel Noddings, *Caring* (Berkeley, Calif.: University of California Press, 1984), pp. 7–29, 175–182; Morton T. Kelsey, *Care* (New York: Paulist, 1981), pp. 148–154; Milton Mayerhoff, *On Caring* (New York: Harper & Row Perennial, 1971), pp. 5–18; Martin Heidegger, *Being and Time,* trans. John Macquarrie and Edward Robinson (New York: Harper & Row, 1962), pp. 225–256; James D. Smart, *The Teaching Ministry of the Church* (Philadelphia; Westminster, 1954), p. 23.

2. James Michael Lee, *The Shape of Religious Instruction* (Birmingham, Ala.; Religious Education Press, 1971), pp. 34–42, 211–213; James Michael Lee, *The Flow of Religious Instruction* (Birmingham, Ala.: Religious Education Press, 1973), pp. 60–65; James Michael Lee, *The Content of Religious Instruction* (Birmingham, Ala.: Religious Education Press, 1985), pp. 18–20, 231–234, 240–241.

MEDITATION 17: PERSEVERANCE

1. This story was told to me, in somewhat different form, by my stepfather, Ernest Lundstrom. Born on April 12, 1901 in the small Swedish town of Sävar near the Arctic Circle, he became at a comparatively young age the captain of a large American luxury liner that sailed the Caribbean before World War II. When war came, he joined the U.S. Navy where he was appointed as master of his former luxury liner, which by then had been converted into a troopship. He and his refitted troopship participated in every major American military invasion of Europe by sea.

2. James Michael Lee, *The Shape of Religious Instruction* (Birmingham, Ala.: Religious Education Press, 1971), pp. 306–313; James Michael Lee, *The Flow of Religious Instruction* (Birmingham, Ala.: Religious Education Press, 1973), pp.

92–93; James Michael Lee, *The Content of Religious Instruction* (Birmingham Ala.: Religious Education Press, 1985), pp. 633–636.

MEDITATION 18: BEING USED

1. An especially lucid account of the incident of the broom can be found in François Trochu, *Saint Bernadette Soubirous,* trans. and adapted John Joyce (Rockford, Ill: TAN, 1957), p. 326. See also Bernadette Soubirous, *Les écrits de Sainte Bernadette et sa voie spirituelle,* 3iéme revue et corrigée, presenteur André Ravier (Paris: Lethiellieux, 1993), pp. 461–526; Jean-Luc Rosselin, *Bernadette Soubirous: Une experience mystique* (Paris: Séguier, 1988), pp. 39–48, 58–66; John W. Lynch, *Bernadette: The Only Witness* (Boston: St. Paul Editions, 1981), pp. 27–44, 121–133, 160–174; René Laurentin, *Bernadette of Lourdes: A Life Based on Authenticated Documents,* trans. John Drury (Minneapolis, Minn: Winston, 1978), pp. 85–114, 171–237; Bernard Billet, *Bernadette: une vocation "comme tout le monde"* (Paris: Lethielleux, 1966), pp. 121–133; Hugh Ross Williamson, *The Challenge of Bernadette* (Westminster, Md.: Newman, 1958), pp. 62–94; Leon Cristiani, *Saint Bernadette,* trans. Patrick O'Shaughnessy (Staten Island, N.Y.: Alba House, 1965), pp. 25–41, 147–164; François Trochu, *Saint Bernadette Soubirous,* pp. 3–70, 100–109, 207–216, 229–329, 352–372; Margaret Trouncer, *Saint Bernadette: Child and Nun* (New York: Sheed and Ward, 1957), pp. 3–68; Marcelle Auclair, *Bernadette* (Paris: Bloud et Gay, 1957), pp. 49–56, 232–244; Michel de Saint-Pierre, *Bernadette and Lourdes,* trans. Edward Fitzgerald (Garden City, N.Y.: Doubleday Image, 1954), pp. 161–182, 195–209, 262–263; Frances Parkinson Keyes, *Bernadette of Lourdes* (New York: Messner, 1953), pp. 9–46, 81–106; Une Religieuse Inconnue, *Bernadette of Lourdes,* trans. J. H. Gregory (Nevers, France: St. Gildard, 1926), pp. 23–57; Jean Barbet, *Bernadette Soubirous: sa naissance, sa vie, sa mort d'après des documents inédits* (Tarbes, France: Barbet, 1923), pp. 13–52, 179–207, 260–285. Perhaps the one book that best conveys the spirit of Bernadette is the historically-based nonfictive novel written by the celebrated Jewish author Franz Werfel, *Song of Bernadette,* trans. Ludwig Lewishohn (New York: Viking, 1942).

2. James Michael Lee, *The Flow of Religious Instruction* (Birmingham, Ala.: Religious Education Press, 1973), pp. 225–229; James Michael Lee, *The Content of Religious Instruction* (Birmingham, Ala.: Religious Education Press, 1985), pp. 240–241; 615–618.

MEDITATION 19: TALKING VERSUS DOING

1. After many days of intense research in which I exhausted all the sources at my disposal, I was unable to find either a citation or an account of the story that I relate at the end of this chapter. Yet I am firmly convinced that I had once either heard or, more likely, read this story. Uncharacteristically, I failed to make notes on it immediately after encountering it. The core of this story as I relate it is true as far as I am aware, though some of the specific details might not be accurate.

Notes

The important thing is that the soul, spirit, and essence of the story is true, as far as I am able to recollect.

I used the following works for the historical account of the life, spirit, and apostolate of Teresa of Calcutta: Mother Teresa, *No Greater Love*, ed. Becky Benenate and Joseph Durepos (Novato, Calif.; New Directions, 1997), pp. 67–73; José Luis Gonzáles-Balado, *Mother Teresa: Her Life, Her Work, Her Message* (Liguori, Mo.: Liguori, 1997), pp. 6–20, 40–74, 111–116, 119–120 (includes an account of a telling dialogue between Teresa of Calcutta and Fidel Castro of Cuba); Kenneth L. Woodward, "Requiem for a Saint," *Newsweek*, 22 September 1997, pp. 22–33; Germaine Greer, "Unmasking the Mother," *Newsweek*, 22 September 1997, p. 33; Andrew M. Greeley, "The Happiest Human," *Newsweek*, 22 September 1997, p. 35; "Mother Teresa, 1910–1997: Seeker of Souls," *Time*, vol. 150, 15 September 1997, pp. 78–84; Peggy Noonan, "A Combatant in the World," *Time*, vol. 150, 15 September 1997, p. 84; Roger Rosenblatt, "An Old Lady and a Young Lady," *Time*, vol. 150, 15 September 1997, p. 116; Renzo Allegri, *Teresa of the Poor* (Ann Arbor: Servant, 1996), pp. 13–24, 33–72; Mother Teresa, *A Simple Path*, comp. Lucinda Vardey (New York: Ballantine, 1995), pp. 31–60, 79–126, 177–185; Roger Royle, *Mother Teresa* (San Francisco, Calif.: HarperSanFrancisco, 1992), pp. 7–34; Jill Wheeler, *Mother Teresa*, ed. Rosemary Wallner (Edina, Minn.: Abdo, 1992), pp. 6–31; Lush Gjergji, *Mother Teresa* (Brooklyn, N.Y.: New City Press, 1991), pp. 7–67; Richard Tames, *Mother Teresa* (New York: Watts, 1989), pp. 4–22; Omer Tanghe, ". . . For the Least of My Brothers": The Spirituality of Mother Teresa and Catherine Doherty*, trans. Jean MacDonald (New York: Alba, 1989), pp. 25–50, 65–78, 95–119; Eileen Egan, *Such a Vision: Mother Teresa—The Spirit and the Work* (Garden City, N.Y.: Doubleday, 1985), pp. 16–44, 211–289, 343–378; Mother Teresa of Calcutta, *The Love of Christ: Spiritual Counsels*, ed. Georges Gorée and Jean Barbier, trans. John A. Otto (New York: Harper & Row, 1982), pp. 6–35; Kathryn Spink, *The Miracle of Love* (San Francisco, Calif.: Harper & Row, 1981), pp. 16–88, 215–239; Desmond Doig, *Mother Teresa of Calcutta, the Love of Christ: Her People, Her Work* (New York: Harper & Row, 1976), pp. 33–43, 63–81; E. LeJoly, *We Do It for Jesus: Mother Teresa and her Missionaries of Charity* (London: Darton, Longman and Todd, 1977), pp. 14–128, Malcolm Muggeridge, *Something Beautiful for God* (New York: Harper & Row, 1971), pp. 65–124.

For some religious instruction treatments of the topic of this meditation, see Dorothy C. Bass et al., *Practicing Our Faith* (San Francisco, Calif.: Jossey-Bass, 1997), pp. 31–32; Charles R. Foster, *Educating Congregations* (Nashville, Tenn.: Abingdon, 1994), pp. 62–79; Sara Little, *To Set One's Heart* (Atlanta: Knox, 1983), p. 76; James Michael Lee, "Facilitating Growth in Faith through Religious Instruction," in *Handbook of Faith*, ed. James Michael Lee (Birmingham, Ala.: Religious Education Press, 1990), pp. 283–286; Charles R. Foster, "The Faith Community as a Guiding Image for Christian Education," in *Contemporary Approaches to Christian Education*, ed. Jack L. Seymour and Donald E. Miller (Nashville, Tenn.: Abingdon, 1982), pp. 59–60; Thomas H. Groome, *Christian Religious Education* (San Francisco, Calif.: Harper & Row, 1980), pp. 63–66; National Conference of Catholic Bishops, *Sharing the Light of Faith: National Catechetical Directory for Catholics of the United States* (Washington, D.C.:

United States Catholic Conference, 1979), p. 49 (no. 86); John H. Westerhoff III, *Will Our Children Have Faith?* (New York: Seabury, 1976), pp. 64–66; John H. Westerhoff III, *Tomorrow's Church: A Community of Change* (Waco, Tex.: Word, 1976), pp. 105–107; David P. O'Neill, *Christian Behavior?: Does It Matter What You Do, or Only What You Are?* (Dayton, Ohio: Pflaum, 1973), pp. 2–11, 89–90; John H. Westerhoff III, *Values for Tomorrow's Children* (Philadelphia: Pilgrim, 1971), pp. 34–45; George Albert Coe, *A Social Theory of Religious Education* (New York: Arno & The New York Times, 1969), pp. 82–84; Marcel van Caster and Jean Le Du, *Experiential Catechetics*, trans. Denis Barrett (Paramus, N.J.: Newman, 1969), p. 222; Frank. W. Gaebelein, *The Pattern of God's Truth* (Chicago: Moody, 1968), pp. 15–16; J. Gordon Chamberlin, *Freedom and Faith* (Philadelphia: Westminster, 1965), pp. 56–68; Alfonso Nebreda, "Living Faith: Major Concern of Religious Education," in *Pastoral Catechetics*, ed. Johannes Hofinger and Theodore C. Stone (New York: Herder and Herder, 1964), pp. 133–141; Congregation pro Clericis, *Directorium catechisticum generale* (Città del Vaticano: Libreria Editrice Vaticana, 1963), p. 25 (no. 16, partes primae et secundae); Philippe André, "Christ's Pedagogy in the Gospel," in *Modern Catechetics: Message and Method in Religious Formation*, ed. Gerard S. Sloyan (New York: Macmillan, 1963), pp. 323–345; Lois E. LeBar, *Education That Is Christian* (n.p. [Old Tappan, N.J.]: Revell, 1958), p. 58; William Clayton Bower, *The Curriculum of Religious Education* (New York: Scribner's, 1925), pp. 55–56; George Herbert Betts, *How to Teach Religion* (New York: Abingdon, 1910), pp. 91–108.

2. James Michael Lee, *The Shape of Religious Instruction* (Birmingham, Ala.: Religious Education Press, 1971), pp. 10–19, 30, 34–42, 81–88, 246–248; James Michael Lee, *The Flow of Religious Instruction* (Birmingham, Ala.: Religious Education Press, 1973), pp. 188–194; James Michael Lee, *The Content of Religious Instruction* (Birmingham, Ala.; Religious Education Press, 1985), pp. 142–149, 292–297, 391–398, 704.

MEDITATION 20: SACRIFICE

1. Joseph Henninger, "Sacrifice," trans. Matthew J. O'Connell, in *The Encyclopedia of Religion*, ed. Mircea Eliade et al. (New York: Macmillan, 1987), pp. 544–557; Stephen D. Jones, *Transforming Discipleship in the Inclusive Church* (Valley Forge, Pa.: Judson, 1984), pp. 39–45; Parker J. Palmer, *The Company of Strangers* (New York: Crossroad, 1981), pp. 111–115; Otto Semmelroth and Leo Scheffczyk, "Sacrifice," in *Sacramentum Mundi*, ed. Karl Rahner et al. (New York: Herder and Herder, 1970), 5: 388–394; Ernest Klein, *A Comprehensive Etymological Dictionary of the English Language*, (Amsterdam: Elsevier, 1967), 2: 1371; Eric Partridge, *Origins* (New York: Macmillan, 1966), p. 579; D. A. Simpson, editor, *Cassell's New Latin Dictionary* (New York: Funk & Wagnalls, 1959, pp. 528–529; *Oxford English Dictionary*, corrected reissue (Oxford: Clarendon, 1933), 9: 17–18; *Latin Dictionary*, rev. ed., ed. Charlton T. Lewis and Charles Short (Oxford: Clarendon, 1879), pp. 1610–1612; Robertus Stephanus, *The-*

saurus linguae latinae, tomus IV (Basileae, Helvetia: Thurnisiorum, 1743), pp. 139–140, 142.

2. James Michael Lee, *The Flow of Religious Instruction* (Birmingham, Ala.: Religious Education Press, 1973), pp. 92–93, 225–229; James Michael Lee, *The Content of Religious Instruction* (Birmingham, Ala.: Religious Education Press, 1985), pp. 269, 709–710.

MEDITATION 21: RENUNCIATION

1. The grinding stone passage cited in this meditation comes from Daisetz Teitaro Suzuki, *The Training of the Zen Buddhist Monk* (New York: University Books, 1965), p. 98. The quotation from the Mahayana School of Buddhism comes from Christmas Humphries, *Zen: A Way of Life* (Boston: Little, Brown, 1962), p. 77 (see also pp. 81–120). The quotation from ancient Zen masters comes from Chang Chen-Chi, *The Practice of Zen* (New York: Harper, 1959), p. 66 (see also pp. 1–40, 45–49).

Sources that I consulted in writing this meditation include Thomas Merton, introduction to *The Golden Age of Zen*, by John C. H. Wu (New York: Doubleday Image, 1996), pp. 11–21; Robert E. Kennedy, *Zen Spirit, Christian Spirit: The Place of Zen in Christian Life* (New York: Continuum, 1995), pp. 24–42; Kazuaki Tanahashi and David Schneider, *Essential Zen* (San Francisco, Calif.: HarperSan Francisco, 1994), pp. 135–144; Kevin Fauteaux, *The Recovery of Self: Regression and Redemption in Religious Experience* (New York: Paulist, 1994), pp. 110–115; Benjamin Radcliff and Amy Radcliff, *Understanding Zen* (Boston: Tuttle, 1993), pp. 3–135; Frederick Franck, *Zen Seeing, Zen Drawing: Meditation in Action* (New York: Bantam, 1993), pp. 21–31, 123–138; Padraic O'Hare, *The Way of Faithfulness: Contemplation and Formation in the Church* (Valley Forge, Pa.: Trinity, 1993), p. 1–22; Master Hsu Yun, *Master Hsu Yun's Discourses and Dharma Words*, 4th ed., ed. and trans. Lu K'uan Yü (Hong Kong: Buddhist Book Distributor, 1993), pp. 1–30; Phillip Olson, *The Discipline of Freedom: A Kantian View of the Role of Moral Precepts in Zen Practice* (Albany, N.Y.: State University of New York Press, 1993), pp. 1–23, 44–59, 131–141; David Scott and Tony Doubleday, *The Elements of Zen* (Shaftsbury, Mass.: Element, 1992), pp. 2–41, 61–66; "Jesuit Zen Buddhist," *Christian Century*, 109 (15 January, 1992), p. 39; John Carmody, "The Concept of Faith in Comparative Religions," in *Handbook of Faith*, ed. James Michael Lee (Birmingham, Al.: Religious Education Press, 1990), pp. 31–35; Ruben L. F. Habito, *Total Liberation: Zen Spirituality and the Social Dimension* (Maryknoll, N.Y.: Orbis, 1989), pp. 10–24, 43–49; Young Bong Oh and Sun Young Park, "Buddhist Education and Religious Pluralism, in *Religious Pluralism and Religious Education*, ed. Norma H. Thompson (Birmingham, Ala.: Religious Education Press, 1988), pp. 249–270; Heinrich Dumoulin, *Zen Buddhism: A History*, vol. 1: *India and China,* trans. James W. Heisig and Paul Knitter (New York: Macmillan, 1988), pp. 245–261; Carl Bielefeldt, *Dōgen's Manuals of Zen Meditation* (Berkeley, Calif.: University of California Press, 1988), pp. 1–12, 109–160; Masao Abe, *Zen and Western Thought*, ed. William R.

LaFleur (Honolulu: University of Hawaii Press, 1985), pp. 3–24, 127–132, 223–227; Sung Bae Park, *Faith and Sudden Enlightenment* (Albany, N.Y.: State University of New York Press, 1983), pp. 11–42; 105–125; Klemens Tilmann, *Meditation in Depth*, trans. David Smith (New York: Paulist, 1979), pp. 56–59; Marilyn May Mallory, *Christian Mysticism: Transcending Techniques: A Theological Reflection on the Empirical Testing of the Teaching of St. John of the Cross* (Amsterdam; Van Gorcum, 1977), pp. 79–83; H. M. Enomiya Lassalle, *Zen Meditations for Christians*, trans. John C. Maraldo (LaSalle, Ill.: Open Court, 1974), pp. 3–52; Else Madelon Hooykaas and Bert Schierbeek, *Zazen*, trans. Charles McGeehan (Tucson, Ariz.: Omen, 1971), pp. 7–16; Daisetz Teitaro Suzuki, *The Zen Doctrine of No Mind*, ed. Christmas Humphreys (York Beach, Me.: Weiser, 1969), pp. 9–21, 106–141; Niu-T'ou Fa-Yung, "No Mind Is Not Different from Mind," in *Original Teachings of Ch'an Buddhism* [excerpted from *Transmission of the Lamp*], ed. Tao-yüan, trans. Chang Chung-Yuan (New York: Pantheon, 1969), pp. 17–26; Thomas Merton, *Mystics and Zen Masters* (New York: Farrar, Straus and Giroux, 1967), pp. viii- x, 3–44, 235–254; Philip Kapleau, *The Three Pillars of Zen: Teaching, Practice, and Enlightenment* (Boston; Beacon, 1965), pp. 26–49; Daisetz Teitaro Suzuki, *An Introduction to Zen Buddhism* (New York; Weidenfeld, 1964), pp. 38–73, 88–117; Paul Wienpahl, *The Matter of Zen: A Brief Account of Zazen* (New York: New York University Press, 1964), pp. 1–5, 39–42, 59–65, 81–94; Aelred Graham, *Zen Catholicism* (New York: Harcourt, Brace, & World, 1963), pp. 76–81, 136–160; Nancy Wilson Ross, introduction to *The World of Zen*, ed. Nancy Wilson Ross (New York; Random House, 1960), pp. 3–14; D. T. Suzuki, *Mysticism: Christian and Buddhist* (New York: Harper & Row, 1957), pp. 3–38, 145–149; D. T. Suzuki, *Zen Buddhism; Selected Writings*, ed. William Barrett (Garden City, N.Y.: Doubleday Anchor, 1956), pp. 3–24, 83–226.

For some treatments of the topic of this mediation specifically by religious educationists or by persons closely related to this field, see Rick Yount, "The Goal of Christian Teaching: Christlikeness," in *The Teaching Ministry of the Church*, ed. Daryl Eldridge (Nashville, Tenn.: Broadman & Holman, 1995), pp. 143–144; James Michael Lee, "The Context of Morality and Religion", *Discipline for Character Development*, by Kevin Walsh (Birmingham, Ala.; R.E.P. Books, 1991), pp. 147–149; Carol Lakey Hess, "Educating in the Spirit" (Ph.D. diss., Princeton Theological Seminary, 1990), pp. 234–241; Gabriel Moran, *No Ladder to the Sky* (San Francisco, Calif.: Harper & Row, 1987), pp. 4, 155–156; James Michael Lee, "Lifework Spirituality and the Religious Educator," in *The Spirituality of the Religious Educator*, ed. James Michael Lee (Birmingham, Ala.: Religious Education Press, 1985), pp. 7–42; Donald E. Bossart, *Creative Conflict in Religious Education and Church Administration* (Birmingham, Ala.: Religious Education Press, 1980), pp. 64–66; H. Schultze, "The Man of God Thoroughly Furnished," in *Fundamentals of Christian Education: Theory and Practice*, ed. Cornelius Jaarsma (Grand Rapids, Mich.: Eerdmans, 1953), pp. 159–182.

2. James Michael Lee, *The Flow of Religious Instruction* (Birmingham, Ala.: Religious Education Press, 1973), pp. 223–225; James Michael Lee, *The Content of Religious Instruction* (Birmingham, Ala.; Religious Education Press, 1985), pp. 53–56, 149–154, 233–235, 507–512, 634–657.

MEDITATION 22: INCONVENIENCE

1. *Webster's Third New International Dictionary*, 1981, s.v." inconvenience"
and "inconvenient"; *Webster's New Dictionary of Synonyms*, 1973, s.v. "inconvenience"; "inconvenient" and "inconvenient", in Samuel Johnson, *A Dictionary of
the English Language*, (New York: AMS Press, 1967), 1: 12D; *The Synonym
Finder*, 1961, s.v., "inconvenience" and "inconvenient"; *The Oxford English Dictionary*, 5: 1933, s.v. "inconvenience" and "inconvenient."

2. James Michael Lee, *The Flow of Religious Instruction* (Birmingham, Ala.:
Religious Education Press. 1973), pp. 270–272; James Michael Lee, *The Content
of Religious Instruction* (Birmingham, Ala.: Religious Education Press, 1985),
pp. 80–85, 709–710.

MEDITATION 23: HARD WORK

1. Pat Riley, *The Winner Within* (New York: Putnam's, 1993); Pat Riley, *Show-
time: Inside the Lakers' Breakthrough Season* (New York: Warner, 1988), pp. ix–
xii, 12–16, 40–63, 111–112, 132–136, 258–259.
Other sources that I consulted in writing this meditation include Michael
Bradley, "Riled Up Defenses," *Sport* 88 (June 1997), pp. 57–58; S. L. Price, "Hot
Hand," *Sports Illustrated*, 86 (May 5, 1997), pp. 28–31, Arthur Martin Cooper,
"Most Stylish Man in America: Pat Riley," *Gentlemen's Quarterly*, 66 (November 1996), p. 328; Jackie MacMullan, "Dealing for Dollars," *Sports Illustrated*,
84 (March 4, 1996), pp. 74, 76, 79; Mark Kriegel, "Escape from New York," *Esquire*, 124 (December, 1995), pp. 126–134; Cotton Fitzsimmons, "One Man, One
Hat," *Sports Illustrated*, 82 (June 26, 1995), p. 94; Johnette Howard, "Now Hear
This," *Sports Illustrated*, 82 (May 1, 1995), pp. 24–26, 31; Mike Lupica, "Ma-
harishi Riley and the New Age Knicks," *Esquire*, 120 (November, 1993), pp. 80,
82–83; Hank Hersch, "All About Pat," *Sports Illustrated*, 76 (10 February 1992),
pp. 16–21; David Halberstam, "Character Study," *New York*, 25 (21 December
1992), 80–81, 85; Joe McDonnell, "Pat Riley," *Sport*, 83 (October 1992), pp.
30–31, 34–38; Ken Auletta, "The Life of Riley," *Vanity Fair*, 55 (April 1992), pp.
106, 108, 114, 118, 122, 124, 128, 132; Eric Pooley, "Coach Pat Riley Brings the
Knicks a New York State of Mind," *New York*, 24 (23 September 1991), pp.
118–119; Rick Weinberg and Tom Kertes, "New York Story,", *Sport*, 82 (December, 1991), pp. 55–59; Michael Stone, "A Whole New Ball Game," *New York*, 24
(25 November 1991), pp. 42–49; Jack McCallum, "Giving a Winner His Due,"
Sports Illustrated, 72 (9 April 1990), p. 112; Diane K. Shah, "The Transformation
of Pat Riley," *Gentleman's Quarterly*, 59 (January, 1989), pp. 136–141, 188–190;
Jack McCallum, "The Dreaded R Word." in *Sports Illustrated*, 68 (18 April
1988), pp. 50–54, 57.

2. James Michael Lee, *The Shape of Religious Instruction* (Birmingham, Ala.;
Religious Education Press, 1971), pp. 164–176; James Michael Lee, *The Flow of
Religious Instruction* (Birmingham, Ala.: Religious Education Press, 1973), pp.

89–98, 233–239; James Michael Lee, *The Content of Religious Instruction* (Birmingham, Ala.: Religious Education Press, 1985), pp. 615–618.

MEDITATION 24: MAKING IT PERFECT

1. My mother told this true story to me very often during her lifetime not only as a testimony to her own mother's desire to do things perfectly when one does things for God but also as a motivational force for me to constantly strive to do everything perfectly especially when directly in the Lord's service.

2. James Michael Lee, *The Shape of Religious Instruction* (Birmingham, Ala.: Religious Education Press, 1971), pp. 154–161; James Michael Lee, *The Flow of Religious Instruction* (Birmingham, Ala.: Religious Education Press, 1973), pp. 230–233, 286–289; James Michael Lee, *The Content of Religious Instruction* (Birmingham, Ala.: Religious Education Press, 1985), pp. 617–618.

MEDITATION 25: DOING THE BEST

1. Some books that touch on the main thrust of this meditation, albeit indirectly and around the edges rather than frontally and essentially, are George Plimpton, *The X Factor* (n.p.: Whittle Direct, 1990), pp. 8–17; Tom Kubistant, *Performing Your Best* (Champaign, Ill.: Leisure Press, 1986), pp. 21–48; Jim Wilhoit, *Christian Education: The Search for Meaning* (Grand Rapids, Mich.: Baker, 1986), p. 58; Irene Kassorla, *Go For It!* (New York: Dell, 1984), pp. 79–86; Wayne Dyer, *The Sky's the Limit* (New York: Pocket Books, 1980), pp. xiii, 329–363; David C. McClelland et al., *The Achievement Motive* (New York: Irvington, 1976), pp. 6–96; Abraham Maslow, *Motivation and Personality*, 2d ed. (New York: Harper & Row, 1970), pp. 149–180; Maxwell Maltz, *Psycho- Cybernetics* (New York: Essandess, 1960), pp. 205–224. I wish to thank Paul Blum for directing my attention to the Maltz volume.

2. James Michael Lee, *The Flow of Religious Instruction* (Birmingham, Ala.; Religious Education Press, 1971), pp. 93–94, 249–268; James Michael Lee, *The Content of Religious Instruction* (Birmingham, Ala.: Religious Education Press, 1985), pp. 676–678.

MEDITATION 26: EXTRAORDINARILY WELL

1. The basic source I used for this meditation is Thérèse of Lisieux, *Story of a Soul: The Autobiography of Saint Thérèse of Lisieux [L'Histoire d'une âme]*, 3d ed., trans. John Clarke (Washington, D.C.: Institute of Carmelite Studies, 1996). This English translation was rendered with great care from the thus far definitive French corrected edition of *L'Histoire d'une âme* issued in 1972, and in this sense makes all other previous translations somewhat out of date.

Other sources about the life and spirituality of Thérèse that I consulted in writing this meditation include Conrad de Meester, *Dynamique de la confiance: Genèse et structure de la "voie d'enfance spirituelle" de sainte Thérèse de Lisieux*, 2ième éd. (Paris: Cerf, 1995), pp. 433–453; Jean Guitton, *Le génie de Thérèse de Lisieux, 2ième édition* (Paris: l'Emmanuel, 1995), pp. 53–87; Thérèse of Lisieux, *A Discovery of Love*, trans. John Clarke, ed. and intro. Terence Carey (New Rochelle, N.Y.: New City Press, 1992), pp. 33–97, 112–139; Hans Urs von Balthasar, *Two Sisters in the Spirit: Thérèse of Lisieux and Elizabeth of the Trinity*, trans. Donald Nichols and Anne Elizabeth England (San Francisco, Calif.: Ignatius, 1992), pp. 117–144; Jean Lafrance, *My Vocation Is Love: Thérèse of Lisieux*, trans. Anne Marie Brennan (Homebush, Australia: St. Paul, 1990), pp. 22–27, 103–136; Guy Gaucher, *The Passion of Thérèse of Lisieux*, trans. Anne Marie Brennan (New York: Crossroad, 1989), pp. 48–51, 97–151, 173–179, 215–239; Alexis Riaud, *La science d'amour' en sainte Thérèse de l'Enfant-Jésus* (Montréal: Médiaspaul et Paulines, 1989), pp. 15–20, 87–107; Susan Leslie, *The Happiness of God: Holiness in Thérèse of Lisieux* (New York: Alba, 1988), pp. 57–80; Patricia O'Connor, *In Search of Thérèse* (Collegeville, Minn.: Liturgical Press, 1987), pp. 118–139; Guy Gaucher, *The Story of a Life*, translator not named (San Francisco, Calif.: HarperSanFrancisco, 1987), pp. 138–149, 168–202; Monica Furlong, *Thérèse of Lisieux* (New York: Pantheon, 1987), pp. 1–19, 74–135; Conrad de Meester, *With Empty Hands: The Message of Thérèse of Lisieux*, trans. Anne Marie (Turnbridge Wells, England: Burns & Oates, 1987), pp. 17–26, 50–58, 110–111; Gaston Roberge, *A Little Way to God: St. Theresa of Lisieux and the Sacred Heart of Jesus* (Arnand, India: Gujarat Sahitya Prakash, 1984), pp. 8–25, 52–56; Patricia O'Connor, *Thérèse of Lisieux* (Huntington, Ind.: Our Sunday Visitor, 1983), pp. 50–65, 82–117; Marie-Pascale Ducrocq, *Thérèse of Lisieux: A Vocation of Love*, trans, Robert Jollet (Staten Island, N.Y.: Alba, 1983), pp. 27–53; Bernard Bro, *The Little Way: The Spirituality of Thérèse of Lisieux*, trans. Alan Neame (London: Darton, Longman & Todd, 1979), pp. 1–36, 101–116; John Clarke, introduction to Thérèse of Lisieux, *Last Conversations*, trans. John Clarke (Washington, D.C.: Institute of Carmelite Studies, 1977), pp. 5–32; Peter-Thomas Rohrbach, *The Search for Saint Thérèse* (Garden City, N.Y.: Doubleday Hanover, 1961), pp. 138–198; Dorothy Day, *Therese* (Notre Dame, Ind.: Fides, 1960), pp. 140–171; Vernon Johnson, *Spiritual Childhood: A Study of St. Teresa's Teaching* (New York: Sheed and Ward, 1954), pp. 118–134; Hans Urs von Balthasar, *Thérèse of Lisieux: The Story of a Mission*, trans. Donald Nichols (New York: Sheed and Ward, 1953), pp. 27–39, 102–103, 180–200; Stéphane-Joseph Piat, *The Story of a Family: The Home of St. Thérèse of Lisieux*, trans. A Benedictine of Stanbrook Abbey (Rockford, Ill.: TAN, 1948), pp. 3–181, 224–261.

See also Kalevi Tamminen and Kari E. Nurmi, "Developmental Theories and Religious Experience," in *Handbook of Religious Experience*, ed. Ralph W. Hood Jr. (Birmingham, Ala.: Religious Education Press, 1995), pp. 295–298; Kenneth E. Hyde, *Religion in Childhood and Adolescence* (Birmingham, Ala.: Religious Education Press, 1990), pp. 98–115, 164–246; Jean-Pierre de Caussade, *The Sacrament of the Present Moment*, trans. Kitty Muggeridge (San Francisco, Calif.: Harper & Row, 1982), pp. 5–27.

2. James Michael Lee, *The Shape of Religious Instruction* (Birmingham, Ala.: Religious Education Press, 1971), pp. 164–175; James Michael Lee, *The Flow of Religious Instruction* (Birmingham, Ala.: Religious Education Press, 1973), pp. 31–38.

MEDITATION 27: A MATTER OF LOVE

1. For a glimpse of the Thomas More's spirituality, see Thomas More, *Thomas More's Prayer Book* (New Haven, Conn.: Yale University Press, 1969). For the scene from Bolt's play about Thomas More that I recounted toward the end of this meditation, see Robert Bolt, *A Man for All Seasons* (New York: Random House, 1962), p. 141.

Sources that I consulted about the life of Thomas More include Louis L. Martz, *Thomas More: The Search for the Inner Man* (New Haven, Conn.: Yale University Press, 1990), pp. 3–27, 45–51; Richard Marius, *Thomas More* (New York: Knopf, 1984), pp. 3–97, 217–250, 407–520; Anthony Kenny, *Thomas More* (Oxford, England: Oxford University Press, 1983), pp. 62–104; Alistair Fox, *Thomas More: History and Providence* (New Haven, Conn.: Yale University Press, 1983), pp. 243–255; Jaspar Ridley, *Statesman and Saint: Cardinal Wolsey, Sir Thomas More, and the Politics of Henry VIII* (New York: Viking, 1982), pp. 10–17, 238–284; J. A. Guy, *The Public Career of Sir Thomas More* (New Haven, Conn.: Yale University Press, 1980), pp. 175–203; G. R. Elton, "The Real Thomas More?", in *Reformation Principle and Practice*, ed. Peter Newman Brooks (London: Scolar Press, 1980), pp. 21–31; Judith P. Jones, *Thomas More* (Boston: Twayne, 1979), pp. 15–31, 112–115, 128–139; Germain Marc'hadour, "Thomas More's Spirituality." in *St. Thomas More: Action, and Contemplation*, ed. Richard S. Sylvester (New Haven, Conn.: Yale University Press, 1972), pp. 125–159; E. E. Reynolds, *The Field Is Won* (Milwaukee: Bruce, 1968), pp. 370–371; E. M. G. Routh, *Sir Thomas More and His Friends* (New York: Russell & Russell, 1963), pp. 122–149, 209–236; R. W. Chambers, *Thomas More* (Ann Arbor, Mich.: University of Michigan Press, 1958), pp. 48–86, 291–350; Theodore Maynard, *Humanist as Hero* (New York: Hafner, 1947), pp. 28–48.

For a treatment of the topic of this meditation as it specifically relates to the religious instruction apostolate, see Daniel Aleshire, "Christian Education and Theology." in *Christian Education Handbook*, 2d ed., ed. Bruce P. Powers (Nashville, Tenn.: Broadman & Holman, 1996), pp. 27–28; Wayne Whitson Floyd, "Compassion in Theology," in *Compassionate Ministry*, ed. Gary L. Sapp (Birmingham, Ala.: Religious Education Press, 1993), pp. 44–45, 50–51. 62–63; Gary L. Sapp, "The Psychology of Religious Compassion", in *Compassionatte Mininstry*, pp. 69–70, 75–76; Lawrence O. Richards, *Creative Personal Bible Study* (Grand Rapids, Mich.: Zondervan Lamplighter, 1987), pp. 43–54; Andrew J. Sopko, "Orthodox Spirituality and the Religious Educator," in *The Spirituality of the Religious Educator*, ed. James Michael Lee (Birmingham, Ala.; Religious Education Press, 1985), pp. 154–155; Fritz Oser and Paul Gmünder, *Religious Judgement: A Developmental Approach* (Birmingham, Ala.: Religious Education Press, 1991), p. 174; Morton T. Kelsey, *Can Christians Be Educated?* ed. and comp. Harold William Burgess (Birmingham, Ala.: Religious Education Pres, 1977), pp. 39–75; Randolph Crump Miller, *The Language Gap and God* (Philadelphia: Pilgrim, 1970), p. 95; Donald Gordon Stewart, *Christian Education and Evangelism* (Philadelphia: Westminster, 1963), pp. 135–140.

2. James Michael Lee, *The Shape of Religious Instruction* (Birmingham, Ala.: Religious Education Press, 1971), pp. 18–19, 55–56, 290; James Michael Lee, *The Content of Religious Instruction* (Birmingham, Ala.: Religious Education Press, 1985), pp. 137, 199, 202–204, 209, 229–244.

MEDITATION 28: COST

1. It was from my father, James Lee III, that I first heard this true anecdote about J. P. Morgan and the man who asked the great financier about purchasing his large yacht. My father was fond of frequently repeating this anecdote to me as a pithy and pointed example of what is required of a person to be successful in the spiritual life as well as in the material life. The anecdote made a great impression on me, an impression that has continued to exercise a significant influence on my own personal and professional life. Sources that I used on the life and times of John Pierpont Morgan include Louis Auchincloss, *The Financier as Collector* (New York: Abrams, 1990); Stanley Jackson, *J. P. Morgan* (New York: Stein and Day, 1983), pp. 11–14, 35–63, 112–117, 135–153, 190–224, 308–324; Cass Canfield, *The Incredible Pierpont Morgan* (New York: Harper & Row, 1974), pp. 11–26, 84–164; Herbert L. Satterlee, *J. Pierpont Morgan* (New York: Macmillan, 1940), pp.70–126, 145–339, 369–583; John Kennedy Winkler, *The Life of J. Pierpont Morgan* (London: Knopf, 1931), pp. 11–31, 56–65, 97–157, 222–262, 271–345; Carl Hovey, *The Life Story of J. Pierpont Morgan* (London: Heinemann, 1912), pp. 3–11, 96–120, 278–352.

See also Romney M. Moseley, *Becoming a Self before God: Critical Transformations* (Nashville, Tenn.: Abingdon, 1991), pp. 107–131. An especially celebrated and *au point* treatment of the topic of this meditation is Dietrich Bonhoeffer, *The Cost of Discipleship*, 2d ed., trans. R. H. Fuller, rev. Irmgard Booth (New York: Macmillan, 1963), pp. 45–690.

Some sources directly related to the religious instruction enterprise include Locke E. Bowman Jr., "Challenges Facing the Churches: What Would Happen If . . . ," in *Does the Church Really Want Religious Education?*, ed. Marlene Mayr (Birmingham, Ala.: Religious Education Press, 1988), p.124; James Michael Lee, "CCD Renewal," in *Renewing the Sunday School and the CCD*, ed. D. Campbell Wyckoff (Birmingham, Ala.: Religious Education Press, 1986), p. 244; Craig R. Dykstra, *Vision and Character* (New York: Paulist, 1981), pp. 90–94; James Michael Lee, "Toward a New Era: A Blueprint for Positive Action," in *The Religious Education We Need*, ed. James Michael Lee (Birmingham, Ala.: Religious Education Press, 1977), p. 155; Rachel Henderlite, *Forgiveness and Hope: Toward a Theology for Protestant Christian Education* (Richmond, Va.: Knox, 1961), p. 67.

2. James Michael Lee, *The Flow of Religious Instruction* (Birmingham, Ala.: Religious Education Press, 1973), p. 206; James Michael Lee, *The Content of Religious Instruction* (Birmingham, Ala: Religious Education Press, 1985), pp. 676–678.

MEDITATION 29: GENEROSITY

1. The essence of this story was told by Gareth Byrne in a sermon he gave in the summer of 1993 at the Cathedral of St. Paul in Birmingham, Alabama. Byrne, a highly intelligent Irish priest from the Dublin Archdiocese, had traveled especially from Rome to Birmingham to spend several weeks with me in order to gain firsthand information about my views of religious instruction in general and the spirituality of the religious educator in particular so that he could successfully prosecute his doctoral dissertation at the Pontificia Studiorum Universitas Salesiana in the Eternal City. (On June 23, 1994, Byrne received his doctorate summa cum laude [30/30] from the Salesianum. His dissertation was entitled "A Critical Evaluation of the Contribution of James Michael Lee toward a Spirituality of the Religious Educator"). Upon hearing Byrne's story of the poor man and the grain of wheat, I decided then and there to include it in this book of meditations. I asked the genial Irishman for its source. He told me that he was unaware of any written source, but that various priests in Ireland used the story in their sermons. Byrne himself has told this story in homilies that he has preached in various venues in Europe and the United States. He currently teaches religious education at Holy Cross College, Clonliffe, Dublin.

2. James Michael Lee, *The Shape of Religious Instruction* (Birmingham, Ala.: Religious Education Press, 1971), pp. 49–50; James Michael Lee, *The Flow of Religious Instruction* (Birmingham, Ala.: Religious Education Press, 1973), p. 160.

MEDITATION 30—CONVERSION

1. Augustinus, *Confessiones*, I-IX. Sources that I used about Augustine's life, conversion, and related matters include Robert J. O'Connell, *Images of Conversion in St. Augustine's* Confessions (New York: Fordham University Press, 1996), pp. 9–34, 219–256; Richard Price, *Augustine* (London: HarperCollins Fount, 1996), pp. 1–13; T. Kermit Scott, *Augustine: His Thought in Context* (New York: Paulist, 1995), pp. 57–150; Benedict J. Groeschel, *Augustine* (New York: Crossroad, 1995), pp. 1–40; Mary T. Clark, *Augustine* (Washington, D.C.: Georgetown University Press, 1994), pp. 1–12; Henry Chadwick, "On Re-reading the *Confessions*, in *Saint Augustine the Bishop*, ed. Fannie Le Moine and Christopher Kleinhenz (New York: Garland, 1994), pp. 139–160; John M. Quinn, "Mysticism in the *Confessiones*: Four Passages Reconsidered," in *Augustine: Mystic and Mystagogue*, ed. Frederick Van Fleteren, Joseph C. Schnaubelt, and Joseph Reino (New York: Lang, 1994), pp. 251–286; J. J. O'Meara, "Augustine's *Confessions*: Elements of Fiction," in *Augustine: From Rhetor to Theologian*, ed. Joanne

McWilliam (Waterloo, Ont.: Wilfred Laurier University Press, 1993), pp. 77–95; James E. Reed and Ronnie Prevost, *A History of Christian Education* (Nashville, Tenn.: Broadman & Holman, 1993), pp. 97–100; Margaret R. Miles, *Desire and Delight; A New Reading of Augustine's Confessions* (New York: Crossroad, 1992), pp. 17–38, 67–99; Vernon J. Bourke, *Augustine's Love of Wisdom* (West Lafayette, Ind.: Purdue University Press, 1992), pp. 117–141, 202–209; Colin Starnes, "Augustine's Conversion and the Ninth Book of the *Confessions*," in *Augustine: From Rhetor to Theologian*, ed. Joanne McWilliam (Waterloo, Ont.: lWilfred Laurier Press, 1992), pp. 51–65; Karl Joachim Weintraub, "St. Augustine's *Confessions*: The Search for a Christian Self," in *The Hunger of the Human Heart: Reflections on the* Confessions *of Augustine*, ed. Donald Capps and James E. Dittes (n.p.: Society for the Scientific Study of Religion, 1990), pp. 3–30; Colin Starnes, *Augustine's Conversion* (Waterloo, Ont.: Wilfred Laurier University Press, 1990), pp. 213–276; Georges Tavard, *Les jardins de Saint Augustin* (Montréal: Bellarmin, 1988), pp. 41–73; Gerald Bonner, *St. Augustine of Hippo: Life and Controversies*, 2d ed. (Norwich, England: Canterbury Press, 1986), pp. 36–156; Marcel Neusch, *Augustin: Un chemin de conversion* (Paris: Desclée de Brouwer, 1986), pp. 13–39, 81–101; Warren Thomas Smith, *Augustine: His Life and Thought* (Atlanta: Knox, 1980), pp. 13–102, 169–171; Howard Grimes, "Augustine." in *A History of Religious Educators*, ed. Elmer L. Towns (Grand Rapids, Mich.: Baker, 1975), pp. 54–59; Peter Brown, *Augustine of Hippo* (Berkeley, Calif.: University of California Press, 1967), pp. 19–211, 427–433; Eugene Kevane, *Augustine the Educator* (Westminster, Md.: Newman, 1964), pp. 43–49, 113–148; 341–380; F. van der Meer, *Augustine the Bishop*, trans. Brian Battershaw and G. R. Lamb (London: Sheed and Ward, 1961), pp. 3–15, 129–274; Romano Guardini, *The Conversion of Augustine*, trans. Elinor Briefs (Westminster, Md.: Newman, 1960), pp. 159–253; Henri Marrou, *St. Augustine and His Influence throughout the Ages*, trans. Patrick Hepburne-Scott (New York: Harper, n.d. [1957]), pp. 5–45; Fulbert Cayré, *La contemplation augustienne*, 2ième éd. (Paris: Desclée de Brouwer, 1954), pp. 83–91, 211–219; A. D. Nock, *Conversion* (London: Oxford University Press, 1933), pp. 259–266; Eleanor McDougall, *St. Augustine: A Study in his Personal Religion* (London: Student Christian Movement Press, 1928), pp. 23–81.

See also Marcel J. Dumestre, *A Church at Risk: The Challenge of Spiritually Hungry Adults* (New York: Crossroad Herder, 1997), pp. 95–97; Ralph W. Hood Jr. et al, *Psychology of Religion: An Empirical Approach*, 2d ed. (New York: Guilford, 1996), pp. 273–299; Raymond F. Paloutzian, *An Invitation to the Psychology of Religion,* 2d ed. (Boston: Allyn and Bacon, 1996), pp. 139–174; Frederick J. Gaiser, "A Biblical Theology of Conversion," in *Handbook of Religious Conversion*, ed. H. Newton Malony and Samuel Southard (Birmingham, Ala.: Religious Education Press, 1992), pp. 93–107; V. Bailey Gillespie, *The Dynamics of Religious Conversion: Identity and Transformation* (Birmingham, Ala.: Religious Education Press, 1991), pp. 3–60; Romney M. Moseley, *Becoming A Self Before God: Critical Transformations* (Nashville, Tenn.: Abingdon, 1991), pp. 88–106; Chana Ullman, *The Transformed Self: The Psychology of Religious Conversion* (New York: Plenum, 1989), pp. 3–25, 45; Walter Conn, *Christian Conversion: A Developmental Interpretation of Autonomy and Surrender* (New York:

Paulist, 1986), pp. 212–268; André Godin, *The Psychological Dynamics of Religious Experience: It Doesn't Fall Down from Heaven*, trans. Mary Turton (Birmingham, Ala.: Religious Education Press, 1985), pp. 73–84; William James, *The Varieties of Religious Experience* (Cambridge, Mass.: Harvard University Press, 1985), pp. 157–209; James W. Fowler, *Becoming Adult, Becoming Christian: Adult Development and Christian Faith* (San Francisco, Calif.: Harper & Row, 1984), pp. 138–141; Susanne Johnson, "Religious Experience as Creative, Revelatory and Transforming: The Implications of Intense Christian Experience for the Christian Educational Process," (Ph.D. diss., Princeton Theological Seminary, 1983), pp. 261–335.

For some religious instructional treatments of the topic of this meditation, see Virgilio Elizondo, "Benevolent Tolerance or Humble Reverence: A Vision for Multicultural Religious Education," in *Multicultural Religious Education*, ed. Barbara Wilkerson (Birmingham, Ala.: Religious Education Press, 1997), pp. 401–403; Les L. Steele, *On the Way* (Grand Rapids, Mich.: Baker, 1990), pp. 110–112; Mary C. Boys, *Educating in Faith* (San Francisco, Calif.: Harper & Row, 1989), pp. 203–207; Robert W. Pazmiño, *Foundational Issues in Christian Education: An Introduction in Evangelical Perspective* (Grand Rapids, Mich.: Baker, 1988), pp. 51–54; Daniel S. Schipani, *Religious Education Encounters Liberation Theology* (Birmingham, Ala.: Religious Education Press, 1988), pp. 219–222; Piere [*sic*]-André Liégé, "The Ministry of the Word: From Kerygma to Catechesis," in *Sourcebook for Modern Catechetics*, ed. Michael Warren (Winona, Minn.: St. Mary's Press, 1983), pp. 320–323; Kenneth O. Gangel and Warren S. Benson, *Christian Education: Its History and Philosophy* (Chicago: Moody, 1983), pp. 100–104; Kenneth R. Barker, *Religious Education, Catechesis, and Freedom* (Birmingham, Ala.: Religious Education Press, 1981), pp. 207–208; John H. Westerhoff III, *Inner Growth Outer Change: An Educational Guide to Church Renewal* (New York: Seabury Crossroad, 1979), pp. 17–28; Larry Richards, *How I Can Experience God* (Grand Rapids, Mich.: Zondervan,. 1979), pp. 77–92; François Coudreau, *Basic Catechetical Perspectives*, trans. John Drury (Paramus, N.J.: Paulist Deus, 1969), pp. 23–47; George M. Schreyer, *Christian Education in Action* (New York: Comet, 1957), pp. 84–85; Harrison S. Elliott, *Can Christian Education Be Christian?* (New York: Macmillan, 1949), pp. 317–321; Edwin Diller Starbuck, *The Psychology of Religion* (London: Scribner's, 1901), pp. 408–420.

2. James Michael Lee, *The Shape of Religious Instruction* (Birmingham, Ala.: Religious Education Press, 1971), pp. 3, 55–65, 298–314; James Michael Lee, *The Flow of Religious Instruction* (Birmingham, Ala.: Religious Education Press, 1973), pp 293–294; James Michael Lee, *The Content of Religious Instruction* (Birmingham, Ala.: Religious Education Press, 1985), pp. 676–678.

Index of Names

Index of Subjects